The Making of a Spy

ALSO BY GERHARDT B. THAMM

Boy Soldier: A German Teenager at the Nazi Twilight
(McFarland, 2000; paperback 2007)

The Making of a Spy

*Memoir of a German
Boy Soldier Turned American
Intelligence Agent*

GERHARDT B. THAMM

McFarland & Company, Inc., Publishers
Jefferson, North Carolina, and London

LIBRARY OF CONGRESS CATALOGUING-IN-PUBLICATION DATA

Thamm, Gerhardt B., 1930–
  The making of a spy : memoir of a German boy soldier turned American Army intelligence agent / Gerhardt B. Thamm.
      p.   cm.
  Includes bibliographical references and index.

  ISBN 978-0-7864-4854-8
  softcover : 50# alkaline paper ∞

  1. Thamm, Gerhardt B., 1930– 2. Intelligence officers — United States — Biography. 3. United States. Army Security Agency — Biography. 4. Military intelligence — United States — History — 20th century. 5. Military intelligence — Germany (West) — History — 20th century. 6. Secret service — United States — History — 20th century. 7. German Americans — Biography. I. Title.
  UB271.U52T47   2010
  355.0092 — dc22   2010002126
  [B]

British Library cataloguing data are available

©2010 Gerhardt B. Thamm. All rights reserved

No part of this book may be reproduced or transmitted in any form or by any means, electronic or mechanical, including photocopying or recording, or by any information storage and retrieval system, without permission in writing from the publisher.

On the cover: American Army Intelligence Agent Gerhardt B. Thamm as German national "Georg Trenker"

Manufactured in the United States of America

McFarland & Company, Inc., Publishers
  Box 611, Jefferson, North Carolina 28640
  www.mcfarlandpub.com

To the very few who fought the Cold War in the murkiness of the clandestine world. Their primary mission was, in Sun Tzu's words, "to know the enemy." They lived lies, received little credit or reward and, as the clandestine service tradition demanded, went unrecognized. Not even their closest family members knew the hazards encountered by those involved in the world's second oldest profession — a profession, some insiders would jest, not as honorable as the world's oldest.

Acknowledgments

There are so many people to whom I have become indebted for support, encouragement and understanding during the course of my unorthodox career.

First and foremost, Erwin Erdmann Erich Thamm, my father, whose love for America compelled him to encourage me to leave family and everything familiar to return to the distant land of my birth.

The Harold Kuehnel family of Detroit; they took me, a total stranger, into their home. For me it was the first of many wonderful experiences of American hospitality.

The U.S. Army that nurtured me and became my surrogate family.

Ann Marie Holstad Thamm, my first wife, who shared with me the initial lean years of army life; who had to endure the tensions inherent in the occupation that had been thrust upon me; who gave birth to our two sons, Erik and Erwin, and our daughter, Renita.

Ann Marie's grandfather, Sigurd H. Holstad, the "Old Viking," who made my father's dream to come to America reality.

The colonel in army personnel — I have long forgotten his name — who propelled me into a lifelong career in foreign intelligence operations.

Manfred "Fred" Herz, aka Doktor Hermann, my long departed friend and mentor in the clandestine service, who taught me the "street smarts" needed to survive in the upside-down world of espionage.

Joe Milewski, my longtime friend, and the many other colleagues who, as tradition requires, must remain nameless; they supported me and made survival in this perilous endeavor possible.

And last only in chronological sequence, but foremost, Suanne Zuzel Thamm, my second wife, who patiently encouraged me to engage in the difficult task of writing, of selecting what can be said and what cannot. She is a supreme editor; she gave this manuscript all the polish it has. She too had to endure the tensions inherent in being married to an intelligence operative. She packed my bags, waved me goodbye, and rarely knew where I went, or when or if I would return. She tried not to pry, although I wonder how often she must have been tempted. She is my wife. She is my best friend, and she made my "third life" worth living.

Table of Contents

Acknowledgments — vi
A Man for All Seasons — 1
Words of Wisdom — 3
A Note About Names — 5
Prologue — A Man Called Trenker — 7

Scared as Hell — 11
Riding the Rollercoaster — 13
Boy Soldier — 15
Strangers in Our Own Land — 18
Life in Post–World War II Germany — 23
Black Market Days — 31
America at Last — 35
You're in the Army Now… — 40
War — Once again — 51
Assignment: The U.S. Army General School — 57
Germany, Here I Come — 63
Something Special — 72
The Visit — 75
Every Man Has a Price — 78
Tattered Cloak and Rusty Dagger — 87
Doktor Hermann and Georg Trenker — 104
The Transformation — 115

Special Operations Team Number Three (SpecOps 3)	120
Special Tasks — German Automobile License Plates	121
Special Tasks — The Proprietary	126
Special Tasks — The Proprietary 2	130
Nosy Old Lady	133
Close Call	136
Special Tasks — The Proprietary 3	143
On the Streets of Berlin	146
Not Quite According to the Rules	152
Ceramics?	154
Problem in the Floor Wax Business	158
Contact Lost	162
Code Name "The Shepherd"	164
Another Busy Day in Berlin	173
Reorganization: The New Boss	180
Wasted Effort	186
The Last Christmas in Silesia	194
New Task — Build a Bolthole	195
Life Is a Gamble	197
End of Tour of Duty	200
Trust, and the Bad Apple	201
Order, Counterorder	205
The Later Years	210
Postscript	212
Notes	215
Index	219

A Man for All Seasons*

A case officer must be intelligent and possess high, but flexible, moral standards. He must be an after-dinner speaker, a before and after-dinner guzzler, a night owl — work all day, drink all night, and appear fresh the next day. He must learn to sleep while riding on trains and on non-pressurized cargo planes. He must exist on one meal a day to make up CIF (Confidential Intelligence Fund) losses.

He must be able to lie convincingly to everyone and in that respect accomplishes the impossible task of lying to his wife without being caught.

He must live his lies, never forgetting which ones he has told to whom, but also remember who he really is, and that he must NEVER lie to higher headquarters even when telling the truth may mean embarrassment to him.

He must be a man's man, a ladies' man, a good provider, a Plutocrat, a Democrat, a Republican, a New Dealer, an old dealer, a fast dealer — technician, electrician, politician, mechanic, polygamist, ambidextrous and a specialist on the black market and various shady dealings.

He must be an expert driver, talker, liar, dancer, bridge player, golfer, poker player, chess player, philanthropist, nudist, and an authority on palmistry, chemistry, archeology, psychology, physiology, meteorology, criminology, international business law, reading tea leaves and crystal balls, blondes, brunettes, and redheads. He must be able to take dictation and type 150 words per minute in English, German, French, Russian, Bulgarian, Chinese, Japanese and Sanskrit, as well as read American Indian sign language, Egyptian hieroglyphics and the deaf and dumb alphabet.

He must have a memory, which is capable of remembering all dates, places, names and other assorted information brought out during three-hour conversations during which no notes were taken.

He must be a naturally gregarious individual, but be capable of working alone for long periods of time.

*Written by a U.S. Army Counter Intelligence (CIC) Agent.

He must be able to establish close personal relationships without becoming involved.

He must love people and be able to make them love him. He must always maintain the proper amount of cynicism and view those who love him in an objective manner, being ready to terminate a relationship without explanation if that relationship is no longer of value to him.

He must be the cosmopolitan type.

He must be comfortable sipping wine in the best restaurants, but also capable of inhaling dust, living outside at 10 degrees below zero, and working all summer without perspiring or acquiring B.0.

He must be able to maintain an expensive wardrobe on a meager salary. He must be methodical and have patience, tenacity, initiative, integrity, but he must not let these traits stand in the way of accomplishing his task in half the time it would take to do it right.

In addition to all of the qualifications, it helps if he is CRAZY.

Old Spooks never die, they...

The Spook — the symbol of espionage — the author's "chop" at upper right.

Words of Wisdom

"If you know the enemy and yourself,
You need not fear the result of a hundred battles.
If you know yourself but not the enemy,
For every victory gained you will also suffer a defeat.
If you know neither the enemy nor yourself,
You will succumb in every battle…"

— Sun Tzu, philosopher-warrior, circa 400 B.C.

A Note About Names

Although this personal narrative speaks of long-ago intelligence operations, I felt compelled to change the names, even some of the cover names, of persons who may still be among the living. I received permission from my good friend Joseph Milewski of Erie, Pennsylvania, to use his name. Joe often helped and encouraged me during the hazardous days of Cold War espionage. I called him my "support agent," although he was much more: He was — still is — my friend; he was my "security blanket."

I have purposely disguised the names of the proprietaries[1]* I operated. Although abolished many years ago, I have even masked their localities for security reasons. However, the operating areas and the various contacts described truly reflect actual events.

*See Notes *beginning on page 215.*

Prologue—
A Man Called Trenker

Berlin/Charlottenburg/Tiergarten, West Berlin
Uhlandstrasse
February 1955

Today you would recognize neither the man nor the scene. But then, on a cold afternoon in early 1955, a man called Trenker stood on Uhlandstrasse a block and a half from the Kurfürstendamm, still Berlin's most elegant avenue, that Berliners lovingly call "Ku'damm."

Trenker, tall and slender to the point of skinniness, appeared to be waiting, cautiously waiting. He wore a typical German felt hat that hooded his watchful eyes yet could not contain his wavy, dark brown hair. His dark eyes fascinated people and seemed to distract them from his large nose, which had been broken at least once. High cheekbones — they came from his mother's side — gave him a somewhat Slavic look. He carried a German *Kennkarte* in the inner jacket pocket of his cheap, post–World War II–vintage German suit. The *Kennkarte*— the identification paper that every German in occupied post–World War II Germany was required to have in his possession at all times, identified him as Georg Trenker, a German citizen living in Frankfurt-on-Main, the American Zone of Occupation, Germany. The drab, slightly too-large suit seemed to hang on his frame.

Others in cheap clothing also lingered on Uhlandstrasse. In those days the corner of Uhlandstrasse and Ku'damm served as a rendezvous spot for small-time black-marketeers, where they exchanged East and West German money, peddled American cigarettes and other difficult-to-get goods from the American military Post Exchange. Often these goods had been "earned" by girlfriends of American occupiers "for services rendered."

Although at first glance the man called Trenker appeared to blend in well with the crowd, appearances were a bit deceiving. Trenker carried, concealed, a .38-caliber Colt Police Special revolver with six copper-coated rounds of ball ammunition in a spring-loaded holster on the left side of his belt — indeed, a strange item for a poorly dressed young German to have in postwar Berlin. Of course, Georg Trenker was neither a German nor a black marketeer. Nor was his real name Trenker. And the Philip Morris cigarettes he smoked were not for sale. In fact Trenker was an American intelligence agent waiting for his East German informant, a man code-named "Landser."

Trenker was twenty-five years old and, as his colleagues would jest, "armed and dangerous." He was armed because the Soviets and their East German surrogates just a stone's throw away across the invisible line that separated East and West Berlin had offered a ten-thousand-dollar bounty in gold for any American intelligence agent brought into East Berlin, preferably alive. He was dangerous because he was determined to kill anyone who attempted to drag him across that East-West line. He had been under Soviet domination once and had sworn never again to become a Soviet prisoner.

The man called Trenker had come a long way.

* * * * *

I am the man called Trenker. The very authentic-looking *Kennkarte* in my inner jacket pocket would convince anyone that I am in fact the aforementioned German citizen Georg Trenker of Frankfurt-on-Main.

I carry two wallets and three additional means of identification. The wallet in my back pocket contains a few dollars and a plastic U.S. Army identification card that declares me to be Gerhardt B. Thamm, Sergeant First Class, U.S. Army. My serial number is preceded by the letters "RA"; they stand for Regular Army. That is my real name and my real U.S. Army serial number, and the few dollars in that wallet are mine.

The wallet in the other inner breast pocket of my cheap German suit contains a large sum of money that is not my own. It is the U.S. government's. In that wallet is another U.S. Army identification that proves

"The Man Called Trenker": The author's special agent credential identification photo.

beyond the shadow of doubt that I am George Trenker, a DAC (Department of the Army Civilian), Grade GS-9, employed by U.S. Army Northern Command, Frankfurt-on-Main.

In my shirt pocket is a fourth identification, the credential of the U.S. Army's clandestine service. This one, in an impressive-looking three-section blue etui, is in three languages: English, French, and German. In fine print it requests anyone to follow the direction or request of Special Agent Gerhardt B. Thamm of the U.S. Army's 522nd Military Intelligence Battalion. It also advises that Special Agent Thamm is authorized to carry a .38-caliber Colt Police Special revolver, concealed.

* * * * *

Standing on Uhlandstrasse, a short distance from Berlin's Ku'damm, I could not help but wonder, perhaps even marvel, about the extraordinary rollercoaster ride that had taken me from pre–and postwar Germany to the United States and back to postwar Germany. Had only ten years gone by since the time I, a 15-year-old boy soldier, sat huddled behind the cemetery wall in Poischwitz, a small village in Lower Silesia, in the hinterlands of Germany?

Scared as Hell

**Eastern Front
Combat Sector Jauer
54th Jäger Regiment, 100th Jäger Division
March 1945**

In early March of 1945 a heavy blanket of snow still covered the land, its whiteness interrupted only by patches of black dirt, the remnants of recent artillery explosions. I was terrified, yet watched in fearful fascination as two Soviet T-34 medium tanks lumbered toward me, their tracks clattering, their diesels roaring, belching black exhaust, the muzzles of their machine-guns flickering, spitting a stream of lead into and over the cemetery wall behind which I had taken cover.

I was afraid to move, yet captivated by the horrendously dangerous spectacle.

Red Army T-34 Medium Tank (from a sketchbook by Wehrmacht combat artist Hans Liska — captured by T-Sergeant Herb W. Owen of General Patton's Third Army. The original is now in the Pentagon Library). The T-34 was the most numerous, most versatile combat vehicle of World War II.

Suddenly two streaks of fire hurtled toward the iron monsters. The fireballs impacted on the glacis of the tanks and exploded. I had not seen that two men from separate foxholes to my right flank had fired their "Hallelujah"[2] weapon, the Panzerfaust antitank rocket. They were members of the 54th Jäger Regiment of the 100th Jäger Division. They had waited until the tanks were a mere thirty yards from their foxholes; then they had launched their deadly projectiles. The heavy warheads penetrated the glacis of these seemingly unstoppable steel monsters. A dual internal explosion turned these two tanks into scrap iron. I saw the turret of one of these iron beasts lazily rise from the body of the tank as if lifted by an invisible hand and then tumble in slow motion into the snow a few yards from the tank. Immediately after the two explosions had destroyed the tanks, a fusillade of fire from hidden machine guns scattered the attacking Soviet infantry — forcing it to retreat.

The "Hallelujah" weapon (Wehrmacht combat photography). The two "old-timers" and the young soldier each carry this short-range, highly effective rocket-propelled antitank rocket launcher also called "Panzerfaust" or "Faustpatrone." It was the only highly effective shaped-charge World War II antitank weapon at infantry squad level.

I was scared as hell and wondered how I ever got into this ridiculous situation. It had not yet occurred to me that I was riding an incredible rollercoaster with heights and depths I never could have imagined.

RIDING THE ROLLERCOASTER

Jauer, Lower Silesia
The 1930s and '40s

This most extraordinary rollercoaster ride started with my birth in Detroit, Michigan, to German immigrants who had come to America in search of the American dream, only to get caught up in the nightmare of the Great Depression.

My father had come to America before the Great Depression, some four years before I was born. Because of immigration-related red tape — the U.S. government considered my mother to be a Polish citizen because she was born in the pre–World War I province of Posen, now located in Poland — my father had to return to Germany to make her a German citizen by marriage. Both then came to Detroit in 1929, the year before I was born.

We lived at 4948 Cabot Street, a few city blocks off Michigan Avenue. My dad thoroughly enjoyed working as a nickel polisher at the big Ford plant in Dearborn. He, along with millions of others, lost his job during the depression of 1929. Our family lived on savings for more than two years. My parents saw friends and neighbors evicted from their homes and forced to live in alleys, their belongings covered with tarps. The thought of having to live in an alley behind our rental house terrified my mother as she saw the family's savings shrink to nothing. With their "last twenty dollars" in their pockets — so the family story is told — my parents decided to leave America, the land of their dreams, and return to Germany, to Silesia, to live on my grandfather's estate. It was humiliating, but not as bad as huddling destitute under tarps in a Detroit alley. Thus, although I was born in the United States, at age two I became a Silesian living in Jauer, Lower Silesia, one of Germany's eastern provinces.

Although life was not pleasant for my father, who worked on his father's farm as a common laborer, or my mother, who had to endure numerous fam-

The author's sketch of Vorwerkgut.

ily squabbles, my early experiences were far from unpleasant. I had lived on my grandfather's city farm (the *Vorwerkgut*) as far back as I could remember. It was a wonderful old place with many nooks and crannies where children could play hide and seek. Life for my young sister Helga, many cousins, and me was full of childhood adventures, typical for those children fortunate enough to grow up in the rural countryside.

However, with the outbreak of World War II, the idyllic life came to a sudden halt. My father, along with his two brothers and many friends and neighbors, became a soldier of the Wehrmacht.

At the very beginning of the war the Nazi government imposed strict rationing along with severe penalties for even the most mundane violation. For us the lack of food was never a wartime concern because we raised the food — potatoes, sugar beets, cereal — and produced the milk and meat. And even though the war raged all over Europe, our town was far from the population centers that suffered Allied bombing. Life in Jauer was by far easier, safer, and more pleasant than in places such as Berlin, Hamburg, or Munich.

Little did we know how quickly it all could change.

Boy Soldier

Lower Silesia, Germany
Early 1945

The world as I knew it started to collapse on the 13th of January 1945. Suddenly, and for us totally unexpectedly, hordes of Soviets broke through the thin German lines in eastern Poland and stormed across the Polish plains toward our home.

Nineteen forty-five had started just right, at least for students at Jauer's middle school. On the first day of the 1945 school year, the principal announced that our school was closed and that all students were to report to city hall. There we received military-gray German Army uniforms; mine was a bit too large, but my classmate Lothar Scholz and I thought these uniforms would make a good impression on the girls. My army-issue laced army boots were of a quality by far better than anything I had worn for many years. Those boots alone made me feel almost like a real soldier.

A town administrator organized the fifteen- and sixteen-year-old boys, I among them, into two alert teams to help unload ambulance trains scheduled to arrive daily from the Eastern Front. Later, when all but one of the town's police officers went to the front along the Oder River, some of he boys, including Lothar and I, became auxiliary police officers armed with Italian carbines. Our families had fled into the Sudeten Mountains only hours before Soviet forces of the First Ukrainian Front captured my hometown in the afternoon on February 12, 1945. On that day we unceremoniously became boy soldiers defending the Sudeten Mountain passes leading into Czechoslovakia. This was the beginning of my short three-month career in the Wehrmacht. The Soviets attempted to advance southward, but a few hastily reassembled Wehrmacht elements stopped this venture. The Sudeten Mountain range favored the defenders; this was definitely not "tank country." The tanks that the Soviets had used to their great advantage in the Polish and Silesian plains were useless on our narrow, curving, twisting mountain roads. The German MLR, the Main Line of Resistance, in fact our only line of resistance, was all along the northern edge of the foothills of the Sudeten Mountains.

Some weeks later, after the front line had further stabilized, a full-fledged division, the 100th Jäger, replaced the hastily assembled units. Lothar Scholz and I landed in a Jäger squad commanded by a corporal — I recall his name as Schwertfeger — of the 100th (Austrian-Silesian) Jäger Division. About one third of the division consisted of German-speaking Walloons from Belgium.

Corporal Schwertfeger walked slightly stooped with a limp — he favored his left leg. He barely tolerated us; it seemed for him we were a big bother. Furthermore, he had to feed us. We ate everything, and whatever was left over by the older soldiers, and still we were hungry. But the corporal needed people with local area knowledge. Thus, the last months of World War II, my classmate Lothar Scholz and I spent our time in the front line just a short distance from Jauer, our hometown, now occupied by the Soviets.[3]

Considering the turmoil of the Soviets rapidly advancing into Germany, our sector of the front was relatively quiet. We had wide minefields in no man's land, both on the Soviet and the German sides of the line. Barbed-wire obstacles covered the entire length of the front line, at least the short distance of

Frontline (from a sketchbook by Wehrmacht combat artist Hans Liska — captured by T-Sergeant Herb W. Owen of General Patton's Third Army. The original is now in the Pentagon Library).

the line we could see. There were the occasional flares fired from both sides, and the occasional artillery round that made impact on our side of the line.

To our rear were some 10 miles of a narrow country road that soon became steep, serpentine mountain road. Short on troops, this area was devoid of people, civilian or military, except for a motley group of foreign volunteers. It was a virtual no man's land patrolled by fierce-looking, heavily armed Croatians dressed in SS uniforms. They were strange men. They sported heavy black beards, rode small, tough mountain ponies, and shot, without questions, any Soviet found behind German lines. Their mules carried machineguns and ammunition boxes in packsaddles. The mules walked tethered behind the ponies. Every so often a Soviet combat patrol went undetected through our thinly manned line to raise havoc in our rear area. The Croatians usually made sure that this was the Soviets' last patrol.

Although I was in the backwaters of the great offensive that would shortly destroy the Fatherland, to a novice fifteen-year-old boy soldier, the fighting in our sector appeared furious — and terribly exciting! Only infrequently did German and Soviet patrols meet. More often than not both sides tried to avoid contact. If contact was unavoidable after a short, heavy firefight, the disadvantaged party withdrew hastily.

I had a slight mishap in late March when Sebastian Trenker, the man in front of me, stepped on a *Schuhmine*, a small, very crude, but also very effective antipersonnel mine.[4]

Three months later, while our families had found refuge in the Sudetenland — now Czechoslovakia — Germany surrendered. The local authorities urged everyone to return to their homes, and we did.

Once home in Jauer we realized that we had become strangers in our own land.

Strangers in Our Own Land

Jauer, Silesia, Germany
or Jawor, Poland
May 1945

In May of 1945 Lothar Scholz and I, along with our families, did not know that we would spend one and a half years as forced laborers in our hometown. Jauer, the idyllic place that we knew as our home, was no longer that; we had become strangers in our own land. The Soviets and the Poles had confiscated our land, grandfather's farm, our horses, our livestock, and all of our personal property — including all watches and valuables, as well as most of our clothing. We stood in total confusion in grandfather's former estate with nothing but some discarded clothing on our backs, stuff the Soviets and the Poles did not want; in an instant we had become impoverished.

In an ironic twist of fate, my entire clan became slave laborers on my grandfather's former farm, now a Soviet *Kolkhoz*[5] that raised food for the local *Kommandantura*.[6] During our three-month absence, Poles had occupied the land and had made it their own.

Life was unfair, unfair for Poles as well as for Germans. The Poles' Soviet friends had expelled them from their ancestral lands in eastern Poland and western Ukraine. In response, I suppose, the Poles did the same, eventually deporting all Germans from their ancestral lands in Silesia, Pomerania and East Prussia, and by ethnically cleansing their newly acquired land to turn it into Western Poland. Ironically, it was the largest United Nations-sanctioned ethnic cleansing operation to date. Some 12.5 million Germans, and God only knows how many Poles, were uprooted and moved from their lands.

The Poles had erased every trace of German property ownership. All the signs over the various stores, street and road signs, and any other vestige of German presence had vanished. Ridiculously, bizarrely, even the names over the stores torched by the Soviets sported freshly painted signs, all uniformly in Poland's national colors, red letters on white backgrounds — phony names that bore no relation to what had been.

Food was scarce. Our German money was worthless. I met Wolfgang Schade, another one of my high school classmates. Together, Lothar Scholz, Wolfgang, and I rummaged through empty houses and through the basements of ruins to bring home anything eatable. For more than a month potatoes were the only food found. There was a shortage of salt. In one of the abandoned stables we found a block of animal salt and, in desperation, our mothers used it as a food supplement. We also stole bags of rapeseed from the Soviet warehouse. Our mothers ground the seeds, steamed them, and extracted the oil.

The Silesia Germans lived precariously. They were virtual prisoners, unable to leave. All Germans had to wear white armbands on their left sleeves, and everyone was afraid to move about. In a curious way our clan, as Soviet slave laborers guarded by Soviet soldiers, found some protection from the arbitrary way in which the Poles treated other Germans. Our guard detachment on my grandfather's farm, now a *Kolkhoz*, consisted of one *starshina* (a senior sergeant) and four to six other ranks. Initially the guards were nervous dealing with Germans. Their famous Soviet submachine guns were always at the ready. The slightest move toward a guard caused the weapon to be aimed at the slave laborer. Everyone became terribly tense. I am sure that although they had all the guns, those young Soviets were almost as scared of us as we were of them.

However, with time the guards and we, their charges, became accustomed to each other. By necessity we shared much of the food from the farm; some guards even shared their tobacco with us. Eventually, the guards became pretty lax. They were correct in the assumption that we had nowhere to go.

In late 1945 our *starshina* ordered some of the laborers on my grandfather's former farm to get on a truck; I was one of the chosen ones. We rode the truck into the foothills and cut trees for firewood. Herr Ehrlich, one of the older men, taught us to look at a tree to determine which way it would fall when cut. Then we went to work with saws and axes. I actually enjoyed cutting down trees and became good in telling where to start the cut so that the tree would fall the correct way. Herr Ehrlich said that I had "the eye" for that. We cut the tree into lengths that we could manhandle into the truck. Even our three guards tried to help. Then we remounted the truck and drove back to the farm.

The next day we came to a different section of the woods to cut another tree. We spotted piles of already-cut timber. Herr Ehrlich thought it was timber for the Upper Silesian coal mines — the timbers were straight and cut into even length. My cousin Klaus, who spoke some Russian, suggested to our guards that it would be quicker to load this timber than cutting our own. The guards agreed. We had just completed loading when three Poles came down the road, shouting at the Soviets. One of our guards terminated the shouting match by waving his PPSh (submachine gun) at the Poles. Admittedly, we thoroughly enjoyed this confrontation. Along the way we and our guards, had become a sort of team. They were a bunch of young guys, and so were we. During one of our firewood hunting trips, one of the three guards thought the truck cab too small; he handed the PPSh to me and told me not to drop it. Thus, five or six Germans, one with a submachine gun, and three Russians cruised through the villages on our return trip to the farm.

Also in late autumn of 1945, a new guard came on duty. Ivan spoke fluent German with a pronounced Swabian dialect. Lothar Scholz thought Ivan was a Volga German.[7] Apparently, he had been assigned to this *Kolkhoz* because he was a moonshiner. Ivan came to the *Kolkhoz* just after the sugar beet harvest. He asked where he could get distilling tools to make vodka. Lothar remembered our high school physics laboratory and Ivan took us to find glass retorts, glass pipes, containers, etc. At the *Kolkhoz*, with the blessing of "higher authority," Ivan assembled the still. He then taught us how to make "good" vodka from shredded sugar beets, barley or rye, and old sourdough bread. He mixed all the ingredients with water and let it sit in an old zinc bathtub in the laundry kitchen; it had all the other necessary equipment to distill alcohol — a large built-in kettle over a stove. There Ivan let the disgusting-looking mixture ferment. Then he scooped the brown sugar and sourdough residue into grain sacks. We placed the sacks into a sugar-beet press and extracted the juices. Ivan let the juices rest overnight to allow the impurities to settle to the bottom; then he carefully poured the liquid, filtered through a rag, into the retort, and the distilling began.

Ivan's secret for making good vodka was minimal heat. He insisted the liquid had to simmer, never to boil. He was the expert; Lothar and I soon became Ivan's expert helpers. Ivan would carefully place two or three pieces of split wood on the fire. When the fire became too hot he removed one or two burning embers; he would even spray a bit of water on the fire to reduce the heat. We had the vodka still simmering day and night. Ivan slept on a cot upholstered with straw, and Lothar and I shared the "duty"; Lothar fetched wood and fed the fire for twelve hours, and I did the same thing for the other twelve. As fellow moonshiners we soon acquired many friends, mostly other guards, but also other visiting Soviet soldiers, even an officer or two. The suspicions that we would harm each other had long ago vanished. Now the guards and slave laborers had a common goal: endearing themselves to the *Kommandantura*, and vodka was their entrée. The visitors would even bring presents—cigarettes for Ivan, a loaf of bread, a hunk of sausage, a cut of cheese for us; it paid to be moonshiners.

For many months we did not know what was happening elsewhere. Germans in Silesia were in an information vacuum. After almost a year of living in ignorance of world events, my friend Wolfgang Schade—we had always thought him to be a mama's boy—stole a small radio from inside a Soviet military security compound. It all happened when our guards ordered a group of Germans, including Lothar, Wolfgang, and me, to clean a villa next to grandfather's former farm. The villa became quarters and office for a Red Army security unit. We had scrubbed, cleaned and polished all day long. The Soviets, in appreciation, had fed us a meal of noodles fried in sunflower oil. Toward late afternoon they released us. We filed out of the building, and when we were out of sight of the Soviets, Wolfgang nudged me and opened his coat jacket. There Lothar and I saw the *Volksempfänger*—the Peoples' Radio from Nazi times.

Lothar and I, almost in union, shouted, "What in hell did you do that for?"

Wolfgang gave us his usual sheepish grin when he was caught in a stupid situation. "It was there for the taking."

Lothar screamed, "You idiot! You could have gotten us killed."

Now Wolfgang became smug. "But they didn't catch me, did they?" And we all laughed. Wolfgang did not know that the radio was broken. However, he managed to repair it from various pieces of salvaged electronics.

Once in a while, when I managed to leave the confines of the *Kolkhoz*, I visited Wolfgang to listen to the radio. Our Russian guards seemed not to care; I just had to be careful not to be caught by the curfew patrol. We thought that listening to broadcasts was prohibited and listened to transmissions coming out of the other parts of Germany rather carefully—clandestinely. From snatches of broadcasts we learned of curious happenings in the western part of Germany—strange words such as "war crimes trials," "occupation zones," and "food rationing." Apparently in other parts of Germany the victors treated Germans rather benevolently—far different from the treatment dished out by the Soviets and the Poles.

After seventeen months of incredible hardship the Polish authorities posted deportation notices. They ordered all Germans to report to the railroad station. Unfortunately, that order did not include those of us in Soviet labor camps or working on the *Kolkhoz*. However, a quirk of luck made our departure possible.

My rollercoaster ride continued.

At the time the Poles deported the Germans, the *Kommandantura* moved to another town; the cows and other farm animals had already moved with the *Kommandantura*. Ivan, along with more than half of the guards, had already transferred to a new location; the other guards apparently did not care whether we stayed or left. So in the confusion our entire clan, along with Herr and Frau Ehrlich, the Scholz family, and the other slave laborers, left the *Kolkhoz*. We walked to the railroad station and climbed into the waiting cattle cars. Our luggage was light. With just a few remaining keepsakes, a shirt or dress or two, and the clothes on our backs, we climbed into cattle cars at the railroad station. When night fell the train left Jauer.

* * * * *

Darkness had cast a benevolent shroud over Jauer as the boxcars rolled slowly westward from our railroad station toward Liegnitz. Through the open door of the car we felt more than saw the all-so-familiar road that led from the back gate of Grandfather's farm into the fields, the fields he had tended so diligently for more than half a century. Only the faintest outlines of the barns, stables, and the residence were visible, but one window, the kitchen window on the second floor, was lit. Then the Thamm family's farm slowly faded forever into darkness. I shall remember this last view of my home for as long as I shall live.

The train rolled westward and then proceeded in a northerly direction. Rumor spread: The transport was going to Russia — to Siberia. As so often there was some truth to the rumor: We were indeed rolling northward, but only because the German Army had blown up the railroad bridges across the Neisse River at Görlitz. Eventually the train turned westward again and crossed the Görlitzer Neisse at Kohlfurt. There, to everyone's surprise, another train awaited us, this one guarded by British troops. After another day's journey we arrived in Detmold, a small town in the British Zone of Germany. We had lost our home and "Germany's richest and most beautiful land" forever. In retrospect, however, it was the best thing that could ever have happened to us.

LIFE IN POST–WORLD WAR II GERMANY

British Zone, West Germany 1946–1948

Continuing the fantastic rollercoaster ride, our train came into the British Zone of Occupation, in the northern part of West Germany. Many of our friends and neighbors resettled in the Soviet Zone — not exactly a haven of liberty and freedom. We arrived in Detmold under British Army escort in September or October of 1946.

Most Germans of my generation and those before me remember an old song about the ancient principality of Lippe, "Lippe-Detmold, eine wunderschöne Stadt, da 'drinnen ein Soldat." It tells of the quaint principality of Lippe-Detmold, a beautiful city that had an army consisting of a single soldier. Detmold, known far beyond her city limits as a romantic place, had received its distinction a time long before the creation of the Second German Empire in 1872, in an era when each principality had its own army.

Our reception was understandably less than lukewarm. German authorities, under British occupation edict, forcibly quartered refugees from the "Eastern Territories" in all private residences. At best it was an awkward situation for the residents as well as for the refugees. We thought, "Hell, we all lost the war, but they still had their homes and all their belongings — we lost everything. How lucky were those folks."

However, for the locals it was another matter. Here came total strangers from the east. Some thought we were Poles, because we spoke a harsh, strange, Slavic-accented German. It was an alien dialect to West German ears. Also, we came with absolutely nothing but the few clothes on our backs and thus received priority ration stamps for everything: clothing, kitchen utensils, bedding, etc. For the indigenous people it was another national emer-

The author's sketch of Saxon farmhouse.

gency, as if the German people had not already suffered enough national emergencies.

The officials loaded my mother, sister Helga, our grandmother, Preuss Oma, and me on a truck and carted us to Istrup, a small village some miles from Detmold and about two miles from Blomberg, another quaint, medieval town. In Istrup we moved into an upstairs room of an old Saxon framework farmhouse — probably into the family's best bedroom, requisitioned by British occupation edict.

The owners, "good Christian folks" that they supposedly were, had obeyed the letter of the British edict by providing a room. The edict said nothing about furnishings. The four of us walked into a completely bare room: no furniture, no rugs, no fixtures of any sort. We slept on straw. We scavenged some wooden crates to serve as our table and chairs. These conditions were particularly harsh for 80-year-old Preuss Oma, our mother's mother, who had great difficulty sitting on those low crates, and who needed our help to get down on the straw-covered floor to sleep each night. But she managed, and we survived.

We had never previously lived in such an old-fashioned wooden house. The farm had no running water. The toilet was a three-holer in the stables next to the pig sty — quite an experience when one had to go to the toilet at night. To get there from our upstairs room we walked downstairs, then through a large *Diele*, a sort of barn floor. The *Diele* served as a central entrance to all the rooms and the stables, as well as the stairs to the second floor. I had learned about such houses in history class, but never thought I would have to live in one. Under different circumstances it could have been an adventure. But for me, suffering from a bad case of dysentery, this was just one more indignity to be endured.

Slowly things normalized. But we could never become a normal family again until we were reunited with our dad, whom we knew had survived the war. It seemed almost a miracle that despite all the chaos surrounding war, Soviet occupation and preparations for deportation from our home in old Germany/new Poland, we had received a letter from Dad with an American APO postmark addressed to the family farm in Jauer. This letter had been forwarded to us at the Red Army *Kolkhoz* before we left on our journey west, probably because some German working for the now Polish Post Office knew of our family and our circumstances. We knew that Dad was alive, but we had no way of letting him know that we, too, had survived the war.

All during the war Mother and our aunts had drilled into their children the address of Mother's brother Karl, who lived in Berlin, Steglitz, Birkbuschstrasse 82a. It was understood that Karl would serve as the family's control center for communications and keeping track of everyone's whereabouts. So as soon as we got settled in Istrup, Mother wrote to both the Red Cross in Hamburg and Uncle Karl in Berlin, seeking information on Dad's location.

Dad had served in the German Army, first in the Silesian 461st Infantry Regiment in the Polish campaign, and then on the Western Front, where he was severely wounded during the breakthrough of the Maginot Line. No longer fit for infantry service, he was transferred into the Luftwaffe as a crew chief on a heavy antiaircraft artillery gun. In May 1945 he was captured by the U.S. Army in Linz, Austria. The Americans had released him shortly thereafter, after having determined that he had no record of activities with the Nazi Party. He became a civilian employee of the U.S. Army motor pool, first in Linz, and later as a houseman in Augsburg, in the most southern part of West Germany. Through the Red Cross and Uncle Karl we were able to make contact with Dad via mail, although our actual reunion would take a little longer.

Uncle Karl was proving to be a very effective missing persons bureau. Mother's other brother, our Uncle Willy, also learned of our location through Karl. Imagine his surprise to discover that his mother and sisters lived only some 40 miles away from his village of Gross-Hilligsfeld. Willy, a decorated veteran of World War I and an ardent foe of the Nazis, had served in law enforcement before, during and after World War II. He came by motorcycle to visit us in Istrup. After seeing the conditions under which we were living, he urged us to move closer to him. He promised to supply us with bread and other foodstuffs. This was an offer we could not afford to refuse.

Uncle Willy had already enabled "Aunt" Emma Raasch, a distant relative connected to Mother's family, and her daughter Irmgard, "Irmchen," to leave the Soviet Zone and resettle in his police district. Aunt Emma and Irmchen lived in a small, second-floor room of a farmhouse in Klein-Hilligsfeld. A few weeks later we moved to nearby Gross-Hilligsfeld, a village near the city of Hameln, made famous by the Pied Piper. This time we had two furnished rooms: one on the ground floor and one in the attic of a brick house situated very close to some heavily used railroad tracks. Preuss Oma slept in the ground floor room heated by a wood-burning stove, while Mother, Helga and I slept in the attic, terribly cold, but adequately furnished with two beds. I slept in one, Mother and Helga in the other. This house also had an outside toilet. My first late-evening visit to the rickety one-holer was one I'll never forget. As I went about my business, I heard and felt the rumbling of an approaching train. The beam of the train's headlight grew brighter and stronger as the train seemed to be hurtling directly toward the outhouse at a terrifying speed. I almost jumped through the closed door before I realized that I could not possibly be sitting on the tracks. The outhouse shook on its flimsy foundations as the train whooshed past. Ah, the stories that I could tell about that outhouse! But that problem paled in comparison to the other problems we encountered in trying to resume a normal life in West Germany.

We refugees had difficulty blending into the new life. All the natives had "connections." They could obtain extra potatoes, bread, or firewood from friends. Despite Uncle Willy's help, we had to supplement our food ration with mushrooms collected in the forest north of Gross-Hilligsfeld. A shortage of coal and firewood forced us to roam farther into the forests, where we hunted dead tree branches. It was against the law to cut live branches from trees. To enforce this law, the county had appointed a forest warden who would confiscate any cutting tool used in violation of this law. The local warden was a little old man who seemed to enjoy exercising his authority to the fullest extent. The fear of losing our only cutting tools made us scour the forest floor, picking up any branch or twig that might be used to fire a stove. By late 1946 Germany's woods were about as clean of debris as any well-maintained park.

My high school education had been interrupted by war and imprisonment. I had left school in Jauer at the age of fourteen in late 1944. Now in 1946 at the age of 16, I returned to school, joining my cousin Joachim, Uncle Willy's son, at Hameln High School. Each morning Joachim and I walked two miles on a country road to the nearest railroad station where we boarded the train to Hameln. Most afternoons we walked the entire way home, because the evening train left Hameln so late in the afternoon.

Each afternoon, following my return from classes, Mother, Helga and I walked into the forest hoping to collect at least enough wood to cook the evening meal and next morning's breakfast. Aunt Emma and Irmchen often joined us.

Uncle Willy had presented us with an axe that I carried hidden under my coat. I used this instrument only occasionally to cut branches that had fallen to the ground to make carrying them easier. One afternoon I spotted a large dry branch still attached to a tree. It was simply too good to be left for someone else. I climbed that tree and whacked away until the branch crashed to the ground. Mother and Helga were overjoyed. Suddenly the forest warden burst upon the scene and began to scold Mother. He apparently had not noticed that I was still in the tree. I quickly clambered down the tree to join in our defense. Spotting the axe in hand, the warden demanded that I hand it over. I replied with the German equivalent of "over my dead body" as I advanced toward him. Truth be told, I only wanted to convince the warden that the branch in question was dry and would have eventually fallen to the ground, but the little old man saw this six-foot long-haired wild man with an axe walking toward him and took off in a flash. We laughed that evening when Uncle Willy, who knew our story, informed us that he was investigating a murderous, long-haired wild man who had threatened to kill the forest warden. I thought it wise to have my hair trimmed to a short military version, because my friends told me that word of a "long-haired wild man with the axe" had already made the rounds among the refugees.

As winter approached, I was forced to supplement our firewood supply via more creative and daring "firewood acquisition." As our supplies dwindled and the woods were swept clean, I found myself venturing along the dark roads, where I "found" logs, railings, loose boards, anything that burned. Since I had become an expert in night actions as a boy soldier on the Eastern Front, no one ever caught me in the act of "firewood acquisition." But some people seemed to have their suspicions. With a twinkle in their eyes the old couple who owned the house we lived in remarked that the small bridges local farmers had built across drainage ditches to reach their fields were mysteriously disappearing. Being day-laborers, they also were "outsiders"; they never mentioned my nightly scavenger trips to anyone else.

Firewood was not the only necessity in short supply. There also was a severe shortage of margarine in postwar Germany. We heard that for several pounds of beechnuts collected in the forests around our village we could receive ration stamps for one pound of margarine. Harvest time for beechnuts was in late fall. Mother, Helga, and I, along with Aunt Emma and Irmchen, now ventured into the forest to collect beechnuts, in addition to mushrooms and wood. Eight-year-old Helga was the premier beechnut collector, much to my chagrin. Everyone accused me of falling down on the job, definitely a slight to my teenage ego. Only much later did I learn the reason for my poor performance: I was partially colorblind and could not differentiate between the various shades of brown on the forest floor.

Christmas 1946 was a joyous one. A few days before the holidays, Dad arrived. As Helga rushed toward him he dropped a few small parcels on the floor and then lifted Helga with one of his powerful arms and embraced Mother with the other. I stood almost in embarrassed wonderment not quite knowing if a man-boy should hug his father like in the olden days, or just shake hands.

During all this euphoria Preuss Oma had busied herself lighting the fire in the stove to boil tea water. After what seemed an eternity Dad released Helga and Mother. He turned toward me. I did not quite know how to handle this reunion, but Dad grabbed me and embraced me. With that it seemed as if two years of depravation, of slave labor, of threats to life and limb had been washed away by a huge flood. It was as if no time had passed between Christmas of 1944, when I had last hugged Dad, and this wonderful day before Christmas of 1946. Time had vanished. All the troubles of the last two years forgotten. All was well again. Once again, we were one family.

Just then Dad seemed to become aware that Preuss Oma was fussing with tea the hot water kettle, poring water over peppermint leaves. He walked over to her and, just as in the olden days, they formally shook hands. Finally, Dad started to unwrap his parcels. He presented Preuss Oma with a can of American coffee and a small tin of powdered tea. He gave Mother a woolen scarf, Helga received a small teddy bear, and I received a U.S. Army khaki shirt. I had not seen such a high quality shirt, ever. I promised to wear it every day — unless, I quickly added, it was in the laundry tub.

As we finally settled down, Preuss Oma started to pour peppermint tea. For what seemed like an eternity all was quiet, then everyone started talking at once. There was so much to tell: Father's last days of the war, his time as an American POW, and his current life as an employee of the U.S. Army in a Augsburg ... and more. We told him of our time during the last three months of the war and what Jauer looked like on our return, the *Vorwerkgut*, the loss of all we owned. I told him how gut-wrenching it was to see our horses led away never to be seen again, and then our almost miraculous journey from Silesia to the British Zone. Talk went on until the late hours.

Helga had already fallen asleep. Mother suggested that I sleep in the warm kitchen because there was just so little room in the sleeping attic. I arranged some pillows and blankets near the stove — this would be the first time in a long time that I would be sleeping in a heated room. Dad carried Helga as he and Mother climbed the stairs to their sleeping quarters.

Whether it was designed to coincided with Christmas or not, our season was made even more joyous when we were given an allocation for firewood. The authorities designated one big maple tree as our tree, meaning that instead of having to wait for dead branches, we could harvest a living tree. There would be enough wood to last a whole year. All of us, except Preuss Oma, went into the forest to cut our assigned tree. Mother told Dad how Herr Ehrlich had proclaimed my tree-felling talent. She convinced Dad that I "had the eye"; he let me survey the tree and decide the best way to cut to ensure that it fell in the proper direction.

For a small fee a farmer carted the logs to our lodgings. There Dad and I cut and chopped enough firewood to last several months, with logs left over for the rest of the year.

Shortly after New Year's Dad returned to Augsburg with the promise that he would attempt to get permission — and an apartment — for us to join him. We knew it would take time, but just the thought of living together as a family made was enough to lighten our hearts.

Shortly thereafter, thanks again to Uncle Willy, we moved to larger, better rooms at a farm in the middle of the village. Mother, Helga, and I now slept in a relatively warm room on the ground floor, while Preuss Oma lived in the large second floor room that also served as our living room and kitchen. Alas, the toilet again was located in the pig sty. But by now we were becoming accustomed to the primitive amenities. And again, the pigs grunted when someone disturbed their siesta.

In the meantime, Irmchen and I had become partners in the daily quest for beechnuts. I was sixteen going on seventeen and Irmchen was in her early twenties. We enjoyed each other's company. In the late afternoon, after we had turned over our stash of beechnuts to our mothers, who traded them in for margarine ration stamps, we joined my cousin Joachim — Uncle Willy's son — to play board games in our upstairs kitchen. Joachim never had to collect beechnuts because his father received little presents from farmers, a loaf of bread here, a chunk of ham there, or a bag of potatoes, while on patrol through the neighboring villages.

Late in the evening, when we tired of our games, I escorted Irmchen to her home in Klein-Hilligsfeld, a short walk through the fields from our village. In those days it was thought unwise for females to walk alone on dark country roads. We played tag, running until we tired; we hugged and kissed — playfully. It was a great game. Somewhere along the way we discovered a mutual need — we kissed and caressed each other. We fell in love. It was at best awkward and terribly secretive. We knew that it could not last, since my parents, especially my father, were planning for me to return to America. Outwardly Irmchen and I pretended to be just good friends, but we in truth enjoyed a special relationship during a tumultuous time in our lives. No one had ever discovered our nocturnal adventures.

My love life was progressing more smoothly than my school days. I had a ghastly time at high school and did not last very long. In an argument over who had talked in class — I had not — the teacher threatened to slap me. I told him if he touched me I would blow out his lights. I was called to the principal's office. There, three stern men, one my teacher, stared at me. The principal asked if I had threatened the teacher. I admitted I had, but said that I had not talked in class.

"Sir," I said very respectfully, "I told my teacher that I was not the talker, but he hauled off to hit me anyway."

"Begging your pardon, sir," I continued, "before I came to West Germany I had spent three months as a boy soldier on the Eastern Front and sixteen months as a Red Army slave laborer. After all the mistreatment I received from the Commies I promised myself never to get beaten again. And, sir, with all due respect, the teacher's threats triggered my reaction."

But I was nevertheless duly expelled.

Black Market Days

Augsburg, American Zone, West Germany
1947

Following my expulsion from school, my parents began to worry about my future. It was fairly obvious that I could never return to being a carefree German schoolboy. Yet I also realized that I needed to do some growing up. Together, we decided that the best course of action was for me to move to Augsburg and live with Dad. Thus, in early summer of 1947 I moved to Augsburg. The move took some pressure off of feeding the rest of the family, while I could provide Dad with a companion to share his solitary life. Alas, there was only one bed, and we shared it.

Today this is difficult to accept, but life in post–World War II Germany was most difficult. Most Germans just sort of hunkered down and waited. For city dwellers and the refugees from the eastern territories, it was especially difficult to get enough food to still their hunger. Those who had lived in western German cities, and did not have their houses or apartments bombed, traveled into the countryside with items to trade: carpets, silver cutlery, fur coats, family jewelry, etc. Farmers, the producers of food, became wealthy beyond their dreams. They filled their houses with luxuries, with paintings, covered their bare wooden floors with expensive Persian rugs, and dressed their wives in furs and silks.

The under-the-table economy flourished, aided by the inexpensive postal mailing fees and rail travel. For a package of American cigarettes I could travel back and forth across Germany — but passenger and freight trains were loaded to capacity: standing room only. I rode just short of 20 hours on a journey of 400 miles all the way from Hanover in northern Germany to Augsburg in Germany's south.

However, there were no overnight accommodations to be had along the way. The occupation forces had taken over most hotels. Refugees, and those who had lost their homes during six years of Allied bombing raids, crammed into those facilities not used by the occupation forces. Even with ration coupons much food was unavailable, and basic commodities such as bread, flour, sugar, or margarine were available only in limited quantities. In postwar Germany it was impossible to go into a restaurant to buy a cup of coffee or a bowl of soup. Each person received coupons for one pair of shoes per year — shoes of rather poor quality; even shoelaces were rationed and difficult to get. The lucky ones found good string to tie their shoes.

German bureaucracy complicated travel. One had to document a "need to travel"; it involved registration at the local police office, obtaining permission to exchange your local food stamps for "travel food stamps," and registration at the police office of your destination — not much of a change from the old Nazi population-control days.

When Dad had arrived in Detroit in 1926, he began a lifelong love affair with America. He admired America and Americans. He had worked as a nickel polisher for the Ford Motor Corporation in Dearborn, Michigan, and often told me that the difference between working for a German and an American boss was like being in hell or in heaven. Even during the war he spoke lovingly of America; his comrades in the Luftwaffe often cautioned him to be careful about voicing that admiration, yet frequently asked him to describe life in America.

Now he urged me to contact the U.S. Consulate about the "Return of U.S. Citizens" program. Shortly after my arrival in Augsburg I contacted the U.S. Consulate in Munich about the program. Augsburg was a mere hour's train ride from Munich. Over a period of six months I had several meeting at the U.S. Consulate in Munich. I had to provide my birth certificate and letters from my American sponsor — Harold Kuehnel, a family friend. I had to certify that I was able to pay the fare from Bremerhaven to New York and deal with the many other details associated with travel to the United States.

Dad quickly found me a job as an employee at the U.S. Army Commissary, where I worked in the warehouse loading and unloading crates of food — wonderful food. The sergeant, supervising me and two elderly Germans, permitted us to eat anything from damaged cans. As a skinny runt, six feet tall, weighing about 95 pounds, I was always hungry. I soon found that condensed milk cans were easily "damaged" and I drank the milk straight from the can. I also ate string beans and other canned vegetables straight from the can. I truly believed I had found paradise.

Unfortunately, living in paradise made me careless. I should have known better, but on the Friday before Easter 1947 I decided to surprise Dad with a little present. Just before closing, I pocketed a small, 2.5-ounce can of instant coffee. We warehouse workers had never been searched before, but this Friday before Easter the Military Police searched all employees leaving the quartermaster depot. When the MPs met us as we dismounted from our truck, I knew immediately that I was in big trouble. To my complete embarrassment, and that of our sergeant, the MPs found the coffee. They arrested me and locked me up in a military jail to await trial. I found myself in an overcrowded cell along with blackmarketeers and one war criminal. The blackmarketeers told me not to be concerned, that this sort of thing happened all the time, and that there was not enough space in jail to house everyone. But the war criminal was not at all reassuring. Next morning after a sleepless night filled with dark thoughts about my possible fate, I stood at attention before a military judge. I pleaded guilty and expressed my sorrow. Sentencing took about 30 seconds. I did not quite understand what my sentence was, but one of the German court employees told me it was "fourteen days suspended."

I made my way home to my worried dad. This was my worst Easter holiday — ever. Worse yet, I was now unemployed.

An opportunity presented itself unexpectedly when I read in one of Irmchen's letters about a severe sanitary napkin shortage. When a local pharmacist told me that sanitary napkins could be provided in exchange for paper, any kind of paper, I hit upon an idea to make my fortune in the German economy. I knew that Dad cleaned out the day rooms in the U.S. Army garrison as part of his houseman duties. He agreed to save all the newspapers and magazines that the soldiers threw in the trash. Dad brought me heaps of papers and magazines for my new business. But as a person who had always loved to read, I couldn't get down to the business of sanitary napkins until I first read through all the interesting and exotic magazines and comic books; I devoured them. I studied wonderful advertisements in *Life* magazine that encouraged young Americans to join the National Guard. I wondered if maybe, just maybe, I could join the National Guard when I got to America.

But in the meantime there was the sanitary napkin business. I had already secured an exchange agreement with the pharmacist and carried some forty to fifty pounds of paper to his store. In return I received a large carton of sanitary napkins. These I shipped to Irmchen, who in turn traded them for other difficult-to-obtain items, like food ration stamps, some of which she then mailed to me. I mailed most of them to Mother, saving some to supplement our rations in Augsburg. Now Dad and I could eat an extra meal whenever we wanted — a true luxury.

Shipping parcels via the German postal system was inexpensive. For the price of an American cigarette I could send a large carton of sanitary napkins to northern Germany and still have change left over.

There was a high demand for American cigarettes; this would be my other economic enterprise. Almost weekly, Dad received a pack of Camels from one of the GIs for extra services, such as spit-shining shoes and boots, polishing brass belt buckles and insignia. Dad never opened these packs — he smoked hand-rolled cigarettes from butts soldiers left in the day room's ashtrays. Most evenings Dad brought half-smoked cigarettes to our room. We peeled off the paper, place the tobacco into a bowl, mixed the tobacco a little, and then rolled new cigarettes with a small "cigarette-maker" tool. Dad's friends enjoyed the occasional smokes; they in turn gave us other, difficult items. Bartering in postwar Germany had become an institution.

One of Dad's friends was a big-time blackmarketeer. He became my middleman in the American cigarette circuit. Thus, between sanitary napkins and black market cigarettes, our economy flourished. After several months of trading and bartering I had accumulated so many German D-marks I did not know what to do with them. During a visit to Gross-Hilligsfeld to personally deliver to Mother some American foodstuffs I had bought on the black market, my cousin Joachim suggested what today one would call "money laundering."

He advised, "Why don't you buy German commemorative postal stamps? They never lose their value." I thought this to be sage advice, and the following day Joachim and I traveled to nearby Hameln where I bought some two thousand D-marks' worth of stamps. I have always wondered why the shop owner went along with this transaction masterminded by what looked like a couple of kids with way too much cash on them.

Although my private enterprise thrived, I soon had to retire from it; the time had arrived for my next adventure — moving to America.

America at Last

Bremerhaven, American Sector, West Germany
Port of Embarkation
February 1948

For some months Dad had been in touch with Harold Kuehnel, the son of old friends in Detroit. The Kuehnels had an old-time affiliation with our family in Jauer — Harold's grandfather, one of my grandfather's neighbors, had emigrated to America at the turn of the century. During the late 1920s and early 1930s Dad and Mother were neighbors of the elder Kuehnels. Harold Kuehnel remembered my parents from his boyhood days, and Dad asked him if they would sponsor me since I was a teenager. Harold and his wife Ann kindly agreed. The Kuehnel family lived at 5742 Lonyo Street, Detroit, Michigan.

Dad and I returned to Gross-Hilligsfeld to celebrate Christmas 1947. Shortly before Christmas I received the most precious Christmas present ever. I received word that I was to leave Germany for America in February 1948. Dad was overjoyed, but he returned to Augsburg while I remained in Gross-Hilligsfeld.

Irmchen and I enjoyed a few weeks of total happiness; then it suddenly became time for my departure. We thought we would never see each other again.

There was little packing to do, as I had only one small suitcase. Mother and I left for Bremen in early February for processing at a camp at Bremen-Fegesack. We overnighted with one of Mother's distant Preuss relatives in Bremen-Fegesack. The next day Mother and I went to the processing center. We hugged a last goodbye, not knowing when we would ever see each other again. I was ambivalent, an eerie feeling of wanting to be in two places at the same time. I wanted to stay where I knew everyone. I was uncertain what the future would bring, yet we all thought that life in the United States of America would be better than anything we could expect in postwar Germany. I am sure Dad had hoped that eventually the family would again be united in the wonderful America he had never wanted to leave.

On 10 February 1948 I boarded the United States Lines' SS *Marine Tiger*,[8] formerly a military transport, now filled to capacity with orphaned Jewish children and a few "returning U.S. citizens." Notes from my diary, February 1948:

S/S Marine Tiger, February 10, 1948.
We departed from the Bremerhaven Columbus pier at 1500 hours. SS Marine Tiger is a not exactly large steam ship. I do not know the exact tonnage. We have to get used to the ship and run up and downstairs until we drop in our bunks in the evening.

S/S Maine Tiger, February 11, 1948.
We are in the North Sea, light wind and light sea. The passengers of the various organizations receive $1.00 to $10.00, only the U.S. citizens get no money. 1500 hours, we are passing through the English Channel under the coast of Dover. We can see a bunch of sunken ships. We pass a fishing fleet — among others, the Concordia out of Copenhagen. At night, at 2400 hours, we set back the clocks by one hour.

S/S Marine Tiger, February 12, 1948.
We are in the Bay of Biscay and encountered heavy seas. Most are seasick; it has caught me a little. I ate, but had to lie down right afterwards. By the way, today is Irmchen's birthday. We had a ship's drill at 1500 hours, all had to assemble at the lifeboat with life jackets. The stewards, the waiters, the kitchen personnel, and the sailors, men, women, and children, everyone is running around with life jackets.

S/S Marine Tiger, February 13, 1948.
I am still a little seasick, but I have not yet thrown up.

(End of notes)

I arrived in New York on a cold February 21, 1948. New York City was wintry and dreary, but a kind lady from Traveler's Aide made me feel at home. She had arranged for me to stay in one of those inexpensive hotels near the waterfront. I also received a few dollars to buy breakfast at a local hole-in-the-wall eatery. I remember sitting at the counter wondering how to order food. I noticed the man next to me having "eggs sunny side up," and I indicated to the cook that I would like the same. Actually, I preferred eggs over light, but it was the first time in more than three years I had seen fried eggs, along with two slices of crisp bacon — a first for me, and beautifully toasted white bread — another first. I sat on the stool at the counter in amazement. Then I devoured it all — "eggs sunny side up," slices of crisp bacon, beautifully toasted white bread, and an unlimited supply of butter and marmalade. I ate so fast, to those watching it must have appeared that I was afraid someone would take it away.

The next morning another customer ordered "eggs over light," and I ordered my eggs that way. The day following my "eggs over light" lesson, the Traveler's Aide lady told me that she had reached my sponsor, the Harold Kuehnel family, in Detroit, and that I would be leaving the next morning.

* * * * *

Ever since I had boarded the *Marine Tiger* in Bremerhaven I felt as if I was in some kind of fog. I knew what was happening, but I just seemed to glide along the path on autopilot. Even on the train to Detroit — I cannot remember boarding or exiting the train — it seemed strange. I could barely grasp what people around me were saying. I do remember arriving in Detroit, walking into the cavernous train depot hall, and somehow, I do not know how, Ann Kuehnel spotted me and escorted me to her car. I have vague memories of arriving at the Kuehnels' residence, a fine brick house.

Luggage tag for SS *Marine Tiger*.

They had a young son. In the evening I met Harold Kuehnel, a big bear of a man with large hands, a kindly man, a working man. He owned a lucrative gas station in Dearborn near the entrance to the Ford factory.

* * * * *

The Kuehnels took me into their home on 5742 Lonyo Street. I am sure they did not know what to expect; nor did I, but they were ever so kind to give me time to recover, to get over the culture shock. For me, Harold and Ann Kuehnel represented America, the most wonderful country on this earth.

Coming from a Europe in ruins to America was a thrilling, even shocking experience. Whereas in Germany everything was rationed, including food, clothing, shoes, and fuel, Americans had everything — food clothing, automobiles, everything. Americans could even travel anywhere without police permission.

What a great country!

Coming to America was akin to going to heaven. I ate as I had never eaten before. The Kuehnels were simply wonderful; they let me eat all the

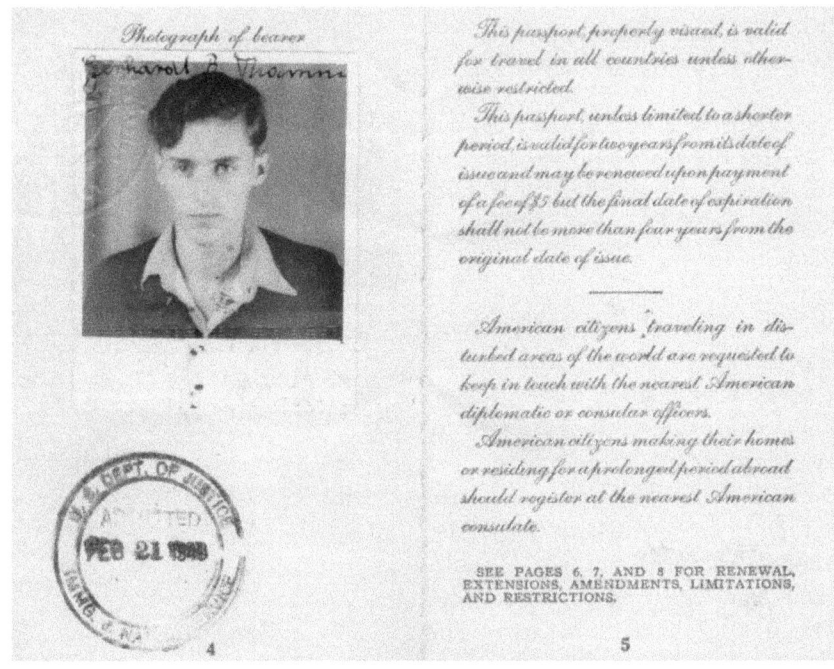

Author's passport photograph, 1948.

bananas and all the other wonderful foodstuffs that I had not seen for many years, if ever — I remember eating "tons" of bananas. I spent the first three weeks with the Kuehnels. They introduced me to several of Dad's old friends from the 1920s, and I quickly became acclimatized to this great country called America.

I met Billy Cunningham, one of my parents' neighbors in Detroit, who, as a young boy, had baby-sat me. He picked me up one morning in a red Ford convertible. Despite the cold February weather he drove with the top down. Billy parked his car in a no-parking zone on Michigan Avenue and took me shopping. He bought me a pair of shoes, socks, underwear, a couple of shirts and a warm zippered jacket. Although he was an Irishman, Billy spoke some German. As we returned to the convertible a police officer passed and greeted Billy. They shook hands and Billy introduced me.

Strange, I thought, *that he did not ticket Billy's car.* But this was Detroit, and Billy was a well-known personality.

That afternoon I met two of Billy's aunts — also friends of my parents. I told them of Billy's kindness. The chuckled, "Oh, Billy, he is our boy. A good boy. Always helping others."

Back at the Kuehnels' home that evening I mentioned that the policeman did not ticket Billy's car. Harold said, "I grew up with Billy, but we went different ways."

I did not quite understand this and asked what Harold meant, but Ann interrupted, "Billy is a gangster." Harold just lifted his arms in apparent resignation. I thought, *Billy is the kindest, nicest gangster I have ever met.* Of course, Billy was also the first and only gangster I had ever met — at least knowingly.

Although I appreciated the Kuehnels' kindness, I did not want to be a burden. I remembered the advertisements in *Life* magazine that Dad had brought home from the army garrison and the pictures of happy National Guard soldiers, the call for enlistment. But as I recalled the bitter cold of days spent in foxholes on the Eastern Front, I changed my mind. The navy would be the life for me. So on the 15th of March 1948, Ann Kuehnel dropped me off at the recruiting station in Dearborn, Michigan. There I found the navy recruiting line. It was long, but I had time, so I waited. As I stood with others, a navy petty officer parted our line. He said something I did not understand. Since most of the men moved across the room, I moved with them.

As I discovered later, the navy recruiter had filled his quota for the day. Since I spoke and understood precious little English, I did not realize that I had moved into the army recruiting line. Thus, once again, I unwittingly became a soldier. Instead of sailing the seven seas in a fast frigate, I was destined once again to dig foxholes.

You're in the Army Now...

3rd Armored Division
Fort Knox, Kentucky
Early to Mid-1948

The army must have been in dire need of recruits, because I qualified when I passed the IQ test by spelling the word "country." Lucky for me, it was one of the very few words I could spell; I barely spoke any English at all. After a very preliminary physical examination and a brief recording of personal data, an officer swore us in and we became soldiers of the United States Army. Late in the afternoon we boarded an overnight Pullman train to somewhere; I did not know the destination, nor did I much care.

My rollercoaster ride continued with the most wonderful train ride I have ever made: imagine, I slept in a Pullman sleeper. What a marvelous change from having ridden in German trains packed to capacity, standing all the way from Hanover in northern Germany to Augsburg in southern Germany.

Our destination turned out to be Louisville, Kentucky. There we boarded buses for Fort Knox. In 1948 Fort Knox was the home of the 3rd Armored Division; it was the 5th U.S. Army Basic Training Center. I received my basic training with the 54th Armored Field Artillery Battalion.

Although I spoke little English, I found soldiering easy. While everyone complained about the food, I found army food good and plentiful. I think the mess sergeant liked me because I ate everything he produced without ever complaining. I obeyed drill commands by watching those around me. If they turned right, I turned right; if they marched or halted, I marched or halted, and if the man next to me made a wrong move, I made a wrong move. My English improved steadily, and after a few weeks I understood most of the commands. One day, already well in advance of the training cycle, we received orders to disassemble the M-1 rifle. I must have gotten ahead of the instructor. He came to my table and shouted, "God damn it, soldier, by the numbers! I said by the goddamned numbers!" He looked at what I had done, and then said something like, "Okay, wise guy, now put it back together." I understood from his motion that I was to reassemble the M-1, which I did — rather quickly.

He looked at me in puzzlement, shook his head, and returned to the podium. From then on he watched me closely, and I was very careful never again to be too eager — from then on I did everything "by the goddamned numbers."

On long marches and on the rifle range I excelled; my three months on the Eastern Front were finally beginning to pay off. I had a friend named Rice, a giant of a man, but totally unaccustomed to the physical demands of a rifleman. Returning from one of our night exercises he stag-

Private Gerhardt B. Thamm, Battery B, 54th Armored Field Artillery Battalion, 3rd Armored Division, Fort Knox, Kentucky, 1948.

gered along — I was afraid he would collapse. I grabbed his rifle and his field pack and carried them back to camp. We became the best of friends, and because his friends had observed my attempt to help him, I became a member of a group in the first platoon that ate together, went to the movies together, and went to the snack bar together. Being a member of a group made army life particularly pleasant for me; I may have talked "funny" but suddenly I was no longer an outsider.

The final check before graduation from basic training was on the rifle range, firing on moving targets. Of course we recruits were unaware that our division's commanding general was visiting the company to observe our target practice. I had so much fun firing and knocking down targets as fast as I could that I was unaware of a gaggle of men behind my foxhole until I heard someone say, "Good shooting, soldier." I looked around and saw my company commander, my platoon sergeant, and another officer with stars on his lapels. All the others, aside from the man with the stars, stood in frozen attention. I thought, *Maybe I had better do what the others are doing.* I flipped on the safety of my M-1 rifle, placed it on the sandbag pointing downrange as taught, rose and came to attention. For good marksmanship, I became a Pfc., a private first class, one of two or three in the battery promoted during basic training. The instructor sergeant, the one who had previously chastised me for not going "by the goddamned numbers," now proudly pinned the stripe on my sleeves — with a paper stapler. The rest of the troops had to wait until the end of boot camp before they made private first class. Being a recruit Pfc. did indeed have some benefits. If I recall correctly, a Pfc. did not have to "pull KP" — kitchen police, in other words peel potatoes, scrub the mess hall, clean the kitchen, and wash the food trays. Soon, too soon for me, basic training ended and the trainees transferred to other duties.

During the latter part of basic training there had been a call for volunteers to become paratroopers with the 82nd Airborne Division at Fort Bragg, North Carolina. I volunteered. The $50 parachute pay greatly influenced this decision. Those selected had to pass rigorous physical tests — no mental tests required for jumping from airplanes. From our battery, only nine trainees made the grade; I was one of them. At basic training graduation parade we received our orders. Eight of the 82nd AB volunteers went to Fort Bragg. To my extreme disappointment I did not.

I received orders to report to "So. Post Ft. Myer, Va. for duty with GMDS, The Pentagon, Washington, DC."

I had absolutely no idea what this meant, or where it was. I had never heard of So. Post Ft. Myer, or GMDS, or the Pentagon.

* * * * *

After a long, pleasant train ride through America's heartland, I arrived at Washington, DC's, Union Station. The military police — in those days the army had a permanent MP station at Union Station — arranged for a sedan to deliver me to South Post Fort Myer, Arlington 8, Virginia. Imagine if you will, I, the poor kid who just a few months ago had ridden in a German train packed like a sardine, now rode in a chauffeur-driven sedan through the capital city of the United States of America: totally unbelievable. This was one hell of a ride, and I was still on the rollercoaster, still holding on for dear life — not knowing where or when the rollercoaster would stop.

It was one of those gorgeous early summer days. Washington, DC, bathed in brilliant sunlight, looked absolutely beautiful. We drove through the city I would learn to love, the city that would become my hometown. We crossed a great river into the Virginia countryside. Finally the driver stopped before a typical old, one-story, wooden army barracks; it was the Orderly Room of Headquarters Company, United States Army. A few days later my first sergeant ordered me to report to GMDS at the Mall Entrance of the Pentagon; a sergeant would escort me from there to my duty station. It was another one of those beautiful days in the middle of June. Dressed in a heavily starched and well-pressed khaki uniform, my brass shined, wearing spit-shined low quarter shoes, I walked through the tunnel that led, under a Virginia highway, to the Pentagon. The Pentagon, the largest building I had ever seen, sat in grounds beautifully landscaped with lush bushes and manicured flowerbeds. I walked through the huge brass doors of the Mall Entrance and came into a reception area richly decorated in dark wood. There Staff Sergeant Walter Wende awaited me. To my utter surprise he greeted me in fluent German.

He laughed, "Wait till you get to the office." We walked along a wide corridor toward the center ring. I glanced in wonderment at both sides of the corridor; they were decorated with large oil paintings of battle scenes and what I assumed to be famous generals and War Department civilians.

As we passed from one corridor to the next, Sergeant Wende explained the layout of the building. "You will hear a lot of jokes about how complicated it is navigating this building. All bullshit. They even have a Pentagon indoctrination film with a mailman trying to deliver a letter. He comes in a young man, walks all over the place and finally delivers the letter as an old man with a white beard. All bullshit."

He laughed, "In the first place no mailman gets into the building; a truck delivers the mail to the military mailroom. There it is sorted and government employees carry the mail to the various offices. But you will find it pretty easy to get around once you get to know the system."

He explained that the center ring was called A-Ring, and the concentric rings outside A-Ring were called B, C, D and E-Ring. He said, "E-Ring is the most prestigious one. That's where all the big shots have their offices with windows overlooking Virginia or Washington."

We arrived at A-Ring, and through large, almost floor-to-ceiling windows I saw a five-cornered park with a gazebo in its center. Onward we walked to the tenth corridor. There we made a slight left turn and entered staircase #10. Walking down two flights of stairs we arrived on the Mezzanine floor. At room MB-1026, Sergeant Wende stopped at a steel vault door guarded by a military policeman. He told the MP on duty that I was a new member of the group and that he would get me documented immediately.

The MP asked for my name and serial number. I answered, "Pfc. Gerhardt B. Thamm," and gave him my Regular Army serial number. He entered the information on his clipboard. Then we walked into an office where Sergeant Wende introduced me to Sergeant Major Ignaz "Iggy" Ernst and to Mr. Brower, a civilian, the boss of GMDS, the German Military Document Section. The sergeant major was a jovial giant of a man from Westphalia. He crushed my hand and welcomed me to his unit, again in fluent German. To me the entire scene was surreal. Here I was, in the center of the United States War Department, and everyone conversed in German. Sergeant Major Ignaz Ernst introduced me to everyone. There were some twenty men in the office and nineteen spoke fluent German. Aside from the old-timers, the World War II veterans, there was one recently arrived soldier, Walter Szopiak, who spoke German, Polish, Ukrainian, and Russian. Only one, Mike Halyshin, a cheerful master sergeant, did not speak German; his language specialties were Russian, Polish and Ukrainian. Sergeant Wende had me properly documented with a photo identification badge — a rarity in those days; only the very few had a military photo identification.

The sergeant major (his friends called him "Big Iggy") assigned me to work with Sergeant Alois Himsl. Sergeant Himsl was a fourth- or fifth-generation American from Minnesota whose family had come from Austria to America during the 1880s. He spoke German with the soft inflection of the Austrians. From him I learned that we would be exploiting German military and Nazi Party documents captured at the end of World War II.

Pentagon ID card

According to Sergeant Himsl, shortly after VE Day,[9] a crafty U.S. Army G2 had lifted some 19 linear miles of German records stored at the Potsdam Archives and had shipped all of it to the United States; the Soviets complained because he had done this "nefarious" act right under the eyes of Soviet occupation forces.

Some of these records were now stored in Room MB 1026 of the Pentagon; the rest was still in wooden crates in a warehouse at Cameron Station in the outskirts of Alexandria, Virginia. German-speaking members of the U.S. Army exploited these records for military intelligence information on the Eastern European territories; they were a gold mine.

Now I knew why we had soldiers who could speak, read, and write German in the Mezzanine basement of the Pentagon. Expertise in the language was the prerequisite for the GMDS assignment. Master Sergeant Halyshin belonged to this unit because the Germans had captured a multitude of Soviet Army records; we had most of the German intelligence files at our warehouse.

The Army needed soldiers, expert linguists, people who could recognize valuable information and could separate the treasure from the trash. The men in the Mezzanine trained me to know what the U.S. Army thought to be important. A few days later Sergeant Himsl told me to bring a set of fatigue uniforms and a pair of service shoes — a cross between low quarter dress shoes and combat boots — during the next few days.

"In a couple of days," Sergeant Himsl informed me, "we'll go out there, to Cameron Station, where most of the documents are. We keep a set of fatigue uniforms here in the office because the warehouse is a work place, rough and dirty."

A few days later a small truck from the Pentagon motor pool brought Sergeant Himsl and a crew of four to the warehouse at Cameron Station. I stood in amazement inside the cavernous repository. There were rows upon rows of wooden crates stacked on wooden pallets, five and six high. Sergeant Himsl asked whether I knew how to drive a tractor or a forklift.

"The only motor vehicle I have ever driven was a tank," I replied.

"That's good enough. I'll teach you how to drive one of these little things. You'll love it." After I had demonstrated to the motor pool sergeant's satisfaction that I could drive one of "these little things," he issued me a military driver's license. For weeks thereafter I used the forklift to pull heavy wooden crates filled with all sorts of papers from the stacks. Sergeant Himsl broke open the crates and he and his helpers sorted through piles of every conceivable thing that our troops had loaded into these wooden boxes. We could tell that they had hurriedly shoveled these documents into the boxes with pitchforks — we saw dirty pitchforks marks on the folders. They had hurried to get them away before the Soviets realized that a vast source of information sat in the Potsdam Archives just waiting to be explored. It was now our task to unload the crates and find the index files for all documents.

We found everything, files deposited by many German agencies and departments. We found all of the German Army officer personnel files, combat situation reports, combat capability assessments, intelligence files on all the "Eastern Territories," including enemy combat assessments of troops and equipment, and geographic/demographic studies of the Soviet Union.

We found battle plans, combat intelligence reports from the Eastern Front, and clandestine reports from *Fremde Heere Ost*[10] — General Gehlen's intelligence specialists deep inside Russia. We had thousands of military situation maps from every German front: East, West, North, South, Africa, the Mediterranean, and southeast Europe. We had three maps of the *Oberkommando der Wehrmacht's*[11] morning, mid-day, and evening reports of the military situation for every day of the war, and for every front. We also had specialty maps for the Mediterranean Theater of Operation and for

Crete, Yugoslavia, Norway and Normandy, etc.—as I said, a treasure chest.

We found hundreds of ingenious little booklets in the MilGeo Collection, the military geography collection. All were uniformly reddish purple and of a size that would fit into the breast pocket of a German Army tunic, designed for company-level officers. There were booklets for every city, town and village in Poland and Russia (up to the Ural mountains) containing a description of the location, a little map of the fastest route through town, all important features, the number of horses and troops that could be quartered in the town, all-important military intelligence information, bridges, river crossings, militarily important geographic features, and more.

We discovered a pile of engineering maps of the Trans-Siberian Railroad. During the 1920s German civil engineers had designed this railroad, and we found construction plans for whole sections of track. Years later, the Central Intelligence Agency picked up these plans and used them, so we learned much later, to calibrate the U-2 reconnaissance aircraft navigation and photography. These maps had their own importance, because, in their paranoia, in their publications the Soviets had offset their map coordinates by several miles to prevent the world from knowing the exact locations of their "strategic" sites. They were not secret to us; we had the engineering surveys.

Other crates contained Gestapo files with indisputable evidence of wartime crimes committed by the Nazis, Nazi Party files, several photo collections, and much more.

We also found files from civilian administrations, from the Gestapo, Nazi Women's organization, scientific research foundations, etc. We found every imaginable printed and handwritten matter, items from before World War I, through the growth of Nazi power, to the very last days of the war.

We had everything imaginable in these crates, except the card files of the Potsdam Archives. Apparently the archives' index files had been in a different office building in Potsdam.

There was much scratching of heads. Without the index files, properly sorting these many documents would be extremely difficult. We had no archivists in the organization to assist. No one had the solution to this momentous problem. Finally, Sergeant Himsl, a good old Minnesota farmer's son, had the answer: "We'll sort all the Leitz[12] folders by the markings on the labels. Sort out all the folders that have red diagonal lines from right to left on one pile, those with the red diagonal line from left to right on another, then those with blue lines, yellow lines, and so on. After we are finished with the Leitz, we'll get to the other stuff."

It was pure genius. Sergeant Himsl, not an archivist, solved the problem in his own unique and efficient fashion. Much later, after Sergeant Himsl's crew had done the groundwork, we would recreate the indexes for the various German departments. In essence, we created a mirror image of the German archival system of indexes — except ours was in English.

Every day was like Christmas. We never knew what morsels we would find when we cracked open a new crate. We opened a set of wooden crates that had neat folders, akin to personnel jackets, all indexed. They were the interrogation records of the *Luftwaffe's Auswertestelle West*[13] — although everyone called it *Dulag Luft West*.[14] All American and British airmen shot down over German territory first came to this POW interrogation center at Oberursel, north of Frankfurt-on-Main, for debriefing.[15] With German efficiency each folder had a letter and a number. The letter identified the type of aircraft, i.e. B-17, B-26, P-51, etc., all filed by sequence number of the shoot-down recorded. We found several thousand folders. Each jacket had everything collected from a particular aircraft — the tail number, description of items and equipment found, and whatever else survived in the crash. Then followed a report of items found on the POWs — whatever the crew carried on them of intelligence value, including the usual photos of girlfriends, newspaper clippings, good-luck charms including the occasional rabbit's foot, communications books, paper, messages found in the aircraft — all the items the crews were warned not to take on the mission.

If the crewmember had a USAAF watch, it was taken for examination. The Luftwaffe recorded the crewmember's complaints, but crews were told the watch was government-issued one, not a personal item. The captured interrogation reports revealed exactly how much each of the men in the aircrew talked. Most often it seemed as if the higher the rank of the flyer, the more he talked. Some entries read, "Young, arrogant second lieutenant, will not say anything except name, rank, and serial number." Others had page upon page of information. It was a rather curious mixture.

I must have mentioned *Dulag Luft* to one of my neighbors in Alexandria, Virginia. He said that he had been shot down over Germany and interrogated in the camp north of Frankfurt/Main. He told me that he had been a gunner on a B-17 and mentioned the date of the shoot-down. The next day I went into the files, located his interrogation record, and found a rabbit's foot in his envelope. Although I knew that it was against regulations, I took the item. I swore him to secrecy when I gave him the rabbit's foot the following evening. He was overwhelmed.

Fred Herz, my future mentor in the clandestine service, would have said, "It's a small world."

After the recently established U.S. Air Force became aware of the existence of these files, it tried to court-martial some members for talking too much. They brought the chief Luftwaffe interrogator, Hanns Joachim Scharff—

the airmen called him "Pokerface Scharff"[16] — to the U.S. He testified, but he accused high officials in the Army Air Corps of being more at fault than the crewmembers. The USAF decided to skip the court-martial idea. I heard the USAF convicted only one officer, one who had defected to Germany. Later the USAF asked, "What was the magic spell or formula used by Scharff which made the prisoners drop their guard and converse with him even though they are conditioned to remain silent?" Pokerface Scharff's methods broke down barriers so effectively that the USAF invited him to make speeches about his method to military audiences in the United States.

We separated books of all sorts that our troops had scooped up along with the documents: cookbooks, children's books, love stories, propaganda leaflets, etc. We stacked them in a corner of the warehouse. In another section of the warehouse we found long, heavy, narrow crates filled with photographic glass plates; they were from Heinrich Hoffmann, the official Nazi Party photographer. It was said Hoffmann had taken some 2.5 million photographs of Hitler, and we had a considerable number of the plates in that warehouse.

The G2 had told us that the files of Reinhard Gehlen's *Fremde Heere Ost* were of primary interest to Army Intelligence, closely followed by the espionage activities of Admiral Wilhelm Canaris,[17] head of *Ausland/Abwehr*.[18] We searched for these files, but had to dig through thousands of Leitz folders to locate them and to organize the files in logical sequence.

After much sorting, arranging and indexing we assembled nineteen linear miles[19] of captured German documents by office of origin and office of responsibility. We eventually stored these documents — still in their original Leitz folders — on steel shelves ten feet high. It was a rather interesting job. I read all that interesting "stuff," but it was not really what had I wanted to do as a soldier — I wanted to be a paratrooper, jumping out of airplanes. However, orders were orders, so I sorted, read, and indexed papers.

For several years we concentrated our research on intelligence matters; later we turned our attention to war crimes. All of us, young soldiers and old alike, found what the Nazis had done to people and to nations utterly disgusting. We could not understand how they had besmirched the whole of Germany for their own shameless ideology. The documentation we had in this warehouse was proof beyond any doubt: evidence written by Germans proud of their despicable acts, of acts which would haunt all Germans into eternity. It made us ashamed of our German roots, ashamed even to be members of the human race.

We found convincing and utterly undeniable evidence of Nazi crimes. For some months it was my task to work through the records of Nazi activity in the Baltic countries. We discovered that the SS had allowed locals, Latvian, Estonians, Poles, Ukrainians, and Lithuanians, to do much of the dirty work. These locals tried to outdo the Nazis in torturing and killing these poor hapless men, women and children. Among the Gestapo files I found a stack of green, linen-covered ledgers from concentration camps in the Baltic counties. Each had, on page after numbered page, in neat handwriting, the names of persons, thousands upon thousands, who had perished in these concentration camps. It listed last name, first name, date of death, and cause of death, *Herzinfrakt*— cardiac arrest — written after each prisoner's name. Some camps provided photos of prisoners undressing before going into the "showers," the euphemism for "gas chambers." A "show-and-tell" sent by these inhuman creatures in fancy black uniforms to their beloved leader, *Reichsführer, SS und Chef der Deutschen Polizei*, Chief of the SS and Head of German Police, Heinrich Himmler, aka the "chicken farmer."[20]

With typical German efficiency, scientists tested the various killing methods. They discarded death by shooting as inefficient, too costly, too time-consuming. These scientists determined that poisonous gases were the most efficient way of mass-killing "undesirables." They tested various chemical combinations on prisoners and finally settled on one that was easiest to administer. Gestapo headquarters then commissioned German architects to design the most efficient gas chambers possible. The architects drew detailed blueprints of gas chambers. Then the mass killing started.

We submitted the evidence to the various war crimes commissions, which tried the guilty parties. They hanged some Nazis, but far fewer than deserved execution. Most of them received long prison terms, later commuted to time served. Many of those executed for war crimes were low-level guards conscripted into the SS, many with prior criminal records.

Under an old German law, certain criminal acts precluded their service in the Wehrmacht, the armed forces. By army regulations dating back to the days of Empire, those convicted of poaching in the olden days not only received prison terms, but "loss of honor" and loss of citizen rights, such as voting, holding public office, and serving in the armed services. Those ineligible to serve in the Wehrmacht found homes, and fancy uniforms, in the *Waffen-SS*, the armed services of the regular SS, Hitler's uniformed henchmen. Many of these low-level concentration camp guards were indeed executed, but scores of high officials had carefully prepared their departure "just in case we lose" and escaped to foreign lands, South America being one of their favorite destinations. From what I saw, it confirmed the truth of a German proverb, "They hang the little ones, but the big ones they let go."[21]

Working in GMDS I came to realize that we must never forget that there is but a thin line between the cultural elite and the mass murderers of yesterday, today and tomorrow.

In recognition for my work I received one set of 42 volumes of the Nürnberg War Crimes Trials; it is now the only German-language set in the Library of the U.S. Holocaust Museum in Washington, DC.

Another part of my rollercoaster ride happened incidentally. In 1948 I met a wonderful girl in Arlington Farms, the dormitories housing women working the for various federal government organizations. Ann Marie Holstad, an American Norwegian girl from Minnesota, had arrived in Virginia about the same time as had I. She worked in the Navy Bureau of Personnel in the Navy Annex, just a short walk from the dormitories. South Post, Fort Myer, my base, was adjacent to the dormitories, and my fellow soldiers and I found it very convenient to meet these young girls. Ann Marie and I were married in April 1949 at the South Post Fort Myer chapel. A year later Erik, our first son, was born, and in 1952 Renita, our daughter, joined us. Sigurd H. Holstad, Ann Marie's grandfather, a very impressive Norwegian-American gentleman, was instrumental in bringing my parents and my sister Helga to the United States. Life could not be more perfect — I was once again rising to the top of the rollercoaster.

But life, the comfortable life, was about to change.

War—Once Again

Camp A. P. Hill, Virginia
Combat training
Mid-1950

Only two years after I joined the U.S. Army, war once again threatened to engulf the world. Tensions had increased in Europe. The Soviets attempted to expand communist influence in southeastern Europe. The United States and her allies had just barely won a bitter Soviet-supported guerrilla war in Greece. The Soviets made another attempt to destabilize Europe by closing off the approaches to Berlin from the Allied Zones of Germany. A determined United States president, in concert with his Western Allies, initiated the Berlin Airlift that defeated that troublesome venture.

In 1950 the Soviets flexed their muscles on the opposite side of the globe. "The Cold War turned into a 'hot' war in the Far East. In June 1950, North Korean tanks rolled across the 38th parallel that had served as a dividing line between the Communist North and the democratic Republic of Korea (ROK) in the South."[22] The Pentagon, primarily concerned with the Soviet threat on Western Europe, had relegated Asia to the sidelines of national interest; they considered the two Koreas on the other side of the globe relatively minor, backwater nations. I was among many Americans who had never heard of Korea. I wondered what made us engage in fighting "to defend democracy" in that faraway place.

Also in 1950, I became a staff sergeant, a four-striper, "three up, one down."

Years later one of my acquaintances at GMDS, a staff sergeant who had been General MacArthur's Order of Battle map plotter, told me that the general had repeatedly ignored available local intelligence of a North Korean troop build-up. The North Koreans made short shrift of those opposing U.S. forces in South Korea. So ill-prepared were they, General MacArthur had to throw his poorly armed, badly trained, insufficiently equipped, and psychologically unprepared Tokyo GHQ "parade-ground" troops into the breech. They were totally unprepared for the rugged, brutal demands of battle.

The United States Army quickly recognized this weakness and started much-neglected combat training. After five years of blessed peace, the army needed several months to gear up for combat. All the "paper pushers" in the Pentagon received remedial combat training. In late July or early August 1950 the first elements of Headquarters Company U.S. Army rode in "deuce-and-a-halfs," two-and-a-half-ton army trucks, over the just recently built Shirley Highway, later designated I-95, to A. P. Hill, Virginia, military reservation. This was the "new" army. The new slogan, at times coming near to inducing nausea, was "You are first a soldier, and only second an intelligence specialist."

Our training at A. P. Hill started with an introduction to artillery support fire. An old lieutenant, a "retread"[23] from World War II, was the officer in charge. His instructions were simple: "Here you get to hear what it sounds like when artillery shells pass overhead." He pointed across the meadow at some woods. "When I give the command, start walking toward this row of trees. When I tell you to stop, stop. Not before. I'll be walking with you. Should I hit the dirt, you too had better hit the dirt, because there may be some shorts."[24]

We looked at the long meadow before us and the line of trees some five or six hundred yards beyond. The lieutenant lined us up in a single assault formation, and at his command, we started walking toward a wooded area. From somewhere behind us we heard the reports of artillery. Most of the "old" soldiers alongside me flinched and threw themselves to the ground. I looked around and observed that only a handful, and the lieutenant, still walked toward the woods.

We heard the old instructors shouting, cursing, and cajoling the troops: "I told you to keep walking. I'll tell you when to stop. Let's not go to sleep. We don't have all day."

For some of us this was old hat. I joined a few of those in front of the others. One of the sergeants said, "Man, do you hear those shells wobble?"

I responded, "Yeah, they must have worn out their barrels in World War II."

He laughed, "Watch out for shorts. They can ruin your whole day." And the rest of our gang joined him in laughter.

The old lieutenant came over and asked, "What's so funny?" One of the other sergeants said, "Sir, just wondering about the barrels on your guns, Lieutenant. Where did you get those tanks from, the National Guard?"

"Okay, men," the old lieutenant replied, "Don't make it look so easy. These others are scared shitless."

We laughed.

The lieutenant walked with us toward the woods. We were about 200 feet in front of the rest of the trainees. Suddenly we heard the wobble of a "short" round and this time we hit the ground together, instantaneously, as a shell exploded about a hundred feet in front of us. The lieutenant chuckled as we brushed the dirt from our uniforms, "I could use you guys to train the rest. I am short of people." Thus our small group became the squad leaders for the next course, "the infiltration course."

Everyone had to go through the infiltration course twice — once during daylight, then again after darkness fell. It was something out of a World War I trench warfare movie. We assembled in a long ditch — not really a trench. Machine-guns fired tracers about three feet above the ground. While tracer rounds whistled overhead, I started to crawl through muck and encouraged my group to follow; most reluctantly did, but I did hear the old lieutenant back in the trench cursing those who hesitated. Every so often a charge exploded to my front or flank. Of course, I knew it was safe as long as we crawled flat on our stomachs and stayed away from the sandbag revetments that contained the explosive charges. For men the noises and smells of war were realistic, but of course, there was no dying — it was somewhat unreal.

Between the day and night infiltration courses we fired our M-2 carbines at moving targets. Along with small-unit tactical training, the army had added a new feature: firing at pop-up targets. The lieutenant formed us "oldtimers" into an infantry assault squad. We stood some distance from the rest of the troops, and the lieutenant instructed, "Listen, guys, here is what I want you to do. Go in squad attack formation. Actually I could use nine guys, but you eight will do."

He selected the oldest sergeant of our group, "You'll be the squad leader. There are pop-up targets out there — spread out so that each of you can get at least three targets. Spread out. I don't have to tell you not to get in front of each other. Fire two or three rounds at each target, just to make it look good, okay?"

He added, "Don't make it look too easy."

He hesitated. "Oh, at the end of the run you get to throw a live a hand grenade at a bunker. I had more trouble with some of these guys with that. I'll give them some serious words on that."

We nodded.

"Okay," the lieutenant continued, "draw two magazines and one hand grenade each. You demonstrate, and then each of you gets his own squad to take through the valley. Make damned sure they maintain fire discipline, and make damned sure nobody gets killed."

We formed a squad attack formation and waited while the lieutenant instructed the rest of the group. Then he ordered the attack. After our demonstration, I led one squad at a time, spread out in attack formation, through a valley. As targets popped up I made sure that everyone knocked down the target before advancing toward the end of the course and the berm from which each would toss a hand grenade.

I was surprised that so few of the older, World War II types had so little combat experience. It turned out that most had never seen combat. I should not have been surprised. Paul Fussell, a professor of English at the University of Pennsylvania and "a superannuated, badly wounded former infantry lieutenant," explained it better than could I. He wrote in the autumn 1996 issue of *The Wilson Quarterly*:

> The truth is that very few people know anything about war.
> In an infantry division, for example, fewer than half of the troops actually fight, that is, fight with rifles, mortars, machine guns, grenades, and trench knives. The others, thousands upon thousands of them, are occupied with ... housekeeping tasks.... For those unlucky enough to be in the forward combat units, the war meant death or maiming, usually in extraordinarily dirty and undignified circumstances.
> At the very least, for most it meant a rapid and shocking metamorphosis from boyhood innocence to adult cynicism and bitterness.... Tolstoy's words are worth recalling: "War," he said, "is not a polite recreation, but the vilest thing in life, and we ought to understand that and not play at war."[25]

On the A. P. Hill training base I realized that of all the folks in uniform, a relative small number serve in the infantry, and of those only a precious few actual see combat in the front line, experience the dirty part of war, the part where killing and being killed is an everyday event. The others, thousands, nay, millions, served in housekeeping, in the all-important support, transport, and administrative functions without which those in the front line could not function.

Our small group of "combat veterans" literally walked hundreds of "old" sergeants through this course. The lieutenant was always there, watching, making sure none of his trainees became a casualty. Some panicked at firing "real bullets" or throwing live hand grenades that exploded at the target; my friend Sergeant Richard Bauer did. During the final phase of the course I had to physically throw myself on top of him so that he would not point his loaded weapon at my squad.

When dusk broke over the fields we came to our final exercise: the night infiltration course. While we were at the infantry squad combat range, the training commander had pumped several thousand gallons of water from two tanker trucks into the infiltration range. Traversing the course was not difficult, but we came out at the other end covered in mud. According to the lieutenant, however, we made it in record time. Aside from a few barbed-wire scratches, no one was injured.

We arrived late in the evening at South Post, Fort Myer, now classified as "Combat Qualified." We were dirty, with mud-covered uniforms and weapons. At Fort Myer we walked into the showers fully dressed, turned on the water, and peeled off our garments while the mud drained into the sewer. Then we washed our carbines in the traditional way with hot soapy water — and then rinsed them three times in clean hot water.

All in all, I felt great — a good day's work of soldiering.

On April 30, 1951, at the ripe age of twenty, I became a Sergeant First Class — three up and two down, still called by the old-timers "Tech Sergeant."

Sergeant First Class (SFC) Gerhardt B. Thamm, Hqs. Co., U.S. Army.

Headquarters U.S. Army thought it was best to have all the captured German records in one place instead of having some at the Pentagon and the bulk at the Cameron Station depository in Alexandria, Virginia. So during 1952 we moved all the records from the crowded, windowless mezzanine basement of the Pentagon into the old Torpedo Factory on King and Union streets in Old Town Alexandria, Virginia. This move involved much manual labor.

A contractor moved the documents, but we had to file them in the proper order. Luckily, although we never discovered the Potsdam Archives' card index, Master Sergeant Al Himsl had developed one that worked quite well. Thus, with every one of the eighteen soldiers in the document section helping, in just a few weeks we had assembled steel shelving, sorted and filed all the documents, and then arranged our office spaces. Himsl, a Sergeant George Wagner, and I had offices in the storage wing of the organization. These were large, well-lit offices with a view, quite a change from the Pentagon's windowless mezzanine basement. Al Himsl and I had desks near huge windows overlooking the Potomac River. If I craned my neck just a little I could even see the domed building on Capitol Hill.

Life could not get any better — or so we thought. Although the army now thought of us as "Combat Qualified," nothing much changed for the soldiers in the German Document Section.

* * * * *

In October 1952 our daughter Renita was born; life seemed perfect. But the rollercoaster's wild ride continued.

During the first week of December 1952 I received those dreaded orders to report to Camp Stoneman, California, for shipment to Korea. I went through the normal procedures of drawing up my last will and testament, the obligatory photo in uniform, the very complicated "full field inspection" of all clothes and equipment needed in the combat zone, and then the dreaded wait and the anticipated goodbyes.

With all this done, and with orders in hand, I received a telephone call from a colonel at Army Personnel.

"Sergeant Thamm," he asked, "do you speak German?"

"Yes, sir!"

"Sergeant, talk to my lieutenant; he speaks German."

The lieutenant and I spoke at length in German. His German was as fluent as was mine. Then the colonel came back on the line. "My lieutenant tells me that you do speak German. How would you like to go to Germany?"

"But, sir, I have orders for Korea!"

"Never mind that. Would you like to go to Germany?"

"Yes, sir."

"Good. You will receive new orders. You'll first report to the Intelligence School at Fort Riley, Kansas, then move to Military Intelligence in Germany."

I could not believe my ears. I was in "pipeline" for Korea. Old soldiers know that once in pipeline, there is no chance to have your orders changed — ever.

After all the rituals of going to war: photo in uniform for the family (or the obituaries), etc., plus having already been scared to death in one war, I was not about to argue with a colonel to be a hero in another war. It turned out the colonel was the Chief of U.S. Army Personnel Assignment.

Assignment: The U.S. Army General School

Fort Riley, Kansas
January 1953

The U.S. Army General School prepared intelligence personnel for all phases of combat intelligence. My specialty was to be Combat Intelligence, IPW.[26] I arrived at the Junction City railroad station on a bitterly cold winter night in January 1953. It was near midnight. The Junction City rail depot looked like what I had always imagined an old Wild West rail depot ought to be — picture-perfect. At least two feet of freshly fallen snow covered the little town. I rode the last bus with a bunch of merrymakers into Fort Riley. There I moved into a room in an old sandstone barracks built in 1861: a well cared for, comfortable two-story building with high ceilings. Large porches and balconies stretched along the four corners of every building. This was the old, the original, part of the fort. The barracks had served the horse cavalry troopers for almost eighty years. Identical buildings bordered one side of a wide, snow-covered parade ground. Ancient, craggy trees separated my company's billets from those of the neighboring companies.

We had one captain and a lieutenant in charge of two student companies — one of enlisted personnel, the other of commissioned and warrant officers. Since the army was short of officers for the training companies, I became the company commander. My friend, Sergeant First Class Walter "Wally" Szopiak, also from the Pentagon, became my executive officer.

A few days after my arrival — all the students for this course arrived within a few days — training started in earnest. It turned out to be a no-nonsense, intense training course. Our instructors were highly capable, highly motivated, experienced officers. The senior instructor told us that we were here to be educated, that training would be tough, and that those who could not meet expectations would leave immediately for Korea. For the first few weeks we learned the basics of intelligence. First it was all about tactics, how platoon-size units deployed in combat, their missions, movements and armament. Then the instructions moved through company, battalion, regiment, division, all the way to corps-size elements. Then followed details on how infantry, artillery, armor, logistics, medical support, and chemical warfare were used and deployed, including the strengths and weaknesses of each of these elements.

The men in my company were competent and professional — especially those who were drafted. Most of the draftees were former college students and seemed to make the best of a bad bargain. We had weekly barracks inspections, and the captain in charge of the student companies rarely found anything to be corrected. I suppose he must have felt that he did not do his job unless he could find something to "gig" — to find needed improvement. Our barracks, old in the service, had a large spot in the wooden floor of the entrance way. It had been there for decades — someone must have accidentally spilled a large can of gun-cleaning fluid or oil. This spot had passed inspection several times, but suddenly the captain called me in front of my company and, as the old army would say, "chewed my ass, royally."

I knew that any kind of explanation was useless, and anything else would have been insubordination — cause to be kicked out of the school. Thus I "Yes sired" the captain to death, and he departed with a warning that this floor had better be clean in one hour.

My guys knew what had transpired, they knew I had been treated unfairly, but had no thoughts on how to get the oil spot out of the wood. I had a sudden thought. "Get me a couple of buckets of hot water," I ordered.

They looked perplexed. Two of the guys moved lightning-fast and returned with the hot water. I then carefully emptied first one bucket, the another while my friend Walter Szopiak spread the hot water very carefully over the entire entrance of the barracks.

Then we waited.

After some minutes I ordered one more bucket of hot water, and a little while later the entire floor — now soaking wet — had turned the same color as the oil spot. We waited another half hour, then I ordered my guys, who by now had started to admired the even color of the floor, to mop off the rest of the water.

Then we waited for the captain to reappear, which eventually he did. He pranced around, looked left and right, nodded his head, and left. My guys contained themselves just long enough for the captain to be out of hearing range. Then they started snickering, laughing, and finally dancing on the wet floor.

My reputation as a "wise old sergeant" was secured.

At class all went fairly well until we came to the map-reading part of the training, called "Land Navigation." There most of us became frustrated; for most of us, enlisted as well as officers, we just seemed to be unable to grasp even the most basic elements of how to navigate from one point to another using a map, a compass, a protractor, and an aerial photo of the area displayed on the map.

Here again our instructors had anticipated the difficulty and with much patience the Land Navigation instructor, a captain, went through his spiel time and again. I was among those to whom this topic was incomprehensible, and I was not the only one. I remember a lieutenant colonel, a World War II veteran, saying in utter frustration, "I only got through the last war because I had a great executive officer who could read a map." He, I, and many others entered the remedial map-reading class, where we devoted many an evening to studying. Here again a patient but relentlessly efficient army captain instructor made "land navigation" experts out of novices — most of the remedial students appreciated the captain's teaching skills. For me came a moment when suddenly everything the instructor had told me fell into place.

This was the last phase of our general intelligence training. Thereafter we began the specialty training: photo interpretation, intelligence analysis, report writing, communications, and my specialty: Prisoner of War (POW) Interrogation.

Here again, everything we had learned the previous weeks became an important element for us interrogators. The army had geared our training toward interrogating high-ranking officers, on everything officers at division and army corps should know. One of our instructors mentioned that the "new" U.S. Army interrogation method was based on that of German Luftwaffe master interrogator "Pokerface" Scharff; it was the basis of our IPW — Interrogator, Prisoner of War — training.

It's still a small world. I remembered "Pokerface" Scharff from my days at GMDS — the captured interrogation files of *Luftwaffe Auswertestelle West.*

The captain explained that before Scharff started a POW interrogation, he did extensive research into the POW's background. Then he overwhelmed the American or the Brit with his knowledge. He had the latest U.S. and British newspaper clippings in his files; the tail number of the aircraft gave him the location from where it took off, the airbase, and often the squadron number as well as the name of the commanding officer. In the meantime, the POW, still in a fog of being captured, sat in a comfortable waiting room with all the latest American or British magazines and newspapers spread on tables, dreading the anticipated interrogation, the one his intelligence officer in England had told him about in great detail. What really blew the POW's mind was that instead of being tortured by these "terrible Nazis," Scharff treated the POW to a good cup of coffee and light conversation. Scharff spoke fluent English, with a slight South African accent, had a good sense of humor, and treated the POW politely but firmly.

The captain wanted us to learn this method and employ it in our next assignment. Scharff, he explained, faced the POW with all the available information at hand and proceeded to bamboozle the POW. At times Scharff knew more about the airbase and its CO than did the aircrew.

"That," the instructor said, "is how we want you to interrogate your subjects. It'll confuse the hell out of them. And we hope they'll spill the beans."

In field exercises we worked in tents. We had a "POW compound" from which military police escorted "Aggressor" officers to the interrogation tent. The Aggressors wore distinct uniforms, with various insignias, collar flashes, medals, etc. We had an Aggressor Order of Battle book; we had "captured" maps, and all sorts of other helpful items.

The Aggressors had been trained to represent various levels of enemy forces, as well as various personalities — some friendly, others ornery. If we followed what we had been trained to do, if we asked the right question, the Aggressors would answer; if not, at times they would become silent, other times arrogant. Initially every prisoner gave his name, rank, serial number and date of birth, then clammed up, claiming to be under the protection of the Geneva Conventions; the most arrogant would even quoted certain paragraphs of the Convention verbatim.

It was then our task to use what we would later call "The Pokerface Method." First we evaluated the items the POW had on his person, then we did some fast research into the background of his unit, and only then did one of our MPs bring the POW into the tent. We would greet the POW, offer him a cup of coffee and a cigarette, and try some friendly conversation, all the while trying to determine whether or not the POW would say more than just his name, rank and serial number. We tried to impress him with how much we already knew about his unit, his commanding officer, etc. If that did not work we called the MP to escort the POW back to the compound. Of course all this was time-constrained, and the POW would return after a few minutes. Then we tried a tactic that often worked. It went something like, "Oh, good morning, Captain Warsick, how are you? Being treated well? Any complaints? How is the food? Is it better than what you received in your unit?"

That usually brought a response other than name, rank, and serial number. Then, when further probing seemed to come to a halt, we tried the next trick. "Oh, Captain Warsick, I know you have to reveal only what the Geneva

Conventions stipulate, but maybe I could help you a little. From a major in your unit I learned that you are recently married. You must be concerned that your wife does not know what has happened to you. If you give me her address, I can expedite a message via Switzerland to let her know you are okay."

If that did not work we tried a little blackmail.

"Captain Warsick, I heard that you are an exceptionally good soldier and disciplinarian. Is that correct?"

He would usually agree.

"Well, Captain, I also heard that in one of your pep talks to your men, you told them how much you hated Americans, and that you would rather die than being captured by these despicable Americans."

Usually silence.

"I just wonder. We captured you, not wounded, not incapacitated, but in good health. What would your men say if they heard that?"

"I mean, you know how it is, my superiors are pressuring me to produce information. I know you have this information, and I must use every method possible. Now, I promise you that nothing will be revealed about your cooperation, but.... Well, I must do what I must do."

And that usually did the trick. Not always. A few times our interrogation reports read, "Young, arrogant lieutenant. Will say nothing but name, rank and serial number."

It was great training.

By late May 1953 we spent most of our waking hours listening to lectures, conducting practical exercises, or studying; we did our homework late into the night. The final test came just before graduation, "Land Navigation." We rode blind in a tarp-covered "deuce-and-a-half" deep into the outback of Fort Riley. At our arrival at a heavily wooded area, the instructor issued each of us the required equipment, plus a list of magnetic and true north azimuths. After telling us to navigate our course through the thick brush and heavily wooded Kansas gullies, he gave us the departure coordinates from which we all would start our exercise. Then he assigned each of us a different magnetic departure azimuth — all seemingly very complicated, but he had made us experts; all we had to do was put to work what we had learned.

My route led into one of those deep typical Fort Riley washouts: tall trees at the bottom, heavy underbrush near the top. To pass the test I had to locate and record some twenty markers affixed to trees. At each location I had to change course based on the magnetic or the true north azimuth listed in the instruction. I navigated from tree to tree, recording the markers, until I reached an open area on a high plateau. Then one more azimuth reading, followed by a short walk to a telephone pole and a cluster of waiting instructors. It was the last test and a passing grade guaranteed graduation. After the instructor rated the entries, it was back to the fort. This had been land navigation at its best, or worst — a true test of our capabilities.

Finally, after three months of rigorous training, we received our diplomas and our reassignments; mine was to the 513th Military Intelligence Group, Camp King, Oberursel, Germany — "Pokerface" Scharff's old interrogation camp. Most of my classmates were mentally prepared to go to Korea. Upon graduation they had their suspicions confirmed. Only a few of us went elsewhere. Over the last few beers at the old Fort Riley Tap Room I listened to the bravado of those Korea-bound guys. They did not know that I had seen combat in another life, that I knew what it meant to be scared out of my wits, that once I had shared their bravado. I was embarrassed, yet more than a little relieved not to go with them. Only when pressed did I admit that my destination was Frankfurt-on-Main, in the American Zone of Occupation, Germany.

After a much too short a stay with my family, I left for Germany.

Germany, Here I Come

Camp King, Oberursel, West Germany
U.S. Army Interrogation Center
513th MIG.
June 1953

I brought a "packet" intelligence team to Germany. To me those five guys, Pfc. Paul and Pvts. LeVine, Bain, Boley, and Dana, were just about the smartest privates in the U.S. Army. Pvt. Bain was a photo specialist; the other four were area intelligence analysts. All five had just recently graduated from university. They had been members of my training company and graduates of the Fort Riley intelligence school. By prior arrangement we met at Camp Kilmer, New Jersey. In New York harbor we boarded a troop transport for Bremerhaven, Germany. From Bremerhaven we rode a troop train to the Zweibrücken Replacement Depot. I vaguely recalled my father having processed through this facility as a German *Gefreiter*[27] in late 1939 when he had transferred from Poland to the Westwall — the Siegfried Line. My father later confirmed my suspicion.

In the meantime I had a little problem at the replacement depot. I tried to convincing the assignment corporal that he could not assign my team to some engineer battalion, that we had orders he could not change at will. No one had ever questioned his authority before; he apparently thought he was the all-powerful assignment NCO. I tried to be friendly, tried to reason with him, but finally left him sitting behind his desk open-mouthed when I walked into the office of his boss, the officer in charge of assignments. Initially this officer tried to back up his NCO until I pointed out that our orders came directly from the Pentagon and that we already had assigned slots with the 513th Military Intelligence Group at Oberursel.

My five privates just stood there, not quite knowing whether we all would end up in the stockade for insubordination.

Life is rather curious. Imagine, my father had been stationed in Zweibrücken in 1939–40 in the German Army's 461st Silesian Infantry Division. Now, just a few years later, his son, a senior U.S. Army intelligence sergeant, had arrived at the same Zweibrücken barracks.

My five privates were still in shock over my audacity in confronting the replacement depot crew. They had never been abroad and discovered Germany from the windows of the train. They asked a thousand questions. As we passed through the German countryside, I pointed out some of the town and cities they had only known through their geography studies. I told them about the almost total destruction by Allied bombing raids and reminded them that they would see many ruins once we arrived in Frankfurt. Viewing Germany through the train windows gave them a snapshot view of a bucolic countryside untouched by war. Then, as the train passed through a railyard of one of the large cities, of Bremen, Hanover, Kassel, and finally Frankfurt, they saw blasted buildings and hundreds if not thousands of teeming workers energetically rebuilding bridges, terminal buildings, and switchyard towers. I explained that the tall concrete towers they saw along the rail lines had once been flak towers manned by sixteen-year-old boys—boy soldiers. Of course, I never mentioned that, almost in another life, I had been one of those boy soldiers—although in the less glamorous infantry.

Our train pulled into the cavernous, still badly damaged Frankfurt central rail station. The steel skeleton of what had once been the huge, vaulted passenger boarding area stood as a reminder of the many bombing raids; not even a single glass panel remained in the framed dome.

We hoisted our duffel bags on our shoulders and walked along the train to the U.S. Army RTO[28] office "manned" by a friendly German lady. I had a telephone number to call at our arrival at Frankfurt. When I asked her if I could use the telephone to call for transportation she suggested, "Allow me to call. Our telephone system still has a few little hiccups." I told her I wanted Camp King. She looked at a plastic-covered list and dialed the number, then handed me the receiver. Since we had to wait some forty-five minutes for our transportation, I asked the lady whether she minded if we left our duffel bags at her office. "I want to show the boys a little of the rail station," I said.

She asked, "Have you been here before?"

I laughed, "Yes, in another life." She laughed in return as if she had understood.

As we walked leisurely through what had once been a gigantic glass and steel hall that had covered the entire passenger depot, I explained that all the glass, blown out by explosions, was slowly being replaced, and that in maybe a year or so this entire hall would again be protected from the elements. The railyard was a beehive of activity. New rails were being laid, switches installed, new lighting installed, internal structures replaced, and it seemed as if everyone was sweeping, cleaning, and polishing the building — everything inside and out. I pointed to the enormous, neatly stacked piles of used brick: "All recovered from ruins, a hell of a job. In 1945 through 1950 anyone who did not have a job had to demolish ruined buildings, clean and stack bricks for later use. At first there was no reconstruction, only a huge cleanup. Streets, alleys, roads, apartment blocks were all cleaned up by men women and any kid over fourteen years old who did not go to middle or high schools."

It may have been Private LeVine who said, "Sergeant Thamm, that sounds like forced labor."

I said, "Well, not really forced labor. No one forced them. If they failed to report to work they just did not get any ration stamps. You were free to starve to death — or do the black market routine."

The boys laughed.

"Just a note of caution," I said. "There still is a relatively strong black market, especially in American cigarettes. Don't be tempted by a few bucks selling your ration. Especially, being in intelligence, that's strictly a big no-no. They kick your ass right out and you may end up in the goddamned engineer battalion the asshole corporal wanted to assign us to." They looked at me to see whether I was kidding.

"No kidding," I said. "It's not worth it. The few bucks you make, I mean."

As we walked to the plaza in front of the station, I pointed to a cluster of men standing doing nothing. "See those guys over there? They will try to tempt you to supplement your income. Don't fall for their shitty talk that 'everyone is doing it.' You are not 'everyone,' you are special. Either that or you sweated your ass off in Fort Riley for nothing. Besides, believe it or not, it's a federal offense."

They looked again to see whether I had kidded them. I just shook my head. Just then I saw the bumper marking "513th MIG" as a weapons carrier[29] pulled up near the RTO reserved parking sign. I walked over and told the driver that we were his "way-bill" and that we would just get our duffel bags from RTO.

We rode through the city. I pointed to one of the city gates, the *Henniger Tor.* "That's the logo of good Frankfurt beer and the northern gate to the city. Didn't get much scratched by bombs, I think."

The driver looked impressed. "You been here before?" he asked.

"Yes, a couple of years ago," I answered.

I thought they did not need to know that in 1947 I had changed trains at Frankfurt; that I had a long stopover and explored the then totally devastated town; that I had exchanged a couple of packs of American cigarettes for black-market food ration stamps on the plaza near the railroad station so that I could eat dinner.

Then as now, Frankfurt was the center of the black market that thrived in postwar Germany as the only free market — albeit an illegal one. We rode along Eschersheimer Landstrasse. Until we reached open country, there was the occasional ruined apartment house, but damage was not as extensive as in the inner city. Once we had passed through the borough of Eschersheim, this road turned into an old-fashioned country lane. From the back of the vehicle I heard someone ask, "What is there to see around here?"

I laughed, "That all depends what you are looking for. Camp King is just north of the village of Oberursel. There is a direct streetcar line that has a stop right at the gate. It goes right into downtown Frankfurt." I paused and asked the driver, "Has the Autobahn bridge been repaired?"

"Not yet. But they are working on it."

I turned to the soldiers behind me. "A little bit up the road you will see one of the stupid things soldiers do in war. We will go under a bridge that the Germans partially blew up in 1945. It led across the road we are on. It did nothing to stop our army. The engineers just bulldozed a path around the bridge. Now it just delays those going between Wiesbaden and Kassel."

The driver nodded his head. "I sort of enjoy taking the weapons carrier down that slope. Passenger cars have to be a bit more careful, but this vehicle is built for that kind of driving."

I turned once more. "If you are interested in history, you are in the right place. The Romans were here before the birth of Christ. They built the Limes, a fortified wall, to keep out the Germanic tribes. In fact, there is a reconstructed fort a few kilometers from here. You will be surprised; the Romans even had central hot water heating in their barracks."

"Sarge," interrupted the driver, "you've got to be kidding."

"Go out there some day," I replied, "and see for yourself. The hot water boiler for the bathhouse is at the top of the hill and the leftover hot bath water runs in clay pipes under the barracks."

I was not sure whether anyone believed me, so I continued, "Barbarossa made himself Emperor of Germania in the twelfth century. I mean, all sorts of things happened here. In the next town down the road, Bad Homburg, one of Germany's fancy spas, Kaiser Wilhelm II and his cousin Czar Nicholas II of Russia vacationed together before World War I. The Czar even had a little Russian chapel built for his use — it's still there. Bad Homburg also has some great restaurants. That is, if you ever want a change from army chow."

They laughed. I thought the guys would like it here. I knew it would be a real change from Fort Riley, Kansas, for all of us.

We arrived at Camp King on a late Saturday afternoon. The camp, in

The Gate — Camp King, Oberursel, Germany, from *The History of Camp King* by Jack C. Spratt, artist unknown.

the foothills of the Taunus Mountains, had the aforementioned streetcar stop conveniently located directly across the road from the main gate. Pleasant one-story barracks bordered two sides of the camp. The military policeman at the gate checked our papers. "Take them to the transient barracks," he told the driver, who nodded his head. He knew the routine. He drove down the road a bit and stopped in front of one of the barracks. We climbed out of the vehicle, shouldered our duffel bags, and looked around.

Camp King looked different from any army camp we, or at least I, had ever seen. We stood in front of a cluster of relatively new one-story cinderblock enlisted barracks, all brightly painted and surrounded by finely landscaped green spaces. Entering the barracks, we walked on highly polished tile floors. Later we learned that a German houseman polished these floors to high gloss. He also cleaned the latrines and kept the exterior surroundings neat. It was almost like living in a country club.

Camp King was the U.S. Army's strategic interrogation center and the home of the 513th Military Intelligence Group. During World War II this facility had been the Luftwaffe's *Auswertestelle West*.[30] It was there where Germans interrogated all American airmen shot down over German, and German-occupied, territory. It was the place that had created and was the former depository of the records I had examined in the German Military Document Section in the Pentagon. The camp had changed little. For a brief time after I arrived we still had guard towers; they soon became history. In any event, our tower guards kept others out, not us in.

And the occupants? This time Americans interviewed Germans: defectors from the East German People's Police (VOPOs).[31]

Sharp at 0800 hours on Monday morning, our shoes spit-shined, our khaki uniforms well pressed, and our brass shined to high glare, I escorted the five members of my intelligence team to the A Company orderly room. I handed the travel orders to the first sergeant as I reported, "All present and accounted for." My military report seemed to startle the first sergeant. He rose, we shook hands, and he said, "Welcome aboard." Then he ordered another sergeant to have us assigned to our posts.

Although I had enjoyed the company of my packet team, I was happy to be free of that responsibility. After we had completed all the usual paperwork involved, I moved into the NCO barracks, where I shared the room with one other sergeant, an interesting fellow named Harry. It turned out we would work in the same interrogation cottage. He claimed to have been a hobo "riding the rails" before the army drafted him. He never did explain how he learned to speak fluent German.

We had several such cottages, all spread out over a wooded hill site. Each sat in a well-kept grass and stone-wall setting. Flagstone walks led to the rear door of each cottage, which looked like typical quaint Franconian weekend cottages: rustic, dark framework and white walls, high gables, large windows and French doors. They sat skillfully arranged around a knoll overlooking the camp. It was here where we interrogated — interviewed — our charges.

I settled quickly into the interesting and relatively easy routine of interviewing those defectors. We interrogated them in the morning and wrote or reviewed the reports in the afternoon. My fellow interrogators were a congenial, fun-loving bunch; most were sergeants, but we did have a sprinkling of civilians. A wonderful WAC[32] officer — I think she was an English major in college — was our editor. She made our scribbled reports look professional. A small group of college-educated draftees then turned these writings into Intelligence Reports, IRs, along with expertly drawn maps, sketches of facilities, and charts, all to be published and disseminated by the G-2 in the Pentagon. In our archives we had voluminous background information, the type of information that made "Pokerface Scharff" an expert interrogator. Some of our college-educated draftees checked the information against that already collected to ascertain that we had not talked to a "Dangle."[33] We had sketches, blueprints, charts, and descriptions of everything in the East German military inventory. Almost all of our "guests" cooperated in these interviews. Although the army had classified our work as interrogation, it really was more akin to interviewing cooperating subjects. The defectors were deliriously happy at being in an American Army camp. They had not eaten such good food for a long time, if ever. They were eager to tell whatever we wanted to know. There were times when we thought, based on the screening report — a record of everything our source could possibly know — that sources told more than they thought they knew. Once in a while some source suddenly remembered additional details that required an extension of his stay at our camp. In several instances we found that this informant had interrogated others and then presented their stories as his. He did it just to stay a little bit longer in the pleasant surroundings of Camp King. Our WAC officer, who screened all reports, occasionally tipped us off that this had occurred. We then gently informed that person that the time had come for him to leave our camp and join the general West German public.

In retrospect, this was probably the best and the easiest job I have ever had during my entire twenty-plus years in the army. We had some military duties: retreat parade once a week, guard duty — the NCOs served as Officer of the Day, which meant that the officer on duty merely had to be near a telephone in the officers club, the BOQ,[34] or his home. The camaraderie among the troops was the best I had ever experienced. The work was important and totally enjoyable.

While I was still in Ft. Riley, Kansas, I had heard of some rumblings of discontent behind the Iron Curtain. On the 17th of June 1953, only a week after my arrival in Camp King, USAREUR[35] in Heidelberg sounded a high alert. The disgruntled East German people had risen in revolt against their German and Soviet masters. In large cities and small towns, but notably in East Berlin, workers and youths fought against the VOPOs and their heavily armed Soviet brethren. Shortly thereafter East German defectors inundated Camp King. U.S. military and civilian screeners had already separated those who had important information from the run-of-the-mill folks who sought refuge from their Communist oppressors. Among those who came to Camp King were high-ranking VOPO officers who had crossed over with their entire families. Others selected for interview included young soldiers, mostly radio operators or other communications specialists.

The easy routine of the past was gone. Camp King became a beehive of exciting activity. Each Monday morning we met new defectors in the same reception room in which, less than a decade ago, U.S. Army Air Corps POWs had waited to be interrogated.

The old-timers played a little game. They looked with anticipation to see whether we had any Polish defectors. At my first time in the reception area, one of my fellow interrogators said, "We watch to see if we have any Poles in the crowd." When I wondered what that was all about, he explained that one of our best Polish interrogators was a black sergeant first class who spoke the language like a native. A few weeks later we had two Polish defectors in the reception area. There was a large group of men in East German uniforms all sitting in one cluster and two others sitting apart from the rest: the Poles. They appeared to be just a bit uncomfortable.

SFC Thamm, enjoying life at the Tap Room garden at Camp King, Oberursel, West Germany, 1953.

My colleagues educated me. "Everyone knows that blacks can't speak Polish. Watch how long it takes them before they realize that our guy speaks excellent Polish. Usually, once the Poles realize that our guy speaks fluent Polish, he can't do anything wrong. We have three other Poles here at the moment; they hang around him like flies on honey. He has a hell of a time getting away from them. They even want to eat at his table."

Unfortunately for the Poles, but fortunately for our black interrogator, we had a strict non-fraternization rule that prohibited any association with sources outside the interrogation area. Although we all ate in the same mess hall, all the defectors sat in a segregated area. Whenever the black sergeant walked into the mess, the Poles would rise from their table, bowing and waving. I heard that initially it had embarrassed our sergeant, but by the time I arrived he had gotten used to their adulation; he courteously returned their bows and waves with a big grin on his face. By all accounts he was the most popular interrogator in Camp King.

And so it happened. One of our sergeants managed the betting; another had the stopwatch ready. The time count started when the black sergeant started his walk toward the Poles and concluded when one or both of the Poles realized that our black sergeant addressed them in their native tongue. And indeed, the two Poles stared uncomprehendingly, even a bit frightened, as our black sergeant walked toward them. The sergeant, dressed in his best khaki uniform, offered his hand all the while chatting in Polish. The two Poles appeared to be in total puzzlement. After a few seconds I saw their looks turning into wonderment, then into surprise. One, then the other jumped up and they started pumping our sergeant's hand. The timekeeper announced, "Eighteen seconds. Who has eighteen seconds?"

One of the fellows looked at his slip, "I got it."

"Goddamn it, Mike," said the timekeeper, "that's the second time you won the pool."

"Hey, man," said Mike, "I'm part Polish. I have the inside track."

Everyone chuckled, because Mike was actually one of our better German linguists. The winner collected more than twenty dollars — in those days a substantial sum.

I had an embarrassing moment a few weeks after my arrival. The refugee reception officer called to announce that he was sending a Hungarian defector to our cottage. I walked downstairs and told the officer-in-charge of the expected arrival, and then I leisurely walked outside. Near the door, smoking a cigarette, stood a gentleman I had never met. I pulled out a Philip Morris and the gentleman offered me a light. We passed a few pleasantries while I waited for the Hungarian source. After a while the gentleman asked me whether I was waiting for someone. I said, "Yes, some Hunky."

He replied, "Oh, that must be me."

I was totally embarrassed. I apologized and invited him into the cottage. I then asked our captain, the officer-in-charge and a non-linguist, whether he wanted to interrogate a Hungarian defector. He looked questioningly at me.

"Sir," I said, "his English is better than mine." The captain was overjoyed. Although he had completed interrogator training, this was the first time he was able to actually interrogate a real defector.

Aside from all the intelligence duties there was always time for athletics — golf, volleyball, and European soccer. I joined the saber fencing team organized by the recently promoted Pfc. Bain, one of the guys who came with me to Germany. He was an excellent teacher and it was not too long before the Camp King fencing team competed with other U.S. military teams. In essence, this had become an ideal assignment. Only the presence of my family would have made it perfect, but, since there was a nine-month waiting period for government quarters, Ann Marie, Erik, and Renita had to remain in Alexandria, Virginia.

SOMETHING SPECIAL

The Little Red Schoolhouse
Camp King, Oberursel, Germany
October 1953

Some months into autumn of 1953, just as the rush of defectors from the June 17 riots in East Germany had subsided, my section officer ordered me to report for an interview at the *Erholungsheim*,[36] as a house near the camp's main gate was called.

The *Erholungsheim* was one of two buildings off-limits to 513th MIG personnel. The other building was a single-level wooden structure, painted an ugly dark red, situated at the edge of our parade ground.

During World War II, the *Erholungsheim*, a rather large, three-storey house, had been the Luftwaffe DULAG commander's abode. I knew that this place did not belong to the 513th MIG, but no one knew, or would tell, to which unit it did belong. For some unknown reason it was known as the *Erholungsheim*, although the fellows living there did not seem to be in need of any medical or mental recuperation. I heard from old timers that some of the guys from the 513th went there for an interview, lived there for a few months, and then mysteriously disappeared. Many rumors circulated.

At the *Erholungsheim* a very businesslike, yet friendly gentleman greeted me. He was in his late thirties, early forties, of medium height, with thinning light blond hair. He wore civilian attire of seemingly good quality. In fact, he looked like a diplomat: dark blue serge suit, white shirt, and conservative dark blue necktie with three thin white strips near the lower half of the cloth. He talked as if he knew much about me. In my surprise at dealing with a civilian, I did not catch his name. He offered to have me transferred to another unit and mentioned, as a sort of by-the-way, that I would get additional training, yet never saying what type of training, or any particulars about the job I was to get; neither did he mentioned the new unit to which

I was to be assigned. I told the gentleman how much I enjoyed my work here at Camp King, and then I turned down his offer.

When I returned to our interrogation cottage, my fellow interrogators were waiting.

"What is it? What did he say? Did you get the job?"

"No," I replied. "There was some civilian there. He didn't tell me anything about the new job. He just said I get additional training. Hell, I got a job here with you guys and I love it. I mean, we got it made."

They berated me.

Harry, my roommate, chided me with, "Jerry, that's the dumbest thing you ever did."

"Why?" I asked surprised.

"Because, dummy, that fellow you talked with in the *Erholungsheim* is the boss of a special outfit in Frankfurt. Jerry, you just screwed yourself out of a goddamned good job."

"What job?" I was puzzled, "He didn't tell me shit about the job. For Christ's sake, man, I know what I have here. It's the job I wanted, right here."

Harry just screwed up his face in disgust. "Man, you don't know shit. You don't know what you are talking about … great job. I saw one of the guys from here, he got to wear civvies there, and they paid him for 'em. Jerry, think, for Christ's sake, here you have to wear that monkey suit at all times, there you don't. So tell me about your great job."

The rest agreed.

The fact I had to wear my uniform did not bother me at all. In occupied Germany, army regulations called for all occupation troopers to be in uniform at all times while outside the confines of the garrison. I had, by all appearances, really killed any chances of ever leaving Camp King, but it did not bother me. I knew that Camp King was the best station in the U.S. Army.

Frank, one of my coworkers, just shook his head in despair. "You jerk, you should have gone for it; it's something special." He opined that the people living in that house by the gate took their training in the ugly red building at the edge of the parade ground, the barracks that everyone called the "Little Red Schoolhouse."

* * * * *

I recall only one of the sergeants at the 513th MIG who strove to be "something special." It was Sergeant First Class George Trofimoff, a respected multilingual interrogator — Russian and German. He was a handsome, although an arrogant young man. He looked sharp in uniform, but seemed to want to be just a little different from the rest of us sergeants. He worked in my interrogation section at Camp King. It seemed as if he strove to be an outsider. He never joined the rest of our gang at the tap room for an after-duty glass of beer; he never dined with us at our mess table. He was always someone "special."

Trofimoff and two other sergeants had become members of a local German tennis club. Occupation authority regulations permitted wearing of civilian attire under certain circumstances, to include athletic attire when participating in off-base athletic activities. Trofimoff tried to make those in our interrogation section believe that he was skirting army regulations, and that to him it did not much matter.

Barracks life. Camp King, the author at right, 1953.

I often saw Trofimoff and two fellow sergeants leaving Camp King on weekends sharply dressed in civilian athletic attire; Trofimoff wore slacks and a white turtleneck sweater. Little did I know until many years later just how "special" Trofimoff was.

The Visit

Northern West Germany
1953

Shortly before my unsettling interview at the *Erholungsheim* I had submitted a request for a week's leave. I had written my Aunt Kläre, Mother's sister, that I would come for a visit. I packed an "AWOL bag"—what GIs called a small satchel—with a couple of cartons of cigarettes, several pounds of good American coffee, and a bottle of Scotch. Dressed in my best OD winter uniform with my sergeant first class chevrons on my sleeves, I rode the *Bundesbahn* passenger train to Detmold. This would be the first time in seven years that I returned to the area where the refugee train had deposited our family after the Poles had expelled the Thamms from their Silesian homes.

In late afternoon I arrived at the Detmold rail depot and boarded a trolley for Pivitsheide. Here I was, the American senior sergeant riding a trolley packed with German workers returning home—strange, yet so familiar. I knew the route, and I knew the stop where I would detrain for Aunt Kläre's cottage. I had ridden the trolley several times in 1946, but today I was a stranger, an American. The locals, used to seeing British soldiers, viewed this American with curiosity. Two young men in their late teens made some remarks about my uniform. I smiled in amusement. They did not know that this American understood their every word. Some of the other passengers must also have wondered what I was doing on this trolley. I eavesdropped on their chitchat. One of the two young men wondered aloud what all the stripes on my sleeves meant. I laughed, turned and said, "These make me an *Oberfeldwebel*." I used the German word for senior NCO. Then I added. "Just wait, in a few years another *Oberfeldwebel* will chase you across the parade ground."

They stared at me in shock, wondering, I suppose, how this foreigner could speak such fluent German. Two of the older men on the trolley pointed their fingers at the young Germans, "For sure, for sure." They scolded, "You youngsters will get yours. Maybe it will do you some good."

The two young men quickly recovered and, seemingly terribly embarrassed, apologized.

I laughed, "Ah, it's all in good fun."

One of the older men then asked, "You aren't Mrs. Thamm's relative, are you?"

Now it was my turn to be surprised. When I confessed that said that I was, he replied, "Oh, she is expecting you. I am her neighbor. I will tell you when we get to the trolley stop; it's where I get off." Then everyone started talking at once asking questions about my uniform, the meaning of my rank insignia, and how I came to speak such fluent German. I told them that I was born in the United States, but that I grew up in Germany. Suddenly I had become part of their group.

The author with his grandfather, "Thamm Opa," in 1953 at Istrup, British Zone of Occupation, West Germany.

Finally, when Aunt Kläre's neighbor and I detrained, half the passengers on the trolley waved us goodbye. Although I had been at Aunt Kläre's cottage some years ago, her neighbor insisted in escorting me; she already stood in the road awaiting my arrival.

The following day we rented a car from one of my aunt's acquaintances and drove to the other side of Detmold, to Istrup, to visit Thamm Opa — my grandfather — and aunts and cousins. Istrup was the village where the local authorities had dropped off mother, my sister, and Preuss Oma. Although economic conditions in West Germany had enormously improved since last I had been there, nothing much seemed to have changed in the village. It seemed to have been arrested in the 1940s timeframe. All in all, it was a pleasant, memorable visit, but I felt completely out of place. I felt like an alien descending from another planet, or from a future time. No longer the poor German refugee boy scrounging for food, looking for some hand-me-down clothing, I was now an American soldier, a senior noncommissioned officer. Life was great, and I was on top of the world.

After just a brief stay we continued to Gross-Hilligsfeld to visit Uncle Willy and Preuss Oma. But first we stopped off in Klein-Hilligsfeld to visit Aunt Emma and Irmchen. It had been five years since we had seen each other.

"Preuss Oma," circa 1955. In background a photograph of Uncle Arthur—he died in Soviet prison in Siberia in 1946.

Irmchen and I hugged far longer than cousins should have. It was awkward but pleasant; it brought back fond memories. Someone may have wondered why Irmchen had tears in her eyes when we hugged for one last time. The memories triggered by my visit belonged to us and us alone. Somehow we knew that we would never see each other again, making this brief reunion bittersweet.

Aunt Kläre and I continued our journey and visited Preuss Oma, who by now had moved in with Uncle Willy and his family.

Both Preuss Oma and Uncle Willy admired men in uniform. Of course, all their relations had worn uniforms of the Kaiser's and Hitler's armies. However, upon my entrance they greeted me warmly. Preuss Oma especially admired my uniform. She asked what all the many chevrons meant. I told her that I was an *Oberfeldwebel*. She recalled that the only one in our family ever to reach such high rank was her beloved, and long deceased, son Bruno. With that comment I felt redeemed. I told them all the family news from America: that Dad, Mother, and Helga were living in a small apartment in Washington, DC; that they had become well acclimatized to America. I told them about my family, about Ann Marie, Erik and Renita, and that I would bring them for a visit probably during spring of 1954 after they had settled in Frankfurt. After we had our customary family afternoon cake and coffee, Aunt Kläre and I departed. I drove her home and hopped a train back to Camp King.

I spent much of the train journey thinking about the role luck had played in my life. And I had a feeling that luck was not yet done with me.

Every Man Has a Price

Camp King, Oberursel, Germany
October 1953

After my return from North Germany, I started to look differently at the ugly red building at the edge of the parade ground, the barracks that everyone called the "Little Red Schoolhouse." Having been at the camp just a short time I had not paid much attention to that building, but my buddies' talk had aroused my interest.

I thought, *If it was restricted territory, and if there was something highly secretive going on in that building, and, especially if I get to wear civvies and they pay me for them, well, maybe it is something special. Maybe I did shoot myself in the foot.* But it really did not matter, because Camp King had become my home away from home.

A week or so later I again was called to the *Erholungsheim*. The same civilian awaited me. He introduced himself as Colonel — his name sounded German. I thought he said "Colonel Hoff." He mentioned that this training was indeed special, that I would be involved in very important functions that very few are ever asked to perform. Then he mentioned that I would get $300 civilian clothing allowance. Hearing this, I started to pay close attention to what the "colonel" had to say. He must have realized that I suddenly appeared interested and said that most likely I would also get a civilian automobile. That was anything better than I ever expected to have while my family was still in the U.S. He also mentioned that I would be working in downtown Frankfurt, but that did not really matter to me. The $300 clothing allowance and the automobile convinced me to take a chance at the "something special" job.

Later, at the Little Red Schoolhouse, I learned that "every man has a price." I suppose the car and civilian clothing were mine. I still am not sure whether it was the offer of the car or the civilian clothing allowance that tipped that balance and made me agree to the transfer.

It turned out that the Little Red Schoolhouse was the school for clandestine case officers — people who handled spies. I moved from my comfortable quarters at the edge of the camp into even better quarters at the *Erholungsheim*. On our first day there we received strict orders not to associate with any of our friends from our old units. The word was, "You will not have enough time for anything but training and studying."

Our class started with more than one hundred students, mostly officers and enlisted men from the U.S. Army along with several Department of the Army civilian employees. There were maybe ten or fifteen air force intelligence NCOs, and a number of "just getting into the business" from the Central Intelligence Agency. They pretended to be air force, but our air force enlisted students knew better — they had never seen nor heard of them. As one of our air force students said, "These guys don't know shit about our aircraft or the air force."

A crusty old colonel was the only non-student and non-instructor. He was a former OSS[37] agent and in charge of all clandestine instruction. He opened the classroom in the morning and locked it at night. He attended every lecture. He usually sat or stood at the rear of the room watching, always holding a coffee cup and occasionally even drinking from it. A large variety of instructors cycled in and out of the classroom; the old colonel always introduced them. Several times the old colonel mentioned that most of the instructors were men with "street experience." In contrast to the intelligence "boot camp" at Fort Riley, most of the training at the Little Red Schoolhouse was conducted indoors; it was mostly theoretical with just a sprinkle of practical demonstrations to make the instructions more interesting. We had lectures covering the entire spectrum of espionage from ancient history and the days of Sun Tzu to yesteryear's, even yesterday's, events, from stunning successes to utter failures. We became acquainted with the modus operandi of espionage, recruiting techniques, how to behave, how to move in a hostile environment, tactics and operations for training "sources," and the many ways we would be slipping them covertly through the Iron Curtain.

One instructor explained that all espionage, no matter which country conducts it, is performed along similar lines. Over the many centuries, various ways have been tried and, through trial and error, either accepted or rejected. We learned the four phases of recruiting a source: spotting, assessing, vetting, and recruiting.

Spotting is the initial research conducted to detect a potential HUMINT source living, working, or otherwise being associated with the item targeted for collection. Research is conducted in official telephone books and through other open-source exploitation using local newspapers and learned journals, to determine who may have access to classified projects. Often a "spotter," a low-level agent, will attempt to physically identify the potential source.

Much later, long after I had left the clandestine service, I learned that I had been spotted. I was in Military Intelligence Service attending Georgetown University. There were several other army and air force members attending classes. We were all a little older than the rest of the students and naturally flocked together. "Frenchie," another older student, a French-Canadian, joined us presumably because he had similar interests. Soon we went to our favorite watering hole, "The Tombs," across from the School of Foreign Service, for beer and hamburgers and became friendly acquaintances. One morning, just before I left home for class, I heard an announcer say, "Soviet spy arrested," and I saw Frenchie's face on the screen. I was shocked to learn that the FBI field office in Washington arrested Frenchie, that he was the spotter, and that we, the military members at Georgetown University, had been his targets.

Assessing, the next step in this recruitment process, calls for very careful and critical value judgment to determine whether or not the target is worth the effort. It is a decision made by experts; in Moscow it's "The Center," in the U.S. it's at Langley, Virginia. If the assessors agree that the target is approachable, that he has the potential of being a good source, the analysts prepare guidance for the case officer's initial approach.

The initial approach is called "vetting." Vetting is a most delicate operation. Only experienced operatives conduct vetting. Every approach is different. This is what makes this work so interesting. The case officer, or his intermediary, will physically approach the target.

The instructor warned us that this was a critical juncture in the eventual recruiting process, and that we would most likely use an intermediary, a former East German refugee who knows the target, to make the initial approach.

He also mentioned a vetting method perfected by the Soviet intelligence services: sexual exploitation, where a "Raven" or "Swallow" would make the approach. Western intelligence agencies had detected several such approaches to which a number of women and men have succumbed. The "raven" is a handsome male with continental charm who concentrates on lonely women, usually unmarried, thirty-five and older. The "swallow" of course is a good-looking female, usually with an interesting background, nice apartment, and a "job" as a research assistant for a newspaper or learned journal.

"Don't get caught with your pants down," he warned us. "These guys mean business."

Recruiting is the last phase before actual intelligence gathering starts. It can be in one of three basic forms: either the target will not know the true nationality or profession of the case officer, or the target will assume that a friendly office or country needs the information.

"We call this the 'false flag' approach," the instructor added. "If you can handle it, I mean with fluency in the language and a good cover, you can pretend to work for a friend or an ally."

Then he went on to explain that his unit most often uses the "straight punch" recruitment where the target knows who receives the product, gets paid for the product and does not care. He added that this approach works more often than one cares to believe.

The next day another instructor continued the previous day's lecture. He warned us that we would encounter another kind of recruitment.

"Actually," he said, "it's not really a recruitment, but for those of you who work the so called 'safehouses' in Berlin especially..." he paused. "But it could happen anywhere, there are the 'walk-ins,' they always look good, but ... for the case officer the walk-in can be a most frustrating, time-consuming event with little or no payoff."

"Well," he added, "not always. And that's the worst of it. Sometimes a 'walk-in' can be pure gold. His motivation? Money! Or the thrill of stepping out of a mundane life to live on the sharp edge of excitement! But mostly money!"

He also surprised most of us when he informed us that only four to six percent of all intelligence information is collected clandestinely. The rest comes from open source — learned journals, library research, photographic and electronic intelligence collections, attachés, and interviews such as those conducted here at Camp King.

We learned that truly clandestine operations, called Non-Official Cover Operations, or NOC Ops, are rare; that it requires a case officer to be not only fluent in the language of the country in which he operates, but that he must not only have reasonable, valid proof that he is what he pretends to be, but he must be able to blend into the country's milieu, its business, its social, and its geographic environment. In other words he must become what he is not. Most important, he must never dirty his own nest. NOC Ops should never be conducted in the country in which the case officer lives, but should be conducted in a third country for obvious reasons: Everything he does is illegal. Everything he does is against the interests of the foreign country in which the case officer lives; everything he does is in violation of the country's neutrality; everything he does subverts the host country's citizens.

"Aside from that," the instructor added, "the NOC agent is subject to arrest in that third country and he most likely will get little or no protection from the U.S. government."

We also viewed training films of surreptitious surveillance and counter-surveillance, and in what the instructor called "surreptitious entry": burglary, safe cracking, and lock-picking.

Some students thought they had come to Camp King to be entertained. They formed a small group. They moved in a cluster, ate at the same table, and congregated at seats in the rear of the classroom. A young, gregarious army captain became their leader. During the long and admittedly wearing hours of instruction they pretended to sleep and even to snore. Whenever an instructor made even the slightest mistake they would guffaw. Ever more frequently as time passed the young army captain would interrupt the instructor with, "Now, in my opinion..." This happened often enough for the rest of the students to call him "Captain Opinion." These interruptions irritated not only the instructors, but also the rest of the trainees.

Some weeks later a practical demonstration interrupted the theoretical instructions — the aforementioned surreptitious entry. The instructor, a tall blond fellow, carried several "tools" from the storage locker at the rear of the building. He had large plywood mock-up of a combination lock for a safe — cut away to demonstrate how the moving plates interact within the lock. He also had various large key (tumbler) lock models made of wood. He even brought from storage a complete door with doorframe and a normal house or office-type lock. All the devices appeared to be homemade, yet ingeniously designed.

Later, the instructor admitted to having built these devices in the Camp King hobby shop. Much later I learned that the U.S. Army's entire "cloak and dagger" operation, the instructions, the tools, even the actual clandestine collection — recruiting sources, running the agents into East Germany, Poland, and Czechoslovakia — was done on "the cheap." Without a doubt, the instructors had all the experience necessary to train new case officers, but their training aids where homemade. Most instructional aides were hand-made by the instructors, or by friends of the instructors, in the local army hobby shops. Some instructors came into the classroom exhausted from the previous night's operation. But they were the cream of the crop, dedicated; apparently most were great case officers, but many had little or no experience in teaching, lecturing, instructing.

The surreptitious-entry hands-on training was far more fascinating than the lectures. The instructor made it especially interesting demonstrating his skill with his lock-picking tools; he told us that upon graduation each of the graduates would be issued one these tool kits. He made it look easy as he deftly opened the five-tumbler lock on the door. Then he asked for volunteers to "give it a try."

Captain Opinion rose from his chair with, "Nothing to it."

The instructor handed him the tools and the captain made attempts at being funny by weaving back and forth. He tried the "rake and tension" process several times; it did not work. He started to perspire. The instructor stood with his arms folded across his chest and studied the procedure. Some students started to snicker. The captain tried harder, became furious. Finally he threw down the tools in frustration and walked back to his fellow snorers at the rear of the room.

Some of us were almost certain what would happen. We thought all the instructors had gotten together to "sandbag" Captain Opinion, the man who had given most of them a hard time. The instructor looked around; he smiled. "Now folks, one of the first lessons in surreptitious entry is" — he turned the doorknob — "always try the doorknob first. Someone may have forgotten to lock the door." The whole class exploded in laughter. For all the laughter, this was a lesson never to be forgotten.

Captain Opinion became very irritated by the instructor's demeanor. He rose from his seat and started his, "In my opinion..." and the classroom exploded in laughter. The instructor looked at the captain disdainfully. "Captain," he said, "let me make one observation: Opinions are like assholes; everyone has one." Captain Opinion first sat down, and then rose, sat down again, then rose and walked out of the classroom.

Shortly after this hilarious episode our crusty old colonel introduced a young army captain as his "secret unit's" Fiscal Officer. The colonel admonished us to pay particular attention to what the Fiscal Officer had to say, because, "You may think that this cloak and dagger business is all fun and games, but let me tell you, everything in espionage ends up with a money trail." He cautioned that most agents do not get in trouble with the opposition, but with screwing up their accounts. Admittedly, the Fiscal Officer's lecture was not the most exciting one of the courses. It was time again for Captain Opinion to make jest of the man he called "moneybags." Soon his cronies joined him and pretended to sleep — again pretending to snore — during the Fiscal Officer's lecture. The Fiscal Officer was undeterred. He spoke enthusiastically while flashing instructional graphics, slides of forms, graphs, etc., on the screen. He seemed convinced that his was the most important lecture of the entire training course.

Near the end of his instruction he gave each of his students a pamphlet — a set of four or five pages stapled together into a neat little booklet. It had an alphabetical listing of all authorized clandestine services expenditures, each with a corresponding number; everything was cross-indexed. He admitted proudly that it was his creation. "I sweated over this one, gentlemen. I wanted to be sure I had covered all the bases."

The Fiscal Officer explained, "Using the number instead of the actual nomenclature of the expenditure reduces the classification of the accounting sheet from Top Secret to Confidential." He paused for emphasis, "I can only tell you that this is very important. Keep that little booklet in your safe at all times when not in use."

The snorers acknowledge his talk with a loud groan.

Our crusty old colonel watched it all; he never uttered a word.

Much later I realized that this little booklet was indeed a wonderful, very useful tool. The colonel was entirely correct. The "money trail" did follow us wherever we went. My U.S. Army 201 file — the personnel record — was classified Confidential and had to be locked in a safe, much to the consternation of all the personnel officers who had to administer this file for the rest of my army career.

The next lecturer was another administrative type, although he neither looked nor talked like one. The old colonel introduced him as the Source Control Officer, or SCO. He brought no visual aids, only a briefcase filled with forms. According to this officer, there was no function more important than Source Control. "An intelligence operation starts with Form Number One and ends with Form Number Six." We learned that Form One was for a newly recruited, but still untried source — temporary or "T-source."

"I don't want you all to keep your sources as a Form Number One source," he said. "That's only for temporary sources. Fiscal can't give you a lot of money to pay temporary sources. I will not recommend nor approve the payment of large sums to T-sources." He waved Form Number Two. "This is the one that requires work. Only when you have documented the source" — he looked around at the sleepers and shouted, "And you assholes there, in the back, you had better pay attention to what I have to say because if you screw up, I'll be on your ass like white on rice."

The snorers only groaned some more. The SCO plowed all the way to Form Number Six, the form that terminated a source's employment.

After another week of instructions the lecture room seemed to be less crowded — the snorers were gone. No explanation came forth, but one of the sergeants in the front office of the *Erholungsheim* mentioned, "They were determined to be unsuitable for this work." The captain, the leader of the snorers, was one of those missing.

Toward the end of the training the entire student body, plus the crusty old colonel and one of his lieutenants, left by bus for counterintelligence instructions in Stuttgart, the home of the 66th CIC,[38] the European headquarters of U.S. Army Counter Intelligence Corps. There we heard more of counterintelligence than we ever thought possible, or worth knowing. Instructors cycled in and out from early morning to late into the evening. One instructor passed out copies of surveillance reports; we were to use the format whenever we "shadowed" anyone, or thought someone was tailing us. All the visual aids consisted of actual surveillance photographs and films from CIC's operations shadowing Soviet spies. No one went to sleep during these lectures.

One CIC Special Agent started his lecture with, "You must realize ... no, you must recognize that a case officer must operate with the premise that 'Every Person has a Price.'"

"I know, I know," he countered those who disagreed, "but history has proven this to be correct. The price may not always be money, but money works best. It could be travel to exotic places, a relationship with an erotic person, or an expertly written dissertation guaranteed to get you that coveted degree of Doctor of Philosophy."

"Oh, yes," he told those looking surprised, "a good case officer can get you a PhD — if that is your price. It can also be revenge. It can be almost anything you always wanted, but could never obtain or attain."

He went on to explain the revenge is one of the most powerful motivations. He listed the CIC's Penetration Indicators: financial difficulties, loss of family home, bankruptcy, and family separation caused by constant money problems. He also thought abusers of drugs and alcohol fell into the threat category, and that for some it is the thrill of stepping out of a mundane life to ride the sharp edge of utter excitement.

Then he added, "But mostly, it's money!"

Another instructor cautioned us not to correspond with people living in foreign countries. Since most of the students had at least some relatives, aunts, uncles, and cousins living in Europe, he allowed that we should restrict our "correspondence to close relatives, and even here to what we call 'Christmas Card Relationships.' In other words, send letters only on birthdays or holidays."

This admonition would make a considerable impact on me and all of those who had friends and relatives living in Europe. For all practical purposes we had to let all contacts with former classmates, neighbors and friends lapse, all for the sake of security and safety — theirs and ours. A few additional students departed, but by now we were hard-core, tested, observed, poked and prodded, and approved — by the crusty old colonel.

After Stuttgart and the CIC, we were off for two weeks in the Alps and Oberammergau, the home of the Passion Plays. We lodged in the old German *Jäger Kaserne*, the headquarters of the former Wehrmacht's Alpine troops. Through the large window of my room I had a beautiful view of the *Kopfel*, a rock formation — a huge stone pillar. But we were not in O'gau, as the GIs called Oberammergau, to enjoy the Alps. We came to immerse ourselves in East European Area Studies, to learn what makes those folks on the other side of the Iron Curtain tick. This was also the place were we received intensive training in "offensive driving." On the large military police parking lot military police sergeants taught us how to react should someone try to force us off the road; also how to force someone else off the road without getting killed. Needless to say, we wrecked a goodly number of old cars. I think we all agreed that this was by far the most fun we had in this "spy" training. Even the crusty old colonel seemed to enjoy this part of training.

At graduation I became an official members of a small circle engaged in espionage — military front-line intelligence gathering. Out of the original group of about sixty U.S. Army students, I, my friend Joe Milewski, and about three or four others received orders to join the U.S. Army's elite clandestine intelligence unit in Frankfurt-on-Main. Those not selected returned to their parent units — they would be our liaison contacts in the various locations in which we operated.

While the crusty old colonel handed out the assignments he gave us one more bit of advice. "Men," he said, "never do anything you don't want your mother to read in the *Washington Post*." This was without a doubt the best advice I had ever received; I remembered and heeded it throughout my career as an intelligence agent.

TATTERED CLOAK
AND RUSTY DAGGER

Frankfurt-on-Main, West Germany
The House on Wolfgangstrasse
Late 1953

A station wagon with civilian U.S. Occupation Army plates brought my friend Joe Milewski, one other graduate of the Little Red Schoolhouse, and me to an old but elegant, four-story townhouse, the headquarters of our new unit. It was, as the colonel had promised, in a pleasant borough in the northern part of Frankfurt, a part of the city that was barely touched by Allied bombs. To my chagrin I realized that the colonel who had originally interviewed me was now my commanding officer; he was the Chief Clandestine Intelligence Agent — better known as "the Old Man."

The unit had various names. Some knew us as the 7880th Army Unit, Headquarters; others thought we belonged to the Northern Area Command — the element in charge of the area that bordered the British Zone of Germany. Officially — at least as far as official orders were concerned, we also responded to the moniker "7982nd USAREUR Liaison Group." We had other cover names, but I have long ago forgotten them; however, in Pentagon records we operated under our true designation, the *522nd Military Intelligence Battalion.*

The Operations Officer (Ops) integrated the recent graduates of the Little Red Schoolhouse into his operation. Initially some, I among them, stayed at the headquarters building. We were not yet "case officers." Case officers conducted their actual clandestine activities from sites other than this building. My friend Joe Milewski became the unit's sergeant major, and I became the operations sergeant and, for a brief time, the commanding officer's bodyguard. He was a fine officer and gentleman of the old school, intelligent, tough and generous — and a man of very few words. Rumor had it that the Old Man once had a run-in with Soviet and Hungarian agents in Vienna, Austria, and that he had killed one of the Hungarians in self-defense; the Old Man's superiors thought he needed extra protection. Thus, after some additional training, I rotated into this duty.

* * * * *

Actually, I enjoyed being the operations sergeant and accompanying the Old Man on trips to USAREUR headquarters in Heidelberg, or wherever his duties required him to be. His duty driver would pick me up in the morning, and I would escort the Old Man from his quarters to the office. My instructors in personnel security training had emphasized that I was never to take the same route every day, but as in many of these security instructions, there was the theory, and then there was the practical employment of these instructions, i.e. there were just a limited number of ways to get from point A to point B. Aide from that, the Old Man did not like to be chauffeured all over town just to get to his office some four city blocks from his apartment.

The Old Man, being a person of few words, greeted me every morning with, "Good morning, Mr. Thamm, how are your wife and family?"

I would reply, "Quite well, sir. The are still in the States awaiting government quarters assignment."

And every morning he would reply, "Very good, Mr. Thamm. Like to see a man live with his family." When my family finally arrived, I told the Old Man that they had, and he answered, "Very good, Mr. Thamm. Like to see a man live with his family." A man of few words, but a great officer and gentleman.

Although we all wore civilian dress, we were, and the army insisted, first and foremost soldiers. As such we maintained our equipment for deployment into the field just in case the Soviets would invade Western Europe. The "Blanket Roll" was one part of the equipment. It consisted of a shelter half (one half of a tent) and other tent paraphernalia, mess gear, blanket, sleeping bag, and more. Each newly arrived soldier and officer received this unwrapped so that he could inventory the items and sign for them. We kept the equipment on wooden racks in the attic of our office. I had just completed inventory and rolled up the items into a solid, well-formed blanket roll when I heard the newly arrived operations officer, standing next to his pile of equipment, say, "Sergeant Thamm, why don't you make my stuff look just like yours."

I was somewhat taken aback, but recovered quickly by replying, "I am sorry sir, but I do not perform personal services."

The captain turned a bit purple; he knew he had overstepped his authority, and I knew that I would have a superior officer who would never forget. And so it went; he never spoke to me, even relaying his orders to me via our secretary. Soon everyone knew that there was a stand-off in Ops. Several weeks later the Old Man called me into his office and asked what the problem was. I told him that one of the Ops officers and I had a little disagreement. The Old Man pressed for a better explanation, and when I told him that I was reluctant to go into details he said, "Look, Mr. Thamm, I know you. Now tell me what the problem is." He paused, "And tell me before I give you a direct order."

I told him, and less than a week later the captain was no longer in our unit. The Old Man was that kind of officer — not a man of words, but of action.

* * * * *

A few months after I had passed muster at the Little Red Schoolhouse, a gentleman looked through the open door of my operations sergeant's office and greeted me with a friendly "Good morning." He was rather short, in his late forties, well dressed, with slightly wavy, carefully combed, gray hair. With a friendly twinkle in his eyes he extended his hand. "So, you are Gerhardt Thamm?"

I was somewhat startled; I had not heard my name pronounced in such flawless German in some time. As the gentleman reached into the inside pocket of his suit and extracted a dark blue, rectangular etui, he introduced himself, "I am Fred Herz — Manfred Herz." He flipped open his identification credential and closed it so quickly his photograph and impressive blue, official-looking seal were barely visible. With a swift, well-practiced movement Fred had returned the etui to his pocket. We had seen each other during the weekly staff meetings, but had never met formally.

Fred said, "I think 'the Old Man' wants to see us." Thus, the process of merging the old and the new agent began on a Monday morning, after the security briefing.

We walked into the Old Man's office, where I was informed that a recent graduate of the Little Red Schoolhouse, one not fluent in languages, would take over my operations sergeant's job and that I would become a case officer trainee under the tutorship of Special Agent Fred Herz.

The Old Man made it very clear that my first duty was to clear up the administrative side of Fred's operation. He told Fred, "Mr. Thamm knows all the administrative details necessary to streamline your operation." He dismissed us with, "If you have any problems, see me!"

Headquarters watched this merger with some trepidation.

* * * * *

Headquarters knew of Fred's value as a clandestine collector. Of course, they also know that he had never attended any fancy school for spies.

I did not know at that time that Fred had operated alone for years and that he was comfortable operating alone. I also did not know that Fred had had several run-ins with the Source Control Officer, the SCO, because Fred had failed to properly document and record his sources. The SCO, who coordinated all source payments with the fiscal office as well as with Ops, had complained that Fred's sources lacked proper documentation, that source payments were not in the proper format, and that Fred's intelligence reports, the IRs,[39] lacked source numbers and source evaluations, i.e. feedback from the Pentagon.

Intelligence Reports, the formal ones published for distribution, were of utmost importance; it was our unit's *raison d'être*. The information had to be in the proper format submitted to those administering clandestine operations, so that our unit could receive feedback from the G-2 in the Pentagon. Almost equally important as the reports was strict accounting of money spent.

Fred had difficulties in all these areas, and thus had trouble getting reimbursed for money spent. In his own way, he hated to be encumbered by "bureaucracy." It was this lack of administrative skills that would eventually fuse Fred, the old-time clandestine officer, and me, the school-trained agent. In retrospect, it turned out to be a great merging of skills from which we both benefited.

Apparently, the initial meeting was to see whether Special Agent Manfred "Fred" Herz thought he and I were compatible, whether we could form a close working partnership. There could not have been two more different men operating as a clandestine intelligence team. The contrast between Fred and me was incredible. Fred was the son of a wealthy Jewish cloth merchant — a big-city boy raised in Frankfurt-on-Main. I was the son of a Protestant farm laborer — a country boy working during summer vacations on the family farm in Jauer, a small town in Lower Silesia, in the hinterlands of Germany.

Fred's parents had perished in the Nazi Holocaust. My father had been conscripted and served through the entire war in the German Army and the Luftwaffe. My clan, with the exception of one uncle who perished in a Soviet forced-labor camp, had survived World War II — mostly by luck and good fortune.

Fred was university-educated. I was a high school dropout.

Fred fought in the U.S. Army from Omaha Beach into Germany. I fought as a German boy soldier on the Eastern Front.

Fred had years of street agent experience in the field of espionage. I had only the school training necessary to run an espionage operation.

Fred drove a Jaguar. I drove my duty vehicle, an Opel Kapitän that I picked up every morning at the unit's motor pool.

Fred was totally European. He was a native of Frankfurt-on-Main. For several years before World War II he had attended Frankfurt's *Goethe Universität*. Once, in another life, Fred Herz had been a good German. Then the new government decided that only Aryans should attend schools of higher learning. With great difficulty his parents managed to send him first to England, and then to America. They, good Germans, remained in Frankfurt-on-Main and perished in the Austrian corporal's attempt to cleanse Germany of all undesirables.

Fred's father had been a veteran of the Great War. The Kaiser's generals had awarded him the Iron Cross and a number of other medals for valor. Fred, his father and mother were Jews only by Nazi definition; they and their parents had been practicing evangelical Lutherans and valued members of Frankfurt's business community. But most of all they were Germans, as were all German Jews. A large percentage of German Jews were part of Germany's academia, the cream of the intellectual elite of the nation. These are the ones the Nazis eliminated in the most brutal, the most despicable, the most hateful ways. The Nazis filled the vacuum they had created with mediocre Party hacks, opportunists, who then commenced to soil forever Germany's honor.

To me, Fred's parents' disappearance exemplified the insidious nature of the Nazis who always portrayed Jews as being different from "good" Germans.

Our first "clandestine" meeting took place in Fred's government apartment. This was a meeting in violation of all of our security regulations; I would soon get used to that.

Initially, it seemed as if Fred resented the intrusion of a stranger into his domain. However, more even than anyone else, Fred knew how badly he needed assistance in the administrative area of this business — what Fred called "the bureaucracy." Headquarters respected Fred's skills, his talent, acquired not in classrooms, but on the street. His proficiency in recruiting agents was unmatched. But for months the SCO and the Fiscal Officer had voiced their complaints to the Old Man.

Since Fred had worked alone, he had never bothered to establish a satellite office, a safehouse,[40] in one of Frankfurt's boroughs. I entered into this arrangement with trepidation. I realized that I was intruding into Fred's domain, but from the very beginning his wife Martha made me feel comfortable in their home. Since my family was still waiting in the U.S. until I received government quarters, I live in one of our unit's dormitories. Thus, every morning when I arrived at Fred's government quarters, Martha stuffed me with the finest breakfast I ever had. It was a very much akin to a family gathering, as we had breakfast together. Then, when she busied herself in he kitchen, and after we had our coffee in the living room, Fred enthralled me with stories of operating "in the good old days"; he meant 1945 to 1946.

At our first gathering, and after some rudimentary discussions of the way he conducted business on the street, Fred thought it most important that I should have proper documentation. He said I needed the Intelligence Service credentials, a German *Kennkarte* with a cover name, the *nom de guerre*. Fred thought I also needed a fake American identification card with a cover name.

"Pick a good cover name," he said, "some last name that starts with a 'T.'" Fred already had his little brown notepad in his hand, his pen poised at the ready. I wracked my brain in the rush for a last name that started with a T. I could not think of a single name that started with a T, other than my own. Suddenly — memories almost from another life, when I was a German boy soldier, flashed before me — I thought of the man who had stepped on a small mine right in front of me.

Trenker, I thought.

"Sebastian Trenker," I mumbled. "Sebastian Trenker."

"Trenker, great name," replied Fred, "But the first name has to start with a 'G.'"

"How about Georg?"

"Great. I'll get you documented as Georg Trenker. By the way, do you know there is a famous German movie actor, Louis Trenker? I have watched many of his mountain climbing exploits, great movies." Within days I became Georg Trenker, a German citizen living in Frankfurt-on-Main. Fred also procured several U.S. identifications that proved without any doubt that I was actually George Trenker, a Department of the Army civilian, who worked at various U.S. Army installations in the Frankfurt area.

"Not to worry," said Fred, "if someone tries to check on you, your identity will be confirmed — we have an answering service right in the headquarters' building with a single telephone number.

Amazing, I thought, *these things Fred can accomplish without any apparent difficulty; his own paperwork he cannot.* Later I came to realize that subconsciously Fred always fought this "damned government bureaucracy."

Fred interrupted my thoughts. "I should also mention that you should think of yourself as Georg Trenker. Outside, on the street, to me you will always be Georg Trenker, and you better get used to calling me Doktor Hermann. This is not just a game. Those guys on the other side play it rough, and for the sake of our families, our true identities must remain hidden."

With the initial details out of the way I started to arrange all of Fred's notes, his source identifications, source capabilities, and most importantly, his receipts for money paid out either in source payments or other operational expenses, such as taxi, bus, streetcar fares and hotel and restaurant bills. The Fiscal Officer had suggested that I include everything Fred had accomplished during the past two months. I had already copied every IR Fred had written during that time and brought them — again against all security regulations — to Fred's government quarters.

Knowing Fred's unorthodox *modus operandi* I should have been mentally prepared, but I was still flabbergasted when Fred pulled receipts for operational expenditures from his left breast pocket. Fred was a walking security violation. He carried his entire operational, fiscal, and source information — notes of his entire espionage operation — in his pockets. In the left side of his suit jacket he carried, only slightly disguised, the identities of his sources. When I told him that the "source control file" was classified TOP SECRET he just shrugged his shoulder, "That file is safe. I guard it with my life." And I realized he meant every word.

First I arranged Fred's "stuff" in three piles: fiscal, source control, and intelligence reports. These three entities had to be correlated; arranged on the table by date. I placed the IRs in one pile — oldest on top. Then I plowed through crumpled-up hotel, restaurant, and agent-payment receipts, arranged them by date, and did what "Money Bags" had taught at the Little Red Schoolhouse. I pasted hundreds of receipts on eight-by-eleven sheets of typing paper. Then, with the IR in one hand, using much imagination — Fred could not possibly remember which expenditure applied to what source — we matched each receipt with a source number and the date on the IRs that Fred had attributed to the source.

It was akin to working a three-dimensional crossword puzzle. Using the booklet I had received from the Fiscal Officer, I wrote in the left-hand margin the code number that identified the reason for the expenditure. Fred just shook his head in disbelief when I asked him to sign the reconstructed fiscal file; he did, reluctantly.

He worried, "Now Gerhardt, that's not getting us into any trouble, is it?"

In retrospect, Fred had a pretty effective financial arrangement. He had two wallets; one had his own money, the other had C.F. — confidential funds. He advised me to "never mix the two."

After two weeks of creating a financial package that was about as close to reality as possible, he carried the bundle of now well-documented, neatly arranged receipts to the unit's Fiscal Officer. Our new headquarters offices were now in the east wing, on the sixth floor, of the I.G. Farben building — we had just recently moved from our cozy but too-small townhouse into this large complex.

A few days later Fred went to headquarters awaiting the Fiscal Officer's verdict. I sat in the car facing the eastern entrance of the I.G. Farben building, waiting for him to emerge. I could see from his smile as he skipped down

The I.G. Farben Hochhaus. Headquarters, Northern Area Command, and the offices of the Army's clandestine service.

the stairs that we had succeeded. He was as happy as if he had won the German Lotto — in some respects he had. Fred was happy, but most importantly, the Fiscal Officer was happy. As Fred climbed into the car, I asked,

"What did Money Bags say?" I asked Fred.

"Money Bags?" he asked.

"That's what we called him at school."

"Believe me," chuckled Fred, "I called him names worse then that. Of course, never to his face." He settled himself comfortably into the seat. "He loved it. He loved it. Not only did he love it, he sends his compliments to you."

He took a deep breath, "You know, I think he knows we faked some of it, but all the code numbers checked out. I bet he double-checked them with some of the IRs. But, everything is" — Fred used the German words — "*in Ordnung.*"[41] Fred was a happy man.

Having ordered Fred's official finances, I turned my attention to what by now we both laughingly called "Fred's Source Control File." Having completed most of the grunt work, I knew that documenting — maybe creating — Fred's source control file would not be too difficult. I was able to match most of the "Contact Reports" with source identity and the already-submitted fiscal report. In some of these he had enough information, along with Fred's physical description of the source, to make them "permanent" — to Fred's surprise, I filled out several Form 2s that he would submit to the SCO.

Among the helter-skelter of notes I found a résumé of a source code-named "Landser."[42] I sorted through the pages. I thought I had seen the notation "100th Jäger Division." I searched again. This time I saw a familiar name and after the notation, "May 1945, captured near Hirschberg."

I called excitedly to Fred, "Describe Landser." Fred came over, looking surprised.

"Why? What's the matter?"

"Fred, I think I know that man. Describe him to me."

Still puzzled, Fred gave me a detailed description of "Landser."

"Fred, you are not going to believe this, but I know that man. His real name is Schwertfeger. I knew him as Corporal Schwertfeger."

I then told Fred my story. I told him that the person now code-named "Landser" and I had met briefly on the Eastern Front during the waning days of World War II. That Landser had known me under my real name.

I said, "Fred, when I first met Landser I was a fifteen-year-old boy soldier and he was my corporal. I am certain that at that time the older soldier paid little attention to a bunch of boys assigned to his front-line unit; for him we were strictly a nuisance, and besides, we ate too much."

Fred smiled as I continued, "Fred, it was a standing joke; the older soldiers kidded us because we were always hungry. But they needed us. We boys knew the area behind the Soviet line intimately; it was where we had lived all our lives; it had been our homes. In early '45 we led patrols far into Soviet territory to rescue civilians and soldiers cut off when the Soviet swept westward in their January '45 offensive."

I paused, looking at Fred. "What if he remembers me? I mean, he had helped to bandage my knee after the real Trenker, Sebastian Trenker, got his foot blown off."

Another vision flashed through my mind: Sebastian Trenker. I blurted out, "Oh shit, that's the other thing. When you asked me for a name starting with 'T,' the only one I could think of in a hurry was Trenker, the guy who got his foot blown off."

Fred still smiled.

When I was finished telling him the story about the patrol in late March of 1945, the ever-sentimental Fred wiped tears from his eyes. "That was a long time ago," he reassured me, "It's a small world, that's what my dad used to say, it's a small world."

Fred cautioned, "Landser is a good man. Should he ever question you about this, admit that you met before. Even in this business there is a certain integrity that must be observed."

"But Fred," I moaned, "the name Trenker. Why in hell did I ever pick that name Trenker?"

"Well, that's one of those things. I could get you another name, but I'll tell you, Trenker is not an unusual name, at least not in Austria and Bavaria. Let's fly with it."

With this assurance I felt much better.

We started to assemble the last file that had to be carefully matched with the previous ones. Fred continued to be amazed as all this information slowly came together. He kept saying, "Now Gerhardt, that's not getting us into trouble, is it?"

I assumed the "us" meant that I had become part of his team; it made me feel very proud.

"No, I think not. We now have a pretty good package of bios that will make the SCO give you several permanent sources. In a few weeks, in the field, we will document the rest."

Finally, after double- and triple-checking the entries, I decided that this was about the best we could do.

"Fred," I tried to assure him, "I think we have it all covered. If they find errors, I'll just admit that I screwed up. They can't blame you, and I am the new guy; I can still make mistakes. Besides, I think the SCO and the Fiscal Officer still remember me. I asked them some good questions during the lectures. They'll help me — or even forgive me. Now, remember, I could not validate some of your sources. If the SCO asks about them, tell him that we will check their identities during the next contact meetings."

Fred carried the source control file to the I.G. Farben building. A few days later the SCO congratulated us; from now on Fred would be "without sin."

I now had the official credential, the impressive-looking etui similar to the one Fred had flashed when we first met. In contrast to everything else in the army's clandestine operation where all was "done on the cheap," our official credential was of excellent quality, a real work of art: blue leather, or possibly imitation leather; on the outside an impressive gold seal. On the inside a photo with seal impressed upon it, and in three languages, English, French, and German, identifying the bearer of this document as an official agent of U.S. Intelligence.

"When I first received the 'spook pass,'" Fred said, "I thought it was much too fancy for us. Someone must have made a mistake. Either that, or they broke the bank making those things."

Fred advised me to never show the agent credential to anyone unless I was in deep trouble and needed help desperately or, he said with the gleam of a former enlisted man in his eye, "when you need to bump a high-ranking officer off the courier flight to Berlin. Remember, that officer is going to Berlin to have a good time. You are going there to work. If he has orders you have equal status; otherwise you have priority — except generals. They always have priority."

When Fred saw that I carried a .38-caliber revolver, he kidded me, "I carried an M-1 rifle all the way across Europe. Long ago I decided that I never needed one of those little toys."

With his right index finger he tapped his nose, "You must develop a nose for danger. I just never go anyplace where I can smell danger." Apparently he had developed this uncanny sense of being in the right place at the right time. Although I had some unarmed combat training, my .38 was part of me; it gave me a certain degree of confidence and maybe just a wee bit of recklessness.

* * * * *

Headquarters called men like Fred Herz "the first line of defense." Fred saw himself strictly as a "Pointman." He had served as a pointman in the infantry, in the "Big Red One," the U.S. Army's 1st Infantry Division. He had fought his way across Europe from the beaches of Normandy to the foothills of the Alps. His fluency in German had first brought him to the attention of his regimental intelligence officer, the G-2. Later he fell

Agent credential (now with the "retired" addition) of Special Agent Gerhardt B. Thamm, F.O.I. (Field Operations Intelligence).

into the world of clandestine collection by pure accident. The U.S. Army's V Corps, better known as "Vee-Corps," needed information on the Russians in the Soviet Zone of Germany. The U.S. Army had no sources there, and the Russians were mum, so the G-2 asked Fred to get a few Germans to go across the border and report on troop dispositions and movements in East Germany. Slowly his operation, and that of some of his compatriots, became the standard intelligence collection method that gave U.S. commanders sufficient warning of a Soviet assault. Fred's East German sources reported troop movements from the Soviet Union into Germany and from East Germany back into the Soviet Union. Others reported activity of Soviet troop in garrison and the maneuver and assembly areas.

With little formal training, but with much native cunning, a thorough knowledge of the area, and a healthy respect for "the other side," Fred became a clandestine case officer. For some years he stumbled along recruiting agents. He had a love for, and great understanding of, people. Fred operated the spy business the way his father had conducted the wholesale fabric business, with honesty and integrity. He bought information and paid for it what it was worth. He never cheated anyone, and he never allowed anyone to cheat him, or his government. The Austrian corporal had kept Fred away from his hometown for some eight years — now he was back on his turf. During the years he operated alone, Berlin had become "his" city. He had reconnoitered it, ridden its streetcars, subways and buses until he knew every nook and cranny of the town.

Aside from his years of experience, aside from Fred's "nose," his knack for spotting danger well in advance, he had one great advantage over me: he was thoroughly comfortable moving in high society, living in first class hotels, and dining in fine restaurants. I was not — not yet, anyway.

Along with the smooth way Fred moved through the German society, he also had a wonderful capability to identify German wines. Later, as we became better acquainted, I tested his ability to identify wines several times, and Fred always won.

Once, Fred and I drove from Frankfurt to Bonn to testify on behalf of one of Fred's sources so that he could be officially recognized by the West German government as a legitimate refugee from Communism — and receive the financial help that government accorded to this type of refugee. On the way back to Frankfurt we stopped for a late lunch at one of the vineyard restaurants overlooking the Rhine River. We ordered lunch and I took the waiter aside to tell him that I wanted to test my friend's wine tasting ability. I asked the waiter to serve Fred a glass of 1950 Rüdesheimer Berg Schlossberg Riesling Spätlese. Fred looked surprised when the waiter appeared with the wine. He started to protest that he had not ordered the wine, but I interjected that I had done so, and that I wanted to test Fred's ability to identify the vineyard and the year.

Fred smiled, "Oh, well, since you are paying for it, that will be just fine." He lifted the glass, tested the clarity and the bouquet as he always did, then took a small sip, sniffed the wine again, took another sip, grinned, lifted the glass and said, "1950 Riesling Spätlese."

He then took another sip, and declared, "Comes from the Middle Rhine, probably from around Rüdesheim." I admitted defeat.

Fred could identify wines by winery, year, and class — I have never archived this, although I have often tried.

I had tried to emulate Fred and his ways. I was not a wine drinker; I enjoyed the occasional bottle of German beer. Fred loved the wines of the Rhine and Mosel rivers. Much later I developed a taste for the dry wines of the Franconian hills, Frankenwein, but was never able to tell the year it was made, or the vineyard that grew it.

Although Manfred Herz was probably the best agent U.S. Army Intelligence ever deployed in the intelligence struggle against the Soviet Army of Occupation in East Germany, he did have some limitations. Fred moved at a social level far above mine, but no matter how well he spoke German, he could never go into deep cover as a post–World War II German. His period of enforced exile from 1938 through 1945 had robbed him of the bond shared by all Germans: the memories of World War II. He could not walk the walk and talk the talk of a German soldier—a highly important requirement for Germans his age. Thus he would always be the American who spoke fluent German.

I, on the other hand, had spent the entire war in Germany. During that period I had experienced life in Germany as a schoolboy, a teenager who rode in youth equestrian competitions, and a boy soldier in the German Army. While a Red Army prisoner I herded cattle on horseback and worked as a lumberjack. I was a quick learner and would soon become familiar with fishing trawlers and tramp steamers to take on my latest role.

I was well on my way to becoming the "Man for All Seasons."

But Fred performed the transformation from Special Agent Fred Herz to Herr Doktor Hermann far better than I; he did it almost instinctively. While I had to consciously think about what I was doing, Fred became Doktor Hermann in an instant, like my comic book hero Superman, who could walk into a phone booth as Clark Kent and emerge the Caped Crusader without missing a beat. Fred was always the totally confident persona, the Doktor Hermann he represented. He moved through German society with ease. And, it seemed to me at least, that Martha, Fred's wife, carried within her the same kind of confidence. Fred had found his niche at his level, and I would only find mine later working in various levels of deep-cover clandestine operations.

* * * * *

In the meantime Ann Marie and our two children, Erik and Renita, had arrived in Germany. We settled in comfortable government quarters, an apartment house on 52 Hansa Allee, in the northern part of Frankfurt-on-Main. These apartments had once belonged to the I.G. Farben concern, a large chemical entity that had been headquartered in the I.G. Farben Building— now one of our U.S. Army headquarters buildings. The employees had been evicted to make room for the ever-increasing U.S. Army occupation force. We lived on the third floor and had maid quarters on the fourth floor— although we opted not to employ a maid. Each apartment had a somewhat unique central water-heating system that had the furnace in the kitchen. A houseman fed the system with coal. It also had a flash-heat water system— gas fired—that initially scared me to death. The heater located in the bathroom lit up every time someone turned on the hot water spigot. I happened to be the lucky one to use the system for the first time. I was in the bathroom when Ann Marie turned on the kitchen's hot water faucet; it caused the water heater to ignite with a loud whooshing sound and a blue flash — very uncomfortable, but we quickly became used to it. Actually, it was quite an efficient system.

There were three bedrooms, a large dinning and living room, kitchen and hallway. The master bedroom, facing away from the street, had a little balcony.

A few months after we had moved into and become familiar with our army quarters, Mr. West, our chief warrant officer and the unit's adjutant, called for volunteers to host fatherless children from West Berlin for a few weeks during summer vacation. Our unit was selected because it housed a fair number of soldiers who spoke some German. On a Saturday afternoon Ann Marie and I were among many at the officers club parking lot awaiting the arrival of these children. Several buses arrived, and one of them brought "our child," a scrawny, ten-year-old, totally bewildered boy named Hans. Hans carried a cheap little suitcase and was reluctant to leave the other children from the bus. But the kids quickly dispersed as they were matched to their sponsors, and we soon drove home with our charge who, despite his misgivings, seemed to enjoy riding in a "big" American car.

Ann Marie had already prepared a bed in Erik's room and the children quickly settled down. Hans told me, and I interpreted it for Erik and Renita, that he lived with his mother in one of West Berlin's public housing apartments. He did not know who or where his father was — he had never seen him. But his mother had a job, and he attended grade school. After school he came home to do his homework and his chores, cleaning and washing the dishes. He was surprised that we had our own bathroom with bathtub in the apartment. When Ann Marie unpacked his suitcase she found one set of underwear and a pair of shorts neatly folded and wrapped in newspaper.

We decided to take the children for the two-city block walk to the Army Post Exchange on "WAC Circle" to buy some additional underwear and a couple of shirts and an extra pair of pants for Hans. There we met several other couples with Berlin's fatherless children. The kids greeted each other as if they had just met long lost family members. They had that dazed look on their faces of children undergoing a total life reorientation. The salesladies, all German of course, lovingly spoke with the children, switching back and forth into English when speaking to their sponsors. This torrent of two languages flooding between salesladies, the American customers and the children added to the atmosphere of confusion.

Back at the apartment, Ann Marie gave Hans the shopping bag to unpack. She wanted Hans to realize that the clothing was his. When it finally dawned on him that all this was his he shyly, yet formally, shook Ann Marie's hand and said "Danke, danke, danke."

While Hans, Erik and Renita started to become acquainted with each other, Ann Marie prepared dinner. As we sat around the table, Hans seemed ill at ease while he watched us preparing to eat. Finally he asked what was on the table. I explained that this was an Italian dinner: spaghetti, meatballs, tomato sauce and salad with Italian dressing. He wanted to know why we ate the salad first. I told him that we usually did that, but that he could eat it any time he wanted. With that said, he hesitantly attacked the salad. He told us that his mother never served fresh salad; he thought it was too expensive. After dinner he insisted helping Ann Marie to wash the dishes.

As our first evening together came to an end, Erik, and then Renita, showered and prepared for bed. I told Hans that he was next in the bathroom, that he could either fill the bathtub or take a shower. Initially he was reluctant to bathe, informing me that his mother had washed him just before he had left Berlin. It took a bit of convincing, but I insisted, and he finally agreed. He opted for a bath and, once in the water, he had a great time until I told him that it was time to get to bed.

Finally, with the children tucked away in their beds, Ann Marie and I started to relax. I wondered aloud whether or not this had been a good idea, bringing Hans into our household, "He is like a kid from outer space. I hope he gets used to us and our way of life."

I left for work early the next morning. I was somewhat concerned, with the language difficulty, about how Hans and our children would get along together. When I returned in the early evening Ann Marie said that somehow the children were able to communicate far better than adults — and so it was. The next week seemed to pass quickly. We decided to go on a mini-vacation that Saturday. We piled into our Studebaker Starlight Coupe and drove along the Main River to Rüdesheim-on-Rhine in the heart of Germany's wine country, for lunch. Hans jabbered excitedly all the way, pointing out sights, asking what they were. He said that this was the first time he had ever gone on vacation riding in a private automobile. Erik and Renita seemed chagrined; for them it was not a novelty.

I remembered the first time I had driven my own car, this Studebaker. It was on a Saturday in early May, 1950. I had just purchased the car from Lee D. Butler Studebaker in Washington, DC. I had made a small down payment toward the full price of $1,650, and Mr. Butler let me have the car on a handshake.

Although I had operated heavy military equipment, aside from driving a passenger car while taking the driver's test in Virginia, I had never driven an automobile before. Thus, I navigated my brand-new Studebaker along

The author with his 1950 Studebaker "Starlight Coupe."

Washington's Rock Creek Parkway to Irving Street. There I carefully, and with much difficulty, parked the car. I walked the last city block to our Irving Street apartment and told Ann Marie that I had managed to bring the Studebaker into the neighborhood without a scratch.

Then, for the next few weeks, I got used to driving the automobile while Ann Marie looked out of the right-side window. Having driven large tractors and prime movers, I had the tendency to drive toward the middle of the road, although Ann Marie kept reassuring me, "You have plenty of room on this side of the road." It took me weeks, but mentally I finally managed to match the width of my car to the width of the road.

Watching Hans, I remembered how exited I was driving my very own car. I also remember how long ago, I had to ride—the shame of it all—Mother's old-lady's bicycle. Before World War II my parents could not afford to buy me a boy's bike, and I remember Mother telling me sadly, "First you want a bike, then you will want a motorbike…" Wanting to have a car never even came up for debate.

By necessity, I had to travel during the second week of Hans's stay. By the time I returned on the Friday before he was scheduled to return to Berlin, Hans seemed very much the "American" boy. On Saturday Ann Marie packed his suitcase — by now bulging with all sorts of clothes and a long-eared toy dog. The time neared for departure. We drove to the officers' club parking lot. All the children arrived and mingled; only Hans remained close to Ann Marie. He hung at her arms, crying. He did not want to leave. It was heartbreaking. We had written our German address on a 3 × 5 card and tucked it in his jacket pocket. We promised to write, to keep in touch, and finally, he was almost the last to board the bus. The children departed, leaving a saddened group of American families standing in the parking lot waving goodbye.

For several months we corresponded with Hans, but, as time passed, we lost contact. For a few months I had been tempted to visit Hans while I was in Berlin working my informants. However, my security training kicked in, and I never did.

DOKTOR HERMANN AND GEORG TRENKER

Clandestine Operations Area
West Berlin
Early 1954

Initially it was "Exigencies of the Service" that had welded the old Special Agent Herz and me, the brand-new Special Agent Thamm. Later we became friends. We respected the each other's knowledge and used the other's experience to further the art of espionage.

Fred Herz had been an extraordinarily effective teacher. After all the theoretical training at the Little Red Schoolhouse — what one instructor had called, "How to be a spy in three easy lessons" — Fred led me into the real world of espionage, first in small steps, with "hands-on" training.

From the beginning we had already violated a number of security regulations when we straightened out Fred's administrative mess in his apartment. Later we would make additional changes to our "security" rules. Fred insisted on strict compliance with his modus operandi. We always followed his tried and proven sequence. Before we ever ventured out on the street we made a map reconnaissance, then we checked out the area by walking the land: area reconnaissance. Whenever we walked the land we followed a strict countersurveillance protocol — that meant checking for "tails," when on foot or while riding buses or streetcars. Together we walked through Berlin's boroughs; we rode streetcars, subways and buses all over West Berlin, but mostly we walked.

As always Fred, the old rifleman, just mentioned as a by-the-by, "You best get the feel of the land by reconnoitering it on foot looking right and left, looking far and near, and always covering your hind end, your rear." And indeed, I soon recognized the many similarities between being a street agent and a pointman in a rifle squad.

"One difference, though," Fred would add, "a street agent most often operates alone. When I was a pointman in the infantry I always had a bunch of heavily armed buddies backing me up. In this profession you have to get used to working alone."

* * * * *

Berlin was my training ground. Fred called Berlin "the most dangerous chunk of earth in Europe."

Fred may have been born in Frankfurt-on-Main, but Berlin was "his" city. Before he allowed me to accompany him on an actual Treff[43] he introduced me to Berlin's boroughs. We toured Dahlem, Steglitz, Moabit, the Grünewald, Charlottenburg, Neukölln, Lichterfelde and Tempelhof. We approached several points along the East-West line of demarcation. Fred wanted to show me one particular border crossing in the Neukölln borough. At Tempelhof airport we boarded a double-decker bus — Fred led the way to the upstairs seating from which we had a good view of the street. Fred watched me as the bus turned into a broad, straight avenue. He had a devious smile on his face. I suspected some sort of trick. I watched everything very carefully. As we turned into this broad avenue I looked at the street sign; it read "Karl-Marx-Strasse." I looked, alarmed, at Fred.

He still smiled. "Scared you? Did it?"

I nodded my head, speechless.

"Nothing to worry about. It's still West Berlin. You must remember that West Berlin buses do not go into East Berlin. On the bus you are sure to be in West Berlin. Now, on the U-Bahn[44] ... I'll show you that later ... those trains go right through East and West Berlin, same with the S-Bahn.[45] I don't recommend riding the S-Bahn, ever; it's East German territory and patrolled by the VOPOs." A few bus stops later we exited. Fred wanted to show me where the actual border crossing into East Berlin was. Then we rode a taxi back to Charlottenburg. We left the cab a few blocks from our hotel. In the safety of our room Fred pulled out a street map of Greater Berlin.

"Take a look. This is where we were today. Tomorrow," he pointed to a section of the map, "we'll reconnoiter the northern sector: the borough of Wedding." It was another map reconnaissance, almost like at Fort Riley, but in far more comfortable accommodations.

We rode the bus into the borough and walked through the area in which I was expected to work, "walking the land," Fred reminded me, "just like in the infantry."

"Walking the land," Fred continued. "Familiarizing yourself with all the terrain features; here in Berlin it's the ruins, the houses left standing, the empty lots cleared of debris. Also, pay attention to weather and light conditions, all highly important in your movements through enemy territory."

Kaiser Wilhelm Gedächtniskirche at the center of author's Op Area.

He looked at me. I must have looked somewhat incredulous. "Don't forget, even here in West Berlin you are in enemy territory. Remember the Monday morning briefings? Remember those SOBs on the other side pay cash for any one of us delivered." I remembered, and I also realized that the "delivery point" was a short few city blocks from our hotel. Then we returned to map reconnaissance. We reviewed the area we had just covered that day, again using the Berlin city map.

Fred believed, "Before you can operate in relative safety in this town you have to get to know everything of our ops area. He pointed out a local restaurant.

"Come, we'll have a beer." We entered a typical neighborhood *Gaststube*, a combination bar/restaurant. Over beer Fred pointed to the rear. "See the sign pointing to the restrooms?"

I nodded.

"That will be our exit."

We finished our beers and Fred led the way past the restrooms into a dark open storage area cluttered with beer kegs and empty soft drink crates.

He led the way, explaining, "The row of houses behind here became casualties during the firebombing, but this path through the ruins leads to the next street. A fantastic way to avoid just in case someone watched the front door."

We continued our reconnaissance. Fred suddenly stopped and turned around to point out certain "terrain features."

"See this stretch of the street? Straight as an arrow. Easy to spot a tail." Later he stopped before a storefront. "Take a look at this beautiful window. In the reflection you can see everyone on the street and still look as if you were window shopping."

Time and again he would reminisce, thinking of his experience in the infantry during the last war, "You know," he chuckled, "this kind of work always reminds me of my days in the infantry. Before we riflemen entered hostile territory we always made a map reconnaissance. Only when we had the general terrain in memory did we reconnoiter the area on foot, observe it physically."

Fred paused for a moment. "A thought just struck me," he said. "Today I feel far more relaxed with you along. Alone on the streets of Berlin, my gut is cold and tight like a catgut on a violin."

I took that as a high compliment.

After some time, while we again walked, he turned and we started to retrace our steps. "This is a good place to hook back and see if someone is following, or to get into the other guy's rear. All very important if you want to survive in this business."

He tapped his nose, "You have to develop 'the nose,' the nose for danger, and you must avoid dangerous areas, you must not let others lure you into going their way."

Fred knew every corner of the area in which he operated and had fascinating, instructive stories to tell. Only after he felt that I was at home in his city was I allowed to accompany him on my first operational meeting, "The Treff," to meet "Landser," the former Corporal Schwertfeger of the 100th Jäger Division. I met "Landser" with some trepidation. After all, he had been the one who bandaged my leg after Sebastian Trenker, the real Trenker, had his foot blown off by a mine. I hoped that this unfortunate incident would not ignite "Landser's" memory.

* * * * *

Ten years had passed, but I remembered it well. It was in a relatively quiet sector of the Eastern Front, and it was supposed to have been just another routine patrol before midnight in late March 1945. We entered a cleared path in one of our minefields. Our pointman had already cleared the supposedly mine-free alley and taken up a defensive position some 50 or 60 feet away. Suddenly, a bright flash and a dull crack shattered the stillness of the night. The man a bare five feet in front of me had stepped on a *Schuhmine*, a small, very crude, but also very effective antipersonnel mine.[46] The explosion knocked me to the ground. My right leg felt as if a hard brushwood broom had whipped across it. Our patrol leader, Corporal Schwertfeger, whispered — God knows why, everyone within miles must have heard the explosion — for no one to move!

"There are mines all around us. Those Russian bastards must have planted a few shoe mines into our 'mine-free' alley." He crawled toward us, carefully probing the ground for other mines with his bayonet. He looked at the bloody leg of the man who had stepped on the mine. With a pocketknife he cut the soldier's trousers. I saw the man's foot just dangling by a thin strip of skin. The corporal quickly severed the last part of the man's skin. With a dull clunk the foot, still in the shredded boot, fell to the ground. A tourniquet, expertly applied, stopped the bleeding. Meanwhile the corpsman, the last man in the patrol, hastily crawled over us so not to step on another mine. He and Corporal Schwertfeger bandaged the stump. The wounded man started to breathe heavily and moaned; from the medical kit the corpsman took a syringe and injected a shot of morphine. Corporal Schwertfeger again whispered for everyone to keep quiet and asked whether anyone else was hurt. Since my knee had started to ache I looked and saw blood all over my right trouser leg of my white camouflage uniform. I grabbed his arm and pointed at my leg. Before I realized it the pocketknife was back in his hand and he cut away my right trouser leg. For a split second I thought he was also going to cut off my leg, but he just stripped off the trouser leg so the corpsman could bandage my knee. Then he passed word to the pointman that we would retrace our route and return to our lines.

"No sense to go any further," he said, "those bastards know where we are."

The wounded man and I arrived in the Landeshut field hospital for further treatment. My comrade disappeared into the operating room; another auxiliary medic, a cute little teenage blond, brought me a steaming cup of coffee while I waited my turn. She stayed to comfort me; what a wonderful girl.

Well after midnight a doctor looked at my leg and kidded me, "Great, I won't have to cut off your leg; it's not as bad as your buddy's. I'll have that fixed in no time."

The hospital was short on anesthetics. The cute little blond washed my leg with iodine; the biting pain of the disinfectant almost made me shoot through the ceiling. Then the doctor used a pair of tweezers to pick bits of dirt, wood and metal out of my leg without any type of painkiller. There must have been a hundred pieces — mostly wood splinters. An eternity later he told the young girl to again wash my leg with iodine; it did not hurt all that bad this time. Then one of the medics put on a light bandage and placed me on one of the hospital cots to sleep.

My wounds were just shallow scratches from particles that had managed to penetrate the three layers of my clothing — long woolen underwear, heavy gray woolen trousers, and white camouflage coveralls. Around noon the next day I found my fellow patrol member. To my utter surprise, he was in high spirits. He gleefully told me that this was the best thing that had ever happened to him, a *Heimatschuss*,[47] he gloated. He told me he would leave for home in a day or two.

I was startled. How could anyone be happy about losing a foot? Undeterred he continued to tell me that this war had turned to shit, that for him it was the only way out of there. He suggested that when the whole thing blew up, as it would, I should not stop along the way.

"Listen, kid," he whispered, "when this shit is over, make sure to get to Bavaria."

He wrote down his address. "My mother is gonna have a bed for you, guaranteed. Just get the hell out of here." He handed me a slip of paper on which he had written his mother's address in fine small print; Sebastian Trenker came from a small village south of München.

That afternoon the duty sergeant told me to pack my satchel and leave for home in the morning to wait there until my puncture wounds had healed. I wanted to say my farewell to Sebastian, but the sergeant told me he was already on a train for a military hospital at München. His wish had come true—he had gotten his *Heimatschuss*.

With my two-way army transportation chit in my pocket and my haversack filled with bread, sausages, six or seven pieces of chocolate from emergency rations, and a half-pound of good coffee—not the common *Ersatzkaffee*[48]—I headed for the train station. I arrived at Altenbuchen, in the Sudetenland, where my clan had found refuge, in the early afternoon. For my family and friends it was a great surprise. I had not had time to write of my misadventure. My mother and Preuss Oma thought I "had grown a whole head taller" during the past few months.

Since my wounds were mostly shallow lacerations, they healed rather quickly. In less than two weeks, over Mother's strenuous objections, I returned to the front.

* * * * *

In 1954, when I again met Corporal Schwertfeger, now code-named Landser, he was thirty years old; he appeared to be in his fifties. He walked slightly stooped with a limp—he favored his left leg—a war wound. He had curly, prematurely gray hair and deep-set dark eyes; he looked almost fragile.

Doktor Hermann and Landser greeted each other like old friends. Doktor Hermann introduced me as Georg Trenker. When Landser first saw me he turned a shade of gray; he seemed to hesitate before shaking my hand; he looked at me as if he had seen a ghost or something supernatural. Landser shook his head as if trying to wipe out a bad dream or memory. As luck had it, it went no further. The connection between a scrawny boy soldier on the Eastern Front and an American Intelligence agent was simply too remote to even contemplate. Even the name Trenker appeared not to have rung a bell. I had never asked, and Landser had never explained his strange behavior, but something about me seemed to have stimulated a long-suppressed memory cell in Landser.

But, I thought, *maybe the real Trenker had also been a short timer in the corporal's squad.*

As Fred had philosophized, *it's a small world.*

* * * * *

In Schwertfeger's vetting report Fred Herz had noted that Landser had been in the high school class of '43. He graduated with an abbreviated Abitur in late 1942 to enter the Wehrmacht. Shortly after basic training he transferred to "flesh out" a badly beaten-up Panzergrenadier[49] Division at the Eastern Front. He got as far as Kursk when the front line collapsed under heavy attack by Soviet armor. He spent almost his entire army career in a long retreat "to shorten the front line."[50] His division retreated from Kursk to Shostka and from there to Chernogov, where Landser lost part of his left heel. After four months in a hospital in Breslau he transferred to "flesh out" another unit; this time it was the recently reestablished 100th Jäger Division.[51]

Just two weeks before the Soviets captured the German Army corporal, now code-named Landser, had participated in that last offensive action of the 100th Jäger Division during World War II. It was one of the many attacks that meant little or nothing to the participants — except death and maiming. They had followed orders from above.[52]

Landser was indeed a soldier *extraordinaire*. He told Fred that he had tried to reach the "Amerikaners" via the Hirschberger Pass. Alas, it was blocked by heavy snow — I knew this to be true, because Lothar and I had tried to get across the mountains there and failed.

The Soviets captured him outside of Hirschberg. He survived years of Soviet POW camps somewhere between Omsk and Novosibirsk. Many of his comrades died from malnutrition and mistreatment. He suffered, as did others, physically as well as mentally.

For him it was always the same nightmare: *He felt the autumn sun on his legs. The warmth soothed the back of his shaved head, his sore spine, and his weary shoulders; he felt secure, comforted. A faint breeze, more like a slight shifting of air, not nearly enough to disturb the warmth generated by the sun's reddish-golden rays, caressed his bruised body. It was, like eons ago, a lazy summer afternoons in the valley. His subconscious thoughts fled swiftly across the barren tundra to the lush, green floor of his home village in the Silesian Mountains. He was a large bird gliding across this wonderful place he called home. He saw the blue-green waters of the Wütende Neisse River. He skimmed toward the dark blue pine forests that crested the valley and saw the familiar glittering band of asphalt that neatly divided his valley. He surged along the road toward the little side street rarely noticed by strangers; it led toward his mother's house. He crossed the old wooden* bridge under which the gently creek murmured in summer and autumn and roared wildly during the spring thaw. This was his most favorite place on earth — a crystal-clear pool that Mother Nature had carved out of huge, yellow sandstone columns. One part of the sandstone formation still towered high above the pool. The water was just deep enough for those risking the dive from that sandstone cliff. How he had relished the thrill of cutting through the clear waters warmed by the sun into the lower layer, still refreshingly cool water that rushed from its high mountain spring. Ah, the joy of surfacing and allowing the sun's rays to warm his young body. His thoughts roamed from the pool along the narrow road shaded by huge maples and oaks that gave the road an almost cathedral-like reverence. Past Herr Putzker's place, where the exuberant white Spitz greeted well-known faces by joyfully charging the wire fence. At the tall brown stone marker he swerved right along the bumpy track where pale blue morning glories and dark green ivy covered weather-bleached fences. As he had done so often, he stopped at the clearing to longingly scan his valley. Little cottages tucked away among trees like spots of color on soft moss. He had often watched the setting sun from this, his very private place. His eyes followed the thin gray veils of smoke rising into the calm evening sky. Slowly he meandered around the bend where a cluster of poplar trees silently reached into the sky — this was the entrance of mother's home. As always, the gate stood open; he had forever meant to repair the old lock that still hung by the same two rusty screws. It did not matter. Folks here had no need to lock their houses! All summer long his mother left the front and back doors open so that cool mountain breezes fanned her house. Strangers never ventured this far from the public road, and folks from the valley were always welcome to stop and chat.

Stretching himself he felt the roughness of his resting place. He smelled the scent of dry burlap and musty earth, and he slowly came to realize that he was a long way from his valley. At first he did not want to open his eyes; he wanted to linger just a little while longer, but the smell of burlap, of potato sacks, did not permit it; the smell brought with it the reality of rusty barbed wire, tall watch towers, and brutal guards.

He was a long way from his peaceful valley. Life? Was there life? He wondered about that, and about the quietness, the peacefulness of this particular autumn afternoon. Slowly, ever so slowly, he opened his eyes. Before him stretched a row of faded clapboard-covered barracks — empty. Beyond the barracks, outside the rusted barbed wire that surrounded the prison compound, were the horse stables, their dark interior lit little by sunlight — empty. And beyond the wire that hung wearily from tired, discolored posts fence the tall, wooden guard towers; they were empty.

There were no guards; not in the towers, and not at the gate. There were no prisoners anywhere! He was alone! Apprehensively, he raised his head. The rest of the compound was deserted, safe for two or three sparrows in the dust fighting for seeds. For the first time since his arrival the rough, hand-hewn wooden gate of the compound, brittle from years of exposure to freezing Siberian winter gales and a bleaching sun, seemed invitingly friendly. Yes, the towers were deserted; the machine guns stared, unmanned, into the soft blue heavens, and the hated red hammer-and-sickle rag hung listlessly from its flagpole above the gate, and ... the gate was open. My God — could it be?

The gate was open!

With great effort he pushed himself to his feet. His legs were weak, but he knew they would strengthen with exercise during his homeward journey. He would see his valley again — finally.

The gate was open!

Painfully he pushed one foot before the other, then, laboriously, faster, and faster, and faster again, afraid the gate would swing shut again — this time forever. Thoughts of freedom — of life — his breath burst in sharp gasps from his dry throat. His worn, broken boots stumbled as his legs pumped through the red dust.

The Gate Was Open!

He felt the warm autumn sun, and dampness on his forehead, and he felt the cooling air stirred by his movement. He would see his valley again. His feet desperately pounded the red earth. He rushed onward, past the towers, through the gate where the air seemed cooler, cleaner, fresher — freer. Oh God, he was free — he would see his valley again.

THE GATE WAS OPEN!

He did not hear the shrill shouts. He did not hear the dry, exactly spaced, stutter of the PPSh machine pistol. He did not feel the hard hammering of copper-encased lead bullets against his back — bullets that flung him forward and into the dust, the red dust.

Then, as quickly as can be, the scene changed. He saw his mother watering flowers on two graves. His was next to that of his father. He saw his name carved on the granite tombstone, and below it he read, "Our beloved son, died somewhere in Russia for Führer, Volk und Vaterland. Lord, the Almighty, please save his soul."

Then he awoke and he knew that he would never go home again. No one knew that he was alive, and no one cared.

* * * * *

During his recruiting interview, Landser told Doktor Hermann, "For two or three years after I came out of that Soviet POW camp, nightmares prevented me from getting enough rest to study. Three or four times a week I went to school or to work hollow-eyed looking like a man suffering from a perpetual hangover. It was always the same nightmare: I look through barbed wire westward into the setting sun..."

After he had recuperated from the ordeal, Landser studied metallurgy and, while still at the university, worked part-time in a laboratory testing structural steels and other high-tensile metals for reparations to their Soviet "friends," as well as for East Germany's reconstruction industry, high-rise apartments, bridges, and U-Bahn tunnels. He volunteered to help the "Amerikaners" to guard against the Soviets. Thus Landser became one of Doktor Herman's train watchers—people who reported Soviet troop transports crossing the Oder and the Neisse rivers into Poland.

I had promised Fred to turn most of his poorly documented temporary sources into permanent ones. In a few weeks in the field I met these sources. It seemed that after Fred had vetted and recruited them he was reluctant to then ask for their identification cards. I explained to Fred what I planned to do to document each of his first temporary sources.

"We can't do that!" he exclaimed. "I have known that fellow for two years and ... well, I feel very uncomfortable doing that at this stage of the game."

"Fred, we have a good system. I learned it at the Spook School. It will make the source feel that it serves him best to give us the information."

Of course, Fred knew that getting this personal data was important for his future operations, so he agreed.

Near the end of a contact meeting, I mentioned how important it was to have personal data recorded just in case he and his family were forced to flee East Germany. Then I enlarged on it by mentioning the Swiss or Lichtenstein account in a source's cover name, and how important it was to have backup data in our office so that he could contact us directly—we had such a system in place.

Fred had not realized, but I had heard at the Little Red Schoolhouse that most Europeans are used to showing their ID cards to authorities, and in occupied Germany we were the authorities. According to our instructor, every source he had ever processed in this manner had agreed to provide basic data, and more.

I always had my Minox camera handy to photograph the *Kennkarte* and make a close-up photo of the source.

Fred was flabbergasted, at least during the first few times I gave my spiel. But our Source Control Officer was a happy man.

* * * * *

I had one last item to correct. No one knew that Fred carried his "shopping list," officially known as the *Essential Elements of Information*, or EEI, in his right coat pocket. The EEI contained highly classified information intelligence analysts in Heidelberg and Washington needed to write their intelligence assessment. By definition the EEI had items of information about the adversary and his environment, and it was a TOP SECRET document — Fred had just snipped the classification markings from the document.

Just to prevent him from carrying it on his person I promised that I would have the EEI ready and available for his use whenever he needed it. Since Fred did not have an office of his own I had already made arrangements with my friend Joe Milewski, our sergeant major, for a small safe to be placed in his office.

The Transformation

Frankfurt-on-Main, West Germany
The House on Hansa Allee
1954

Little, seemingly innocuous incidents can complicate a married Special Agent's life. When Ann Marie arrived in Frankfurt she wondered whatever happened to my army uniforms; she asked why I wore civilian attire at all times. I explained that I was still in intelligence, but that now my duties required this new mode of dress and that the army had paid for it all. Because I was still, and foolishly, following the strict security rules of classified information that the instructors at the Little Red Schoolhouse had made the students believe were important, I did not reveal any details. Later I also had to explain why I was armed and why I disappeared for days on end. I should have realized that all the older, more experienced Special Agents had told their wives much of what their duties were — of course not the operational secrets, but the routine, everyday activities. I should also have remembered that Fred's wife seemed to be totally at ease when I picked up Fred to fly to Berlin for my training and later, to assist him in filling out the Form 2 source personal data. The wives of experienced case officers knew that we ran agents into East Germany, or Czechoslovakia, or Poland, but I had never told Ann Marie — all for the sake of security.

All went relatively well until, at a unit gathering, a major's wife asked Ann Marie, "Oh, didn't you know your husband is a spy?"

The officer wife's indiscretion caused considerable difficulties in our marriage, accusations that I did not trust my wife as much as other members in the unit trusted their wives. I explained that this woman's "loose lips" constituted a major security violation, that it could endanger all of us working in this profession. Discussions went back and forth until I finally realized that I might just as well clear the deck. I told Ann Marie that I was not a spy, that

I was one who ran spies into East Germany, that this was our unit's mission, and that it was an important mission. Just to forestall any future "collisions" I explained that at times I worked in "deep cover" under a number of different names, but that my main cover name was Georg Trenker, and that I was documented both as the German citizen Georg Trenker and the U.S. Army civilian George Trenker. I also explained that just in case we should run into one of my local contact, I would introduce her as "Frau Trenker." Ann Marie was somewhat perplexed, but she soon recovered. However, I noticed shortly thereafter that she seemed more concerned — frightened even — whenever I left the apartment.

Operating as a clandestine case officer, I remembered many of Fred's lessons and his warnings. One was that in this profession you have to get used to working alone. Another was that "waiting on Berlin's street corners tightens up your gut like catgut on a violin." Fred had failed to tell me about several — I would later learn important — aspects of clandestine agent's life: the physiological and psychological transformation I had to undergo whenever I departed on a missions; the transition from U.S. Army sergeant to German national, from Gerhardt Thamm to Georg Trenker.

It had most likely not even occurred to Fred, because for him it had long ago become second nature. It was not so critical when I lived in a government dormitory, but after my family and I had moved into government quarters the transformation became acute. For me, the new case officer, it came as a total surprise, as a shocking event whenever I departed from the safety of my government quarters, from the warm environment of family, of wife, of children, whenever I had to make the switch to enter the never-never world of deceit, of espionage, of covert operations. At least initially I had not reached Fred's plateau of confidence, and Ann Marie was not as comfortable in the Special Agent wife's role as was Fred's wife. It was, to note the obvious, an extremely stressful period for both of us.

Whenever I left on a mission, I rose early in the morning to prepare myself for the role I would play. I dressed in whatever clothing the mission required — German suit, coat and hat when meeting a foreign government official or businessman, dark woolen trousers, turtleneck sweater, and fisherman's cap when operating out of a Baltic Sea port, sports regalia when the meeting took place in a yacht club or other athletic facility. Indeed, I had become the "Man for All Seasons" and had to dress and behave as — to become — whatever particular persona I represented.

My escort driver would pick me up at my quarters at least two hours before the courier aircraft departed Rhine-Main Air Force Base, or the train left Frankfurt Hauptbahnhof — the central rail station.

I only realized much later that loading and checking my weapon, holstering it in either my shoulder or belt regalia, checking and placing the four means of identification I was required to have on my person, made Ann Marie extremely uncomfortable. She shied away from me when I tried to hug her for one last goodbye. When I saw the vehicle stop at the front door I walked downstairs. I cast a last glance at the living room window. Ann Marie had pulled back the curtain; I momentarily saw her worried face. I waved a last goodbye; she did not respond. She turned away, and the curtain fell back in place, covering the window — in that moment I became that other me.

My physiological condition was particularly noticeable. When I returned from a mission I was unable to eat. My stomach was in knots. I was terribly constipated. The army medical service had a quick solution to that physiological problem: I received a six-ounce bottle of Bella Donna; thereafter I felt no pain. Some months later I discovered that a pint of ice cold milk served the same purpose. Thereafter, psychological transformation did not seem to be a problem for me, but for Ann Marie the fear was ever present. For Ann Marie, these times must have been extremely stressful.

* * * * *

Fred Herz had nurtured me for some six months. Finally he declared me ready for independent clandestine operations.

In 1954 I became one of forty-nine "Special Agents," later called "Case Officers," of the U.S. Army's intelligence service that clandestinely collected information on the Soviet and East German Order of Battle,[53] logistics, transportation, and all those aspects associated with "enemy intentions" essential to our unit's "early warning" mission — early warning so that U.S. Army, Europe, and British Army of the Rhine could move into blocking positions to prevent the Soviets and their puppet regimes from overrunning Western Europe. This was an important and highly essential mission. These forty-nine agents and their sources covered the entire eastern frontier — from Lübeck on the Baltic Sea in the north to Trieste on the Adriatic Sea in the south.

In some respects, because the Soviets moved all their troops, their equipment and all their logistics by rail, it made the early warning mission "easy." Most of our train watchers were former members of the Wehrmacht who knew to differentiate between a tank and a self-propelled gun.

Train watching was an important but not particularly spectacular clandestine operation. Two rivers, the Oder and the Neisse, formed the border between Poland and the German Democratic Republic — better known as East Germany. Soviet trains crossed either the Oder or the Neisse Rivers at Kietz-Küstrin/Oder, Frankfurt/Oder, Forst/Neisse, and Görlitz/Neisse. We had to have at least two, often three independent sources with visual access to each of these sites. Together, yet independent of each other — each source operated as a "Singleton"[54]— they reported movements of troops, equipment

Special Agents Fred Herz and the author (standing), in the "safehouse," Eschersheimer Landstrasse, Frankfurt-on-Main, 1954.

and cargoes crossing from Poland into East Germany or, during the autumn troop rotation, back into Poland. They reported the number of boxcars carrying troops. Through open boxcar doors our sources watched the incoming or outgoing Soviet troops frolicking with girls on street and river crossings, waving their caps, whooping and shouting—typical soldiers in transit.

The "bean counters," the analysts in U.S. Army's Heidelberg headquarters, kept a watchful eye on the numbers of troops and tanks, trucks and aircraft, as well as the size of Soviets' logistic stockpiles in East Germany. They would determine any increase in all these items that indicated possible hostile intention. Someone long ago had realized that the Soviets brought most of their troops and equipment by rail into Germany via Poland. The Red Army had apparently developed quite an efficient system of loading heavy armored vehicles on rail flatcars by backing a line of these flatcars against a loading platform and closing the caps between the flatcars with "bridges." This permitted a quick loading—the tanks just rolled from the last flatcar all the way to the first. They unloaded them by reversing the train the same way they loaded it. Also, they used boxcars to transport troops. They installed triple bunk beds and primitive toilets in the boxcars. Later, I heard from my sources that the method of train travel was relatively comfortable. They had a kitchen in one of the boxcars located in the center of the troop section of the train.

From longtime experience we had learned close to the exact number of troops that each boxcar could hold. Thus, Heidelberg "bean counters" could predict with relative accuracy how many troops rotated into East Germany in autumn and how many left thereafter.

We had other sources living near Soviet bases and their training and assembly areas. These sources reported only when the elements they watched moved from the garrison. Others reported their arrival at the training or assembly areas. The most critical time — the threat time — was in autumn when the old and newly-arrived units conducted joint maneuvers. These maneuvers were held in the assembly areas, which were also the locations from which an attack on Western Europe could be launched. The folks at Heidelberg GHQ had a matrix to determine whether the move was for training or assault, and our sources watched for these indicators — although the sources were never told the exact meaning of what they were supposed to report; each source had only a part of the matrix information required to determine the threat.

Our sources made it possible for Army Intelligence to provide USAREUR with some eight days to two weeks of advance warning of Soviet hostile intentions. In the mid-1950s USAREUR needed only three days' advance warning; U.S. combat elements were well positioned to effectively block a Soviet attack upon the West. Based on the reporting by this relatively small army clandestine element and its train watchers, Heidelberg headquarters transmitted a single-sentence early-morning message to the Pentagon; it read, "No imminence of hostile activities."

Since we did not yet have two-way telecommunication between case officer and source, each report had to be handled individually in either a physical contact meeting or via a mail drop in West Berlin — a very laborious, as well as dangerous, undertaking. Normal contact between case officer and source was prearranged. We only made special contact arrangements when either the source or the case officer deemed it necessary to have an unscheduled meeting. Again, lacking any better method of communicating, the case officers arranged the meeting via clandestinely mailed postal cards. The message on the card contained the dates for the meeting with two alternate ones; the place of the Treff and the hour was always prearranged. I, and the guys before me, had recruited hundreds of train watchers living near these river crossings. We had especially vetted "mailmen" who picked up letters in West Berlin or elsewhere and mailed them in large cities in East Germany. After much trials, Source Control had given these mailmen its special "blessing."

Special Operations Team Number Three (SpecOps 3)

Frankfurt-on-Main
1954

After I had operated in the train watcher mode for several months, the Old Man appointed me Chief of SpecOps 3. Other intelligence teams continued their "early warning," collection, the primary mission of our unit. SpecOps 3 responded only to requests from the Old Man. My team had five agents, all fluent German speakers — they could pass either as German or Dutch nationals — and I also had one administrative support agent. Initially we operated out of a large, two-story house on Eschersheimer Landstrasse in the northern sector of Frankfurt-on-Main. Our safehouse was a comfortable place. We had living quarters for the unmarried men on the second floor and offices on the first. There was also a three-car garage — something unusual for Germany — below the offices, with entrance to the rear of the house. A wide park and playground area separated us from recently built high-rise apartment buildings. Three unmarried men lived on the second floor. They shared the "duty agent" task. One of the three was always in the building. All doors, except the large front door at Eschersheimer Landstrasse, were locked and barred from the inside. We had a heavy wooden desk strategically placed in the hallway some distance from the door; this was the duty agent's station. We had an army-issued .45-caliber Colt automatic pistol on each floor near the apartment door. The duty agent had his automatic on the right side of the desk — we were all right-handed — hidden under the *Stars and Stripes* newspaper. I was the only member who had been issued a .38-caliber Colt Police Special that I carried on my person at all times. Later, a year or so later, all clandestine agents would receive government-issued Colts.

Special Tasks—German Automobile License Plates

Frankfurt-on-Main
1954

After one of our Monday morning meetings, the Old Man called me into his office. "Mr. Thamm, we need a bunch of German license plates. We have only one set here in this building. We need more. Get them. We can't afford driving to clandestine meetings with U.S. plates."

"Yes, sir," I replied, all the while wondering how and where in hell I could get them. I had absolutely no idea how Germans obtained their license plates, much less how I could get my hands on "a bunch" of them. I went back to my safehouse to ask the other team members. Not one of the guys knew anything about license plates.

What a dilemma: The first job and no idea how to even get started. I called Fred Herz; we met at his apartment. But he admitted that this was one problem he had never encountered.

"However," he said with a twinkle in his eyes, "I have a friend, a former Frankfurt high school classmate of mine, who owns a car."

I vaguely remember having documented Fred's support agent and part-time recruiter; it was one of the most detailed Form 2s Fred had submitted. It was another one of Fred's not entirely "by-the-book-recruitments" because the SCO did not know that the man, code-named Anton, had been Fred's old high school classmate. Anton of course knew Fred by his real name. Fred assured me that Anton was totally reliable and that he spoke and wrote English quite well—he had worked for several years as a U.S. Army PX[55] manager.

Fred said, "Let me call Anton. He should know how to go about getting those plates."

The next morning I picked up Fred in my Opel. He gave directions to

Anton's house in the western suburbs of Frankfurt. We arrived at a quaint little cottage with a low wooden fence, faded white paint, overgrown with morning-glory vines in full bloom. A small, two-door, DKW[56] automobile sat in the short cement driveway. Anton had obviously been awaiting us; as soon as we started walking up the driveway he opened the door. He was a skinny man of medium height, partly balding with graying black hair. He accentuated his high forehead by combing to the back whatever hair he still had. He greeted us with, "Good morning, Manfred." He warmly shook Fred's hand, and then turned toward me. "And this must be your Mr. Trenker." As we shook hands I noticed he had the same curious twinkle in his eyes that I had noticed when I first met Fred.

"Come into the kitchen. My wife just went to the bakery to get some sweets. The coffee is brewing, and besides, I got all my files in the kitchen drawer."

The man code-named "Anton."

I thought to myself, *I could get to like this guy. Not an ounce of pretentiousness in that fellow; totally different from the average German; almost like an American.*

The tiny kitchen was brightly lit. We sat at the small table below one of the two kitchen windows. Anton produced three cups and poured freshly-brewed coffee, "Manfred, you like cream and sugar; Mr. Trenker, what will you have?"

"Just cream," I replied.

"That's the way I have mine too," said Anton.

After our first sips Anton busied himself with what he jokingly called his files. He turned to me. "Manfred said you need German automobile license plates. I have a man who can help you, a police Oberinspektor at Frankfurt police headquarters. I met the Oberinspektor[57] in charge of vehicle licenses a little over a year ago when I still ... or was it two years ago?" He laughed. "Time flies when you are having fun. Anyway, his name is Hanke. I looked up the telephone number of the Division for Vehicle Licenses and wrote it down for you. His full name is Eduard Hanke. He is a bit stiff, even worse than most German officials, but once you get to know him he is an okay fellow."

Anton handed me a slip of paper with the data. "His office is in the police headquarters, downtown."

I thanked Anton for the information. "Nothing to it, all part of the Manfred Herz service," he laughed. Just then Anton's wife arrived. She bustled into the kitchen. Introductions were made while she pulled plates from the cupboard and arranged the sweets for us to devour. She excused herself, saying, "While you are stilling your hunger, I have work to do," and disappeared into the living quarters.

Fred and Anton started to discuss some of Fred's next week's operational plans. Fred had received another lead from his contact in Camp King. It was another refugee from the East German/Polish border area who had been resettled into the Nürnberg area. They agreed that Anton would pick up Fred the following Monday at his house. Fred turned to me. "Oh, I forgot to tell you. When I go out for the initial contact Anton drives me in his car. A couple of years ago, when I still worked for Vee-Corps, their G-2 had allocated some money for a down payment on the DKW you saw in the driveway. Anton bought the car and of course it is totally German-owned and documented. That's one of the reasons I never bugged the Old Man for a German license plate — I already had one."

I marveled about the things Fred did without as much as a smattering of involvement of the U.S. Army bureaucracy.

That same morning I called the office of Oberinspektor Hanke. I introduced myself as Inspektor Thamm, of U.S. Army Intelligence. We arranged to meet in the late afternoon. At the safehouse I pulled our leather courier briefcase from the shelf. I loaded it with three cartons of cigarettes, a can of U.S. Army Quartermaster coffee, one bottle of cognac and one of Kentucky bourbon.

I parked the car in front of police headquarters, in spaces reserved for police cars. I placed an official-looking sign on the dashboard that proclaimed the vehicle to be "U.S. Military Police." I carried the sign just for these parking privileges behind the sun visor of my car. One of our support agents had it prepared by our drafting department. On either side of "U.S. Military Police" the artist had drawn the official MP logo: crossed pistols; it looked very impressive and never failed in its intended purpose: keeping me from getting parking tickets.

I climbed the stairs to the fourth floor of Police Headquarters and told the desk sergeant on duty, "Inspektor Thamm to see Herr Oberinspektor Hanke." He ushered me into the inner sanctum of the Oberinspektor. Oberinspektor Hanke was a tall man, my height, over six feet tall, slender, graying hair carefully combed straight back. He wore a gray suit, white shirt, and black tie. He rose and came toward me, hand outstretched. "Inspector Thamm," he addressed me in halting English, "what can I do for you?"

"Herr Oberinspektor," I spoke in German, "I wondered whether you can help me." I presented my fancy blue and gold agent credentials, "I am a representative of the U.S. Intelligence Service."

The Oberinspektor glanced only briefly at the etui and returned it.

"Our organization operates throughout West Germany. As you know, we work at a most discreet level and like to move in and out of areas without attracting a lot of attention. My colonel [I used the German *Herr Oberst*] asked me to procure a number of German automobile license plates for that purpose."

The Oberinspektor nodded his head. "Yes, I understand the *Herr Oberst's* concerns. I think I can help you."

He paused, looking at me somewhat curiously. "Excuse me, Herr Inspektor Thamm, do I detect a Silesian accent? Are you from Silesia?"

I smiled. "Why, how perceptive. My parents came from Lower Silesia."

"I thought I detected a most familiar speech pattern," the Oberinspektor replied. "I grew up in Löwenberg, but as luck would have it, I was captured by the Americans."

"Well, sir, my parents came from Jauer."

"Indeed, Herr Landsmann,"[58] replied the Oberinspektor. "That's just a stone's throw from my hometown." He waved me to an area where several leather-covered club chairs were arranged around an antique coffee table. On the intercom he called for two cups of coffee, and we settled down for a bit of socializing. Almost instantly a police officer appeared with a tray that had two cups of coffee, a small container of cream, and one of sugar. I complimented the Oberinspektor on the wonderful view from his office that overlooked downtown Frankfurt. He mentioned that his division had moved into this complex from rather primitive temporary wooden barracks, "Well, you know ... the war and all the bombings played havoc."

I made a conciliatory comment, partially quoting William Tecumseh Sherman's "War is hell."

He nodded in agreement. For some time we spoke of the world around us, of Silesia, East Germany, and the sad state of East German affairs. He mentioned how lucky West Germany was to have the Americans, the Britischers,[59] and the French instead of the Russians and the Poles as occupiers. Finally we returned to the reason of my visit.

"I think we can be of assistance. How many numbers do you need?"

"Well, my *Herr Oberst* thought that maybe ten would do."

"Ten? How many vehicles do you have?"

"I am not sure, but we must have at least forty or fifty cars."

"How about if I give you twenty numbers?" He continued without awaiting an answer. "You have to go downstairs to a shop in the back of the building to have the plates made." He again called on the intercom for a file he called "old numbers." When the police officer brought a card file box into his office, the Oberinspektor pulled twenty files and wrote numbers on office stationary, then dated, placed his official stamp next to the date and signed the paper. As he handed me the page, he said, "I thought having old numbers, not sequential new ones, numbers that were handed in by folks who sold their cars, random numbers, would be better for you purposes than new, continuous, numbers."

I had not even thought of that security concept. "One thing you must give me, your telephone number, or a number where I can reach you in case there are some problems, tickets, and that sort of thing." I gave him two: the telephone number for my safehouse and the number of the duty agent at headquarters; I also wrote down our unit's cover addresses so that traffic violations could be mailed and quickly adjudicated.

I then pointed at the leather briefcase I had brought. "I brought a little present for the guys in the office. They were all so efficient when I first called to make this appointment. I'll leave the briefcase here and come to pick it up in a few days."

The Oberinspektor thanked me and escorted me out of the office.

The following day I returned to Police Headquarters to have the license plates manufactured. About an hour later I brought a box of these plates, less one set for my own team, to the Old Man. I set the box on his desk. "How many?" the Old Man asked.

"Nineteen sets, sir. I kept one for myself."

"How much did it cost?"

"Well, sir, a half hour of friendly conversation, a couple bottles of booze, and a can of Quartermaster coffee. The Oberinspektor discovered that I was a *Landsmann* from Lower Silesia. My folks came from a town just a few miles from where he grew up."

"Good job."

"Oh, sir? I left two telephone numbers and one of our accommodation addresses with him. He needed them to register the tags, but most importantly, in case one of our guys gets a traffic citation."

The Old Man smiled, "No problem. Give me a *Memo for the Record* so that we can get that thing moving. Good job."

I departed knowing that our first job had paid off big — thanks to Fred Herz and his connections.

SPECIAL TASKS—
THE PROPRIETARY

Frankfurt-on Main
The Atelier
1954

A few weeks later, just as I was on my way out of the weekly Monday morning staff meeting, the Old Man tapped me on the shoulder. "See me in my office." I told my friends to have coffee and donuts in the downstairs snack bar without me and followed the Old Man to his office. He settled himself behind his desk and looked at me questioningly. "Do you know what a proprietary is?"

"Proprietary? No, sir. Never heard of it."

"A proprietary, officially known as a proprietary corporation, is a business that looks from the outside like a private business but is in fact financed by us, the intelligence service. OPS has looked at some of your sources and at least two look like good prospects for a proprietary."

I was still puzzled and must have telegraphed it.

"We need a way to get messages into Czechoslovakia. You have two people, one an artist, his friend a former tour bus operator. Those two have worked for you pretty diligently. The SCO has evaluated them, and I thought they deserve a break. See if you can set up a meeting between yourself and the two sources and see if they are interested."

"Yes, sir."

"If you have any problems get help from Special Agent Herz."

"Yes, sir."

"Give me a report next week."

With my last "Yes, sir" I left his office. My second mission and again I had absolutely no idea what in hell the Old Man wanted, or how he expected me to accomplish this new task. Special Agent Herz was out of town for the next few days. I had to get some idea what this was all about from my old friend Joe Milewski, our sergeant major. Joe was just having his after-meeting morning coffee. He looked up and automatically poured a second cup for me.

"What's up?"

"Joe, do you have any idea what in hell a proprietary is?"

"First heard about it three days ago from Ops; why don't you ask him?"

Ops explained that this proprietary would be a two-way street. "We help Mecklenburger start a business so that we can have a back room of our own. We get a foothold just in case we someday need to run a NOC operation — I mean we need a real, a legitimate address, a real location, to run these non-official contact ops." He went on to explain that the Old Man had plans for at least one other proprietary, and that in the meantime, I could use Mecklenburger's studio as a combination office and travel bureau with his buddy "Westländer," who might possibly get our operation into Czechoslovakia through some kind of tour bus service.

Back in Joe's office I gave him the thumbs-up, and Joe asked, "Are you going to do it?"

"After I know how in hell, I will."

"Nothing to it," Joe advised. "We got the money; you got the bodies. Put the two together and we have a proprietary."

"Shit, man. You are no help at all."

"No, no. Listen. Meet with your source 'Mecklenburger' first. Ask him if he wants to have his own business. If he does, he can get his buddy, the bus driver, into the business. I mean, if I were them I would snap that up in a New York minute."

I looked at Joe. He seemed sincere. I said, "Maybe this could work. Thanks for the coffee. I'll let you know how it comes out."

"Thanks for the coffee my eye, Gerhardt, how about 'thanks for the advice?' Don't I get something for that?"

"Buy you a beer tonight."

"All right, see you tonight." Joe waved me out of his office. He had more important work to do.

* * * * *

The man codenamed Mecklenburger was my artist source. I called him and we arranged to meet at Ristorante Milano, a quiet place on Goethe Strasse, in Frankfurt's town center. Mecklenburger was a slightly pudgy young man. He was almost totally bald; he had just a light fringe of blond hair that he kept combed from the back over his bald forehead. He claimed his baldness did not bother him, but he repeatedly arranged what little hair he had to cover his bare head — alas, most unsuccessfully.

Before his departure from East Germany, Mecklenburger had managed a state-owned artist studio that produced propaganda material for the government. Over time he began to despise himself for producing propaganda material for a despicable government; he decided he no longer could do this work. He told me, "I had become so psychologically depressed I developed psychosomatic illnesses, mostly in the intestinal area. I had to leave to preserve my sanity if not my stomach." He, his wife, and small child fled to the West.

We had a pleasant meal and over a cup of espresso I asked Mecklenburger whether he had ever thought of running his own artist studio.

He looked at me quizzically, then nodded his head and said, "Yes, but..." rubbing his thumb and forefinger together — meaning money.

I asked, "Could you set up a studio if I gave you the money?"

He looked at me, still puzzled. "What do you get out of it?"

I had not thought of that part of the deal. No one at the spy school had ever mentioned proprietary. I had to give it a shot in the dark, "Well, first of all I like to have a place where I can hang my hat without being observed, a place where we could talk without worrying who listens."

I did some quick thinking. "I thought you could rent a place here in town. The front looking like an atelier — no, actually it will be one, and the back room or rooms kind of like storage and office spaces."

"Yes?"

"Well, I could use it as an office, maybe." Then I told him about my plans for his buddy, the bus driver code-named "Westländer," and the tour bus. I mentioned that the atelier could serve as both an artist studio as well as a travel bureau, at least for the very beginning.

"I am interested in tours going to Czechoslovakia. Do you think Westländer could maybe advertise through your atelier tours for Sudeten Germans visiting their former homes?"

"Sure, there is a growing market for that," replied Mecklenburger. "Czechoslovakia and Hungary, even East Germany." On reflection he added, "Although neither I nor Westländer would dare to visit East Germany."

He laughed, "They would cut off our balls if they caught us there."

"Okay. Look into it. Get me locations and prices; write me a plan how you are going to do it, so that I can explain it to the Old Man with the money."

Mecklenburger laughed, "*Jawohl*, Herr Trenker," and he gave me a sloppy salute. We shook hands and, after I paid the bill, we departed.

I suspected that Mecklenburger had long ago made plans to once again have his own artist studio. He just did not have the finances. I was almost sure he already had a plan, that he had been thinking about starting a business here in Frankfurt-on-Main where he could use his artist skills. I was sure that a business plan would soon follow. We arranged to meet at the same restaurant for lunch three days hence.

The spy school would have frowned on having a Treff twice in succession in the same place, but the food at Ristorante Milano was terrific, and they had the best cappuccino in town. Well, actually, in 1954 it was the only place in Frankfurt that served cappuccino.

Mecklenburger appeared excited. Even before we sat down at the table he sputtered, "Herr Trenker, I walked all over town, but I found the perfect place right down the street from here."

I waited.

"Herr Trenker, the place is right here on Goethe Strasse."

"So, what's so perfect?" I wondered.

"It is a little walk-up two-room office, and..." he paused for effect, "it has a back exit that ends in a one-car garage at the alley off Goethe Strasse. When you visit, you don't have to park in the street. You can come right into the garage and walk up the back stairs. You can enter the atelier without ever walking through the front office."

I was more than a little surprised. "That's perfect, Herr Mecklenburger, you are a genius. What's the cost?"

"Here is the deal. As a refugee I get a state grant for starting a business. I'll have to get a bank loan for the rest, about five or six thousand D-Marks. To get the state grant all I have to do is prove my expertise as an artist; I have all the certificates from the schools in East Germany here. I thought I would take out the loan for six thousand D-Marks just to make it look good. I will repay it with your money. Once I have proof of the rental agreement the German government will provide the seed money; I provide the labor."

He then outlined how he would go about setting up the atelier. I took copious notes. Apparently Mecklenburger had indeed thought about running his own business for some time. He just did not know how it would conflict with his work for the U.S. intelligence agency. Now, knowing we were interested, he plowed full-steam ahead.

"Herr Mecklenburger, I will present the plan to the Old Man. I'll get the six thousand D-Marks. In the meantime get the atelier. Get the contract signed. I am sure the Old Man will love it."

As we parted he gave me his usual sloppy salute, with, "*Jawohl*, Herr Trenker." "Good job," said the Old Man when I read him from the notes I had taken. "Write this up as a Contact Report.[60] Then come back and present it to Ops,[61] Fiscal and SCO.[62] After that we'll talk about the 'Post Office.'"

"... Sir?"

Special Tasks—
The Proprietary 2

The Rolling Post Office
Frankfurt-on-Main
1954

The Old Man surprised me—"When you are all finished with the atelier, we want the other source in the atelier, the one you call 'the bus driver,' to run the 'tourist business.' Well, actually, he will be the mailman. He will actually run a post office on wheels going into Czechoslovakia—but he won't know it."

The Old Man grinned. "Two businesses in one office. If the bus driver is willing to operate the tourist service, Ops will buy a used touring bus. One of our technicians[63] will just slightly modify the bus; he already has drawn up a plan to make this bus into a rolling post office. He will attach additional reflectors, you know, for safety," he laughed—the Old Man really seemed to enjoy this. "Two left and right near the front of the bus, two left and right near the rear. Under each of the rear ones he will build a hidden compartment, one on the left side and one on the right, small enough to be disguised, large enough for envelopes and that sort of thing. He has designed a hinge that looks like a reflector and is held closed by a rather strong magnet."

The Old Man was really proud of his technicians. "Give me an update as soon as the atelier is in place. I'll allocate six thousand Marks for the first payment; we also want to make the monthly payments to tie the whole thing into our operation."

Cajoling the authorities with his sad refugee story, Mecklenburger managed to rent the atelier, to get his business and professional licenses and, with our six thousand or so D-Marks, to refurbish the place, paint it, and place advertisements into the Frankfurt newspapers. We also paid for two used drawing tables, several easels, one portable and two for the office. Mecklenburger managed to have a telephone installed — not quickly done in postwar Germany. Westländer, the bus driver, helped with painting and decorating the atelier. He also carried the furnishings into the offices. I visited the place from time to time and parked my car in the garage. Westländer — I kept calling him "the bus driver" — had whitewashed the interior of the garage; he had even installed bright overhead lights. It already had a metal circular staircase leading to the atelier; Westländer had cleaned, and painted it. Mecklenburger, an enthusiastic photographer, had taken numerous photos. I would have a "show-and-tell" at headquarters with the extra set he had made for me.

We popped a bottle of champagne when we opened the atelier.

Mecklenburger had already laid the groundwork for my talk with Westländer. Westländer was large, both in the vertical as well as in the horizontal planes. I had never seen him when he did not wear the same nondescript brown suit that looked as if he had slept in it, with a striped workman's shirt — he never sported a necktie.

Westländer enthusiastically agreed with my proposal to open a tourist bus line — initially with one bus — so that *Sudetenländer*[64] could visit their old homeland. He even volunteered — he was licensed — to drive the bus until he could hire and train a driver. I let it be known that there would be no need to buy a bus. I told him that the Old Man would select one and that the newly formed travel agency would buy it with money provided by the Old Man. I told Westländer that we would also refurbish the bus, make it look like new. I asked Mecklenburger to design the logo for the bus and the office letterhead. Mecklenburger would paint the logo on both sides of the bus. Thereafter we would be in business.

In the meantime Westländer, assisted by Mecklenburger, who could smooth-talk much better than he, obtained the necessary permits, licenses, refueling arrangements in Czechoslovakia, as well as overnight stops at small inns, etc., everything needed for a successful tourist business; the overnight stops were critical to our mail service operation.

Mission "Proprietary" accomplished. All SpecOps 3 now needed to do was maintain liaison with the proprietary — and service the mail drop. Hans Volker, one of my case officers, had already recruited and tested for reliability a source living near the designated bus route stop in Czechoslovakia who would service the mail drop.

When I handed the Old Man the photos Mecklenburger had taken, he called in Ops and the fiscal officer. "Take a look at our proprietary," he said proudly. "This is just the beginning."

He looked around. "Okay, Mr. Thamm, when can we inspect it?"

"Eh, eh," I stuttered. I thought to deflect the question and asked, "Without meeting the sources?"

The Old Man chuckled, "Yes, I guess so. Can you arrange it?"

Always the good soldier, I agreed that I could.

At the next meeting I asked Mecklenburger if he had an extra key so I could visit the atelier when he was not there. "Like this coming Sunday," I suggested.

He reached in his desk drawer and pulled out a set of keys, one for the garage, one for the front door of the building, and a third for the door to the atelier. "I thought you ought to have keys to your office."

"Well, actually, it's bragging time. I want to show the Old Man and 'Money Bags' what they got for their money."

"Money Bags?" Mecklenburger laughed.

"Yeah, that's what everyone calls our accountant."

"Well, I hope they like what they see."

The following Sunday the Old Man, Ops, and Money Bags rode in my Opel. I drove to the back door garage, opened the door, drove into it, and then closed the door. The trio came out just as I turned on the lights. I escorted them up the spiral stairs into the back room.

"That's my office — supposedly. But it's actually a storage room. Let me show you the real atelier.

They oohed and aahed when they entered Mecklenburger's space. In anticipation Mecklenburger had arranged several of his advertisement projects as well as the preliminary logo for the Old Man's bus.

Back at the I.G. Farben building the Old Man complimented me. "Good job." He always was a man of few words, but the fiscal officer was highly impressed. "Did we get all that with a lousy 6,000 D-Marks?" he asked.

"Not really, Lieutenant; Mecklenburger is a thrifty man. He got most of it financed by the German government because he is a refugee."

"Great, I've got to put that in my report — I got to write a chronological history of money spent. I guess for future operations. This will look great."

Nosy Old Lady

Frankfurt-on-Main, West Germany
Eschersheimer Landstrasse
Mid-1954

With our new German automobile license plates, thanks to the Herr Oberinspektor at Frankfurt Police Headquarters, we could finally drive unnoticed among the German population.

I had visited my newly found *Landsmann* at Frankfurt Police Headquarters a few days after I had the plates manufactured to retrieve my courier briefcase. Since the Oberinspektor's department had a coffee mess I thought this time I would make another small donation — I wrapped two large three-pound cans of quartermaster coffee in a brown paper bag. Once again I parked my vehicle in the police squad car spaces with my "U.S. Military Police" sign in the windshield. When I handed Oberinspektor Hanke the paper bag I told him that I wanted to make a small contribution to his coffee mess.

The Oberinspektor escorted me through his outer office. He lifted the two large coffee cans over his had and announced, "Men, Herr Inspektor Thamm's contribution to our mess. With his previous contribution this Friday at closing we will have Coffee Royal. Maybe Herr Inspektor Thamm can join us?" He looked questioningly at me.

I nodded my head.

One of the police officers jumped from his seat and held the door for me. There were smiles all around.

I had arrived. Apparently I was now a welcome addition to their office.

To maintain police liaison and good relations with the Herr Oberinspektor, I had written a *Memo for the Record*. In it I recommended, in case I was unavailable, that one member of my team should visit Police Headquarters before each holiday, especially before Easter and Christmas, and that I would introduce a replacement "Inspektor" before my departure.

A few months later the importance of good police relations became apparent. The Herr Oberinspektor called. "Herr Inspektor Thamm, would you mind coming to my office? I think we have a little problem."

At Police Headquarters the chagrined Oberinspektor told me that he had received a report of "suspicious activity" at a large house on Eschersheimer Landstrasse. He assumed that was my office.

I nodded to confirm.

"Are you changing your license plates in the garage in the rear of your office?" he asked.

"Yes, but I have left strict instructions to always close the doors," I replied.

The Oberinspektor laughed, "There is a nosy old lady on the seventh or eighth floor of a high-rise apartment. Obviously she has nothing better to do. She spies on everything and everyone with a pair of apparently high-quality field glasses. My office took several reports, one about 'suspicious activity,' cars that enter the garage on Eschersheimer Landstrasse with American license plates and leave with German plates."

He chuckled, "Very suspicious."

I swore under my breath, and then I laughed. "Herr Oberinspektor, we both know that these goddamned nosy old ladies can be some of the best informants we ever have." And we both had a good laugh.

"I'll take care of it immediately." I promised. "That old lady will have to look elsewhere for excitement."

"I just thought you wanted to know before you have a patrol officer knocking on your door," replied the Oberinspektor.

We had previously encountered one or two small problems, all connected with our operation run on the cheap. For example, we were not allowed to purchase gasoline on the German economy, from German gas stations. We had two choices, either the U.S. Army motor pool or the PX gas station. Refueling vehicles with German license plates was our first problem, because only vehicles bearing U.S. military or U.S. civilian license plates could gas up at Army or the PX gas stations. Since we had to change license plates before and after fueling up our operational vehicles, we thought it wise to attach the license plates with wing nuts. I had cautioned my guys to change plates only in our garage and the doors shut. Everyone obeyed these instructions meticulously.

I explained our modus operandi to the Herr Oberinspektor. He merely shrugged his shoulders. "But what can we do? Unfortunately, taking her messages has only encouraged her to report more 'derelictions of duty' to my office, all for good public relations. Admittedly, she is a real pain. She also reported that the police officer directing traffic near your office takes a break when there is little traffic. She also complains about police cars parking in front of a small coffee stand near the I.G. Farben building."

I told my boys the "nosy old lady" story when I returned to the safehouse. There was swearing all around, especially when I told the guys that we had to leave our very comfortable abode as soon as possible and that our support folks would find us another safehouse. During the late evening hours the following weekend we moved into a new place at the north side of town, a row house located on a quiet, tree-shaded side street. Alas, it had no garage. We again had an apartment upstairs for the duty agents and offices on the ground floor. This time I positioned the duty agent sitting at a table in the hallway. As always, he had his .45-caliber automatic hidden under a *Stars and Stripes* newspaper on a small table.

We decided that the best way to switch license plates would be on an open country road outside of town. The agent would pull onto the shoulder, open the hood, and pretend the motor had overheated before attending to changing the license plates. The agent would take a smoke break and switch plates. With wing nuts the operation was quickly completed. It turned out to be much better, security-wise, than our previous method — no nosy old ladies with spyglasses. We always made sure not to be near any dwelling.

Although I had established great relations with Oberinspektor Hanke, and although he had declared us to be *Landsmänner*, in true German fashion our conversational mode was always on an extremely formal level. One always addresses another adult person in the formal you, never the familiar thou.[65] Americans find it particularly difficult to maintain this formality. I cautioned those of my agents who had not learned German at home or in-country of this peculiarity; it was one of many important aspects of maintaining good liaison with European officials.

Close Call

Berlin-Charlottenburg, West Berlin
Uhlandstrasse
Late 1954

Before he escaped from East Germany, Mecklenburger, my artist and Frankfurt-on-Main proprietor, had a relatively good position connected with the Saxony state propaganda office managing a state-owned artist studio. He defected to the West, but left behind some wonderful friends in the propaganda arena. They too despised the system and their work, but for family reasons could not leave.

The Old Man decided it would be good to have some informants in Mecklenburger's former ministry to "Maybe beat the East Germans, or maybe even the Soviets, to the punch — propaganda-wise, that is." He suggested that we ought to recruit one or two of Mecklenburger's friends, "just to feel the pulse."

After Mecklenburger had made the preliminary contact, I flew with him to Berlin. Since we were early for the morning courier flight to Frankfurt, I thought I would introduce Mecklenburger to a typical "American" breakfast at the airbase cafeteria: coffee and doughnuts. We waited in the serving line, conversing in German.

One of two young air force captains standing behind the two "foreigners" became irritated. I heard the captain muttering something to his cohort about foreigners not being authorized to eat in the air force cafeteria. He finally tapped me on the shoulder and asked, "Are you authorized to eat here?"

I looked at him in wonderment and asked, "Who are you? Are you the exchange officer?"

The captain became furious and called for the manager.

The German manager viewed the two foreign-looking men with seeming distaste. I knew the manager routinely permitted German employees to eat in the snack bar; it was the nearest eatery for those cleaning the offices.

As the cafeteria manager came closer, I started to smile. I thought, *I bet he thinks he has to throw two of his fellow Germans out of the snack bar; poor fellow.*

The manager hesitated slightly. Apparently he did not quite know how to handled this particular situation. He spoke very apologetically in German, asking to see my identification. I thought about what Fred Herz had told me about using the agent's ID and thought, *What the hell, why not?*

I dug out my fancy etui with the golden badge of the Army Intelligence Service. The manager glanced at it; his eyes widened. He bowed and scraped and apologized profusely. The complaining officer, who had peeked over the manager's shoulder, said to his companion, "You never know who you meet here."

I turned around. "And don't you ever forget it."

Mecklenburger, who understood a little English, appeared suitably impressed that his "protector" had stared down not only two "high-ranking" American officers, but also the German cafeteria manager.

We arrived in Berlin-Tempelhof at mid-morning. I made Mecklenburger wait until most of the courier aircraft's passengers had dispersed because I wanted to leave unobserved via the German employees exit, believing that the STASI[66] had a low-level observer watching the American exit door.

One of our Berlin-based support agents had arranged for modest hotel accommodations in the center of the city. Mecklenburger stayed at a Pension near the corner of Kant and Uhlandstrasse; I registered in another Pension on Meinekestrasse, about four city blocks to the southeast. I had chosen, as Fred Herz had recommended, staying in separate dwellings from those of my source. The only exception to that rule, again on Fred's recommendation, was our association with "Landser." We always felt totally secure with him.

As arranged — via a postal card mailed in East Germany — Mecklenburger met his friend from the Dresden propaganda office in a small restaurant on Meinekestrasse. These initial contact meetings were at best dicey; they were always conducted to look like a meeting between old friends — which in fact they most often were.

I observed from afar, sitting at a corner table near the exit. Mecklenburger had instructions to check out his friend regarding his feelings toward the West, and whether he would be willing to occasionally come to Berlin with reports on East German propaganda, with insider views of the activity of the Socialist Unity Party — the East German communist party. If the friend agreed to work for us, Mecklenburger would make arrangements for another Treff at a time convenient to the man from Dresden. I saw Mecklenburger greet a short, stocky man in his late twenties. Apparently he wore his best business suit — it looked like a well-pressed potato sack. He had dark, wavy hair and a black, Stalinesque mustache.

Apparently all was well.

While Mecklenburger and the man from Dresden ate their dinner, I could not help noticing how shabbily dressed the East German looked compared to Mecklenburger. They appeared to enjoy each other's company. After dinner Mecklenburger escorted his friend outside. I saw them shaking hands, and then the friend departed.

By prior arrangement I met Mecklenburger at one of the quaint cafés just around the corner on Ku'damm. This walk allowed me to make a security sweep to be certain Mecklenburger had not inherited a tail.

"It's in the bag," said Mecklenburger. "You know, he saw all the glittering lights, the store windows filled with everything imaginable — all the difficult-to-get things in East Germany. He first wanted to come across, but I talked him out of it, reminding him that his family would be opposed to leaving their homes. But he is willing to report."

Mecklenburger paused for a moment, seemingly embarrassed. "This was his first time in Berlin, West Berlin that is, and he liked what he saw." He paused again. "I don't know how to say this, but he said he wants money; he wants to build up a nest egg in the West."

Mecklenburger looked at me questioningly.

"What did you tell him?"

"I said it could be arranged at the next meeting. Was that okay?"

"Sure, I will set it up. The longer he stays as a reporter, the bigger his nest egg will be. Next time you, Hans Volker and me — you remember Hans, the fellow who brought the American advertisement magazines and the artist paints to the atelier?"

"Sure, a nice guy."

"He will conduct the business end and the training so that your friend does not spend time at Bautzen."[67]

Mecklenburger laughed, somewhat embarrassed. "I hope it does not come to that."

"Well, you can never be too careful. Hans will tell him what to do, and especially what not to do. Then Hans will set up a 'no name' bank account in either Switzerland or Liechtenstein, and the longer your friend reports the more money will be in the account."

We finished our café royal. It was time to go through the security procedure of approaching the source's abode, or, in the spy lingo, "putting the source to bed." This counter-surveillance procedure would take up to an hour — a lengthy, but necessary course of action.

The evening had turned dark and chilly. Expecting a cool evening, I had zipped in the liner of my trenchcoat. I carried my .38-caliber revolver in the right coat pocket. We left the café and turned in the opposite direction from Mecklenburger's Pension. I planned to walk south on Meinekestrasse to Lietzenburger Strasse; Lietzenburger Strasse was wide and open. It would be easy to spot a tail. We would turn right on Lietzenburger Strasse, walk the short block, and turn right into Fasanenstrasse. Fasanenstrasse to Ku'damm was a conveniently long city block to see whether anyone followed us. It had been Fred Herz's favorite city block for this particular purpose: long, relatively well lit, with few visual obstructions. We arrived at Ku'damm. So far, so good; I had not noticed anyone following us. Actually, we were alone on Fasanenstrasse. At Ku'damm we turned left again and crossed the street, turning right into Uhlandstrasse. It was getting late and I was anxious to get Mecklenburger safely into his Pension. The street appeared to be empty, except for one young couple about three-fourths of the way down the first block of Uhlandstrasse walking toward us on Uhlandstrasse; they seemed to be preoccupied with each other. They passed us, barely giving us a glance.

I saw the overpass for the S-Bahn authority about three-fourths of the way along the first block of Uhlandstrasse — the East Berlin transit system. It was a deep, wide, dark sort of tunnel lit only from the end of the block by the bright lights of Kantstrasse. These S-Bahn bridges always gave me the willies, but I felt reassured by the cold steel of my .38-caliber Colt in my overcoat pocket.

Mecklenburger, still talking about the successful meeting with his Dresden friend, appeared relaxed. I glanced nervously into the darkness of the overpass. I noticed a vehicle parked on the opposite side of the street under the overpass. As we came into the dark area I saw the "IK" preface of the license place — East Berlin. This in itself was not unusual; in those days the traffic between East and West Berlin was unimpeded, but it heightened my anxiety. As we came abreast a man came out of the vehicle and called Mecklenburger by his real first name. I froze. Momentarily I was terrified. I tried not to panic. I thought, *Shit, we did pick up a tail. That guy with the Stalinesque mustache must have suckered us in.*

I moved backward to increase the distance between Mecklenburger and me and to get into a better firing position — should it come to that. Momentarily, I was unsure whether Mecklenburger or the mustachioed bastard arranged this kidnapping, but I was ready to defend myself at all cost, even if it meant to kill both men — one I had trusted almost totally, and one I had never met. There was no way I would ever again be captured by the Soviets or their surrogates. With my hand still inside the trench coat pocket I pulled back the hammer on my .38-caliber snub-nose Colt. From some three or four feet away I looked at Mecklenburger. He stood frozen in his tracks. His face was as pale as mine must have been.

Oh, good, only one to knock off.

As if in slow motion the man came across the street, again calling Mecklenburger's first name, then, "It's me, Franz. Man, what the hell are you doing in Berlin?"

The short skinny man, wearing a dark overcoat, paid not the least attention to me; he walked toward my source with his arms outstretched — seemingly friendly. I became confused when I saw the apparently unarmed man walking toward Mecklenburger. I looked around. There was something missing: Mecklenburger, the skinny guy and I were the only people on the street. I felt kidnapping would involve more than one person. I searched the darkness for others. I thought there had to be at least one more, possibly as many as three other goons in that car, but that man appeared to be alone. A million security warnings flashed through my brain — all totally useless in this particular situation. In the meantime I had distanced myself far enough from Mecklenburger with my .38 still in the coat pocket but now aimed at the skinny fellow. I needed only one threatening move and the man would kiss his ass goodbye.

I heard Mecklenburger, still in shock, mumble something that sounded like, "Shit, that's my former neighbor."

I was still unsure of what was taking place, but having enlarged the gap between myself and Mecklenburger I was ready. I intended to shoot through the trench coat pocket if that man produced a weapon.

The East German, seemingly overjoyed, started pumping Mecklenburger's hand. In the meantime I again checked the entire street visually. My eyes had become accustomed to the darkness; I could clearly see the rail bridge pylons, the East German vehicle and the area up to a city block away. I remembered the young lovers, but they had disappeared in the direction of the Ku'-damm.

We were alone.

Mecklenburger, still frozen in shock, looked uncertain what to do. He appeared completely confused, still shaking a bit. It seemed like an eternity before he found awkward words of greeting. Eventually he realized that he had failed to introduce me. I walked toward the two men, still keeping the muzzle of my revolver aimed at the skinny fellow's gut. Mecklenburger told Franz that I was a fellow refugee from Silesia. I mumbled a greeting. From my Silesian dialect the East German could easily assumed that I was indeed another *Landsmann*. The East German offered to shake my hand. I held out my left one — not unusual in postwar Germany with so many wounded still about.

I now concluded that this was not a kidnapping and forced my trigger finger under the hammer so as not to fire the revolver accidentally. I stood there for a while listening to the two talking about family and friends. I felt a little awkward. I was the outsider. I stepped back again, wondering how to extradite myself from this extremely uncomfortable situation. While Mecklenburger and his former neighbor talked excitedly about their unexpected encounter, I excused myself and walked a few steps away and turned, my right side concealed, as I carefully extracted the revolver from my pocket. With my left hand, I held back the hammer before extracting my now totally numb trigger finger. With the revolver once again securely in my trench coat pocket, I returned to the two neighbors, still deeply engaged in conversation. They seemed not to even have noticed my absence; they were too preoccupied with updating each other's life histories.

I stood there feeling just a little bit stupid and thought to myself, *Damn you, Fred, you with your "It's a small world"— even if it is.*

After what seemed to me like an eternity, I saw Mecklenburger shake his former neighbor's hand; the neighbor waved goodbye in my direction, climbed into his car and departed.

Mecklenburger, pale, still shaking, said, "A thousand curses. I don't think I can sleep tonight. How in hell did this happen?"

I shrugged my shoulders. "What in hell was that guy doing there sitting in a dark car?"

"He said he was smoking his last West Berlin cigarette before returning to Dresden and stashing away packages of West German tobacco he had bought for himself and friends. He did not want the border guards accusing him of smuggling Western items into East Germany."

"For Christ's sake. How paranoid can you get?"

Mecklenburger just smiled. "Herr Trenker, you just don't know. He was not paranoid, just careful."

I shook my head in disbelief, "What a fucked-up world this has become."

Mecklenburger shrugged his shoulders and continued to babble nervously, reviewing the day's events, "This guy, just sitting in the dark ... I told no one where I was staying — the Pension..."

He shook his head, "I don't know about you, but I was scared shitless ... I mean ... no, I nearly pissed in my pants ... could this have been just a coincidence?"

"What did you tell your friend from Dresden?"

"What? Who? You mean Michael?"

I nodded.

"Nothing. He did not even ask. He was so enamored with West Berlin, that's all he could talk about."

"Okay, here is what we'll do. I have already paid for your night at the Pension. We'll tell the lady at the desk that you have a change in plans and must return to Cologne tonight. Then we put you in another hotel. You'll have to register by yourself; that'll speed up the move."

In my address booklet I had a secondary listing of Pensions; one was very conveniently located just a few blocks from Mecklenburger's Pension. After we had walked two city blocks with Mecklenburger carrying his valise, I again made sure there was no tail. I was almost certain no one had followed us. I hailed a taxi and directed the driver to take us to Kurfürstenkeller, a beer and good home-cooking type restaurant. From there we rode another taxi to the corner of Ku'damm and Meinekestrasse and walked around the block — again checking for surveillance — to *Pension Imperator* at number 5 Meinekestrasse. Of course, Mecklenburger did not know that I roomed in another Pension on the same street — I thought that would make the early morning pick-up easier than previously planned.

I told Mecklenburger that he should be safe there, to register, stay at the Pension, and that I would pick him up in the morning for the courier flight back to Frankfurt's Rhine-Main Airbase.

Just before noon the following day we arrived back in Frankfurt-on-Main.

Ann Marie noticed that I was exceptionally uptight — meaning barely able to eat. She asked what had happened. Since we no longer had any secrets about my life as a Special Agent, I told her what had happened the previous night; this only appeared to increase her concern.

Special Tasks—
The Proprietary 3

Wholesale Wax Business
Frankfurt-on-Main
1955

I must have been on a roll. It seemed as if headquarters thought I was the expert on German business establishment. Of course my friend Joe and I knew better; we knew it was all pure luck having a reliable, professional artist as a source. Thus, a couple of months after I had established the first proprietary, the Old Man wanted to see me again in his office.

"Get me a car that has been baptized and blessed in German," he told me.

"This place needs at least one car that is totally German," the Old Man continued. "A car German beyond the shadow of a doubt."

I could not tell him that he already had a car "baptized and blessed in German" but that it was Fred Herz's car. Even when I had straightened out his fiscal and his SCO problems, Fred admitted that it had never occurred to him to include Anton into this audit because the car was not purchased by our unit, that Anton had bought it a few years ago with money provided by the G-2 of V Corps.

However, the Old Man by now considered his special operations team expert on proprietaries. Of course, I could not tell him that I was groping in the dark, that my first shot at a proprietary was just a lucky one. As usual, SpecOps 3 approached the "German car thing" as a team.

One of my guys, Special Agent Carl Schenck, aka Chuck Sattler, a blond, aggressive giant—he looked like the typical Hollywood SS trooper—had a former salesman working low-level contacts in East Germany. He assured me that the man was reliable and "looked like a real salesman." Since he had previously sold floor wax, we thought it best to get him involved in a floor wax business that needed at least one car — preferably a station wagon. The SCO changed the salesman's registration from "contact recruiter" to "proprietary operator," code-named "Waxman." He was a German from Latvia; he claimed that he was a baron from an old German-Latvian family. Our counterintelligence people had not been able to verify that claim, but in the contact reports we had, Waxman looked like as typical German low-level businessman. He was in his middle forties, nearly six feet tall, graying, wavy hair, and, at least in the ID photo, a good dresser. Carl Schenck said that he was a steady worker, reliable, and seemed to have some business experience — at least, he had sub-sources in East Germany who had produced a string of reports.

Schenck arranged for me to meet Waxman at the Hauptwache Café in downtown Frankfurt. Waxman was true to his ID photo and wore a brown-speckled suit. He spoke a slightly Slavic-accented German. He appeared confident and businesslike. Since he was Schenck's source, I decided to let him run this proprietary with me overseeing the operation.

We rented a two-room office in one of Frankfurt's finest office buildings, near the prestigious *Frankfurter Hof* hotel. Several weeks later, we also had an Opel station wagon and a small basement warehouse full of floor wax. Waxman, the proprietor, conducted the wax business in the outer office; SpecOps 3, actually Schenck, had the other room with a separate entrance from the corridor. As a security measure we had installed a heavy ceiling-to-floor curtain to soundproof the room.

A few weeks after I had met Waxman, Schenck and I sat in our safehouse drinking our morning coffee — I usually had an informal morning meeting with those not out of town. Schenck mentioned that he felt a little uneasiness with Waxman running the proprietary all by himself.

"I am not sure, but I just have this feeling that Waxman loves to be a big shot. Nothing, really, just a gut feeling." He looked at me.

"What do you mean by that?" I asked.

"Nothing positive. I know that our reports received fair evaluations, and all that…" Schenck raised his hands in a gesture of helplessness.

"You mean money?"

"Well, I don't know. I just don't know."

I thought a while. I ran mentally through what would be best for all the options — there were not many.

"Carl, we have to get someone into his operation. A German. A reliable person who can keep an eye on Waxman."

Schenck nodded, "Yeah, but who?"

"Let me ask you: Is the business doing well?"

Schenck again nodded. "Better than well. It really took off. I think the baron must have a good line of shit selling that wax. Either that, or there is a definite shortage of that stuff. You know," he added, "we have three kinds of wax, the regular stuff used by office maintenance workers, then a medium-quality one that the average German housewife uses, and lastly a high-grade wax, I mean it is really good stuff, that is used in executive offices and high-grade hotels like the Frankfurter Hof across the street from Waxman's office."

"Okay, first I have to talk with Fred Herz. He has just the man we need, a guy code-named Anton. Anton, Fred Herz's number one source, but if Fred agrees, we can have Anton permanently employed, and Fred can still use him as contact agent."

I thought this through. "Fred will like this, because Anton will get a pretty good raise — he'll get two paychecks, one from Waxman, the other from us. On top of all that, it will not cost Fred a penny; I think he'll agree."

I met with Fred and Anton at Anton's house. I had become much less concerned with all these so-called security violations after the "loose-lips" major's wife who had told Ann Marie that I was a spy.

Fred had already agreed to that arrangement, and Anton also agreed to work for Waxman. I had briefed Anton about the job, and the real job, i.e. keeping an eye on Waxman. I told Anton that Fred would get him a new *Kennkarte* with a cover name and cover address, and that he would work as an under-cover agent for us.

I told Schenck that I had worked with Anton, that Fred had vouched for him as "one hundred percent honest," and that Anton was already fully documented: a permanent intelligence source. Also, Anton was a lifelong resident of Frankfurt-on-Main, friendly, hard-working, always cheerful.

I said, "Just the kind we needed to keep tabs on Waxman."

Schenck wondered aloud, "But how are we going to get Anton into the proprietary?"

"That's your job. Make the Herr Baron feel that he is too good to do all that manual work. Now that the business has taken off, he should not be doing menial work stocking the warehouse, loading the station wagon. He should not even deliver the wax. He should concentrate all his time and talent selling wax and maintaining a good front."

Carl laughed, "That'll do it. He can now be the big shot he always wanted to be."

"However," I added, "you will insert Anton under cover. I will have him documented as Anton Hauser. Fred will get the documentation, and we will have Anton supposedly living somewhere in one of our covert addresses."

It was even easier then Schenck had thought; in no time at all we had "our man" Anton in the proprietary.

Less than three months after we had opened the business, we gave the Old Man a ride in his Opel, "blessed and baptized in German."

On the Streets of Berlin

Berlin/Charlottenburg/Tiergarten West Berlin
Uhlandstrasse
February 1955

Everything considered, establishing and operating a proprietary was not an especially difficult task once we had learned the basics. The essential ingredient of course was having an honest and knowledgeable operator, someone akin to Mecklenburger; with him at the artist atelier, everything went smoothly — except for that little excitement after the Treff with Mecklenburger's former East German neighbor.

However, with new assignments come new problems. This became obvious in late 1954 or early 1955 when the Old Man ordered my team to penetrate the East German scientific and technical community. Someone in the Pentagon wanted to know whether German scientists and engineers conducted research, experiments, or tests to advance the level of Soviet technology. As always, the folks in the Pentagon had little concern about how complicated and dangerous a simple request like that can be.

During the course of the next year, we established a network of agents probing East Germany for sophisticated scientific and technical testing or research facilities, those that were thought to be suited to assist Soviet technology. Once again Fred Herz helped us in this venture. Among others he offered us one of his most valuable sources, "Landser," the metallurgist, and the man who eons ago had been my German Army squad leader.

That was why I stood on the corner of Uhlandstrasse and Ku'damm on that miserable on day in February of 1955. The lousy Berlin weather made waiting extremely uncomfortable. I tried looking as inconspicuous as possible. There were others standing, milling around, waiting — black-marketers. I tried to look like one of them while watching everyone approaching from the main road.

Trenker — I had started to think of myself no longer as Sergeant Thamm, but as Georg Trenker — waited for his East German source.

The light drizzle made waiting unpleasant. The mist gave Berlin the then-familiar musty smell of old ruins, repaired tenements, and tarred-over, shell-cratered streets, mixed with the all-too-familiar sweet smell of not-yet-recovered rotting corpses deep under ruins of apartment buildings, corpses still patiently awaiting burial. Some, along with a large number of unexploded 500- and 1,000-pound bombs, had been there for more than a decade. I started to check my wristwatch, but I could readily see by the clock in the jeweler's store window that I had been here only three minutes. By the school solution I was to wait no longer than five minutes. Then I was to go to the next proposed meeting place, the next Treff.

Bored waiting, I thought about those endless instructions and school solutions. *Blend into the scenery — the only reason I wore that God-awful suit; make sure you are not followed; make sure your spook has not been followed; be sure you are not being set up by your spook for a kidnapping to the East.* I knew that the rules for "spying in three easy lessons" were important — some were designed for pure self-preservation. Even at the Little Red Schoolhouse, students questioned some of the wisdom the instructors dispensed, such as, "Always be the last one off the subway, bus or streetcar; never take a waiting taxi — always hail a cruising one."

One of the students had asked, "Just imagine, there are ten taxis waiting at the taxi stand, and you hail a cruising one. Or, you are waiting for a bus or streetcar; it arrives. You wait leisurely while everyone else gets on the bus. Then you swing aboard at the last second. Now, do you think that's not suspicious?"

Most agreed that it was almost impossible to spot a "tail" on the busy Berlin sidewalks. We had found out how difficult it was during our training exercises in Frankfurt-on-Main. The instructor answered honestly. "When you are on the street you can make your own rules. We tell you what is best, not what is wisest under different conditions."

I remember he snickered, "Let's face it. That's not exactly the safest nor the easiest job in the world." Then continued more factually, "There are no easy answers. When you operate alone, it's damned dangerous. You have to watch not only your back, but left and right and front. You have to know at all times where you are, where you came from, and where you are going. That is especially true at night — and most of the time you will be operating in the late afternoon into the evening, and into the night."

At night especially, the streets of Berlin were indeed dangerous, at least for U.S. intelligence agents. According to our sources, the STASI had offered $10,000 "in gold" for any U.S. agent delivered to East Berlin. In the mid-1950s that was a whole lot of money, for any German — East or West. In those days Berlin, though divided, had no barriers. Taxis, the U-Bahn and the S-Bahn traveled freely between East and West Berlin.

By far the most dangerous ride was by taxi. When traveling from my normal operation base in Charlottenburg to Tempelhof airport, the taxi passed one city block away from Potsdamer Platz and East Berlin territory. Potsdamer Platz jutted out into West Berlin territory, and the main road to Tempelhof Airbase passed it only one wide-open block away. I preferred riding the city bus along that stretch, but when I had to catch the early-morning courier flight I had to use the Berlin taxi service.

As Fred had cautioned me, "Be aware of where you are at all times." Thus, I checked the route the taxi used to Tempelhof very carefully. I had my .38-caliber Colt in my coat pocket, ready to use should the driver make an unscheduled left turn on the road leading past Potsdamer Platz — East Berlin. Long ago I had promised myself never to be captured by the Red Army or her surrogates. I was mentally, as well as physically, well prepared that in extremis I would shoot the driver in the head and roll out of the moving taxi before it reached East Berlin. Quick action was necessary. At thirty mph, it takes only a few seconds for the taxi to traverse one block. I thought, *a hell of a decision for a young guy to make.* But self-preservation is always number one, and I would have killed the taxi driver without even the slightest hesitation or remorse.

I now thought longingly of those wonderful days at the Little Red Schoolhouse — a comfortable cross-country streetcar ride from the center of Frankfurt-on-Main. There it was dry, warm and comfortable — and safe. Here in Berlin I missed the camaraderie of my fellow soldiers, the secure feeling of being among men I trusted.

The cold drizzle had started to penetrate my clothing. The wetness reminded me of long-ago cold and wet weeks on the Eastern Front. I became uncomfortable, uneasy, impatient, standing and watching the busy afternoon's pedestrian traffic funneling in from the Ku'damm, Berlin's answer to New York's Fifth Avenue.

My informant was late. This was not particularly unusual. The rail traffic in East Germany tested everyone's patience. One of the lessons taught at the Little Red Schoolhouse was, "Patience is one of the great virtues in the espionage business." But this waiting… I thought, *what did Fred Herz say about waiting on Berlin's street corners? "It tightens up your gut like catgut on a violin."*

Good old Fred, I thought. *I wonder on which street corner he is waiting today?*

I did not know it just then, but in more ways than one, that day and the next would not be my most comfortable ones.

My informant did not show. We had agreed on an alternate Treff two weeks hence; same place and same time; there would be no problem. We had contingency arrangements just for such an event. It was just one of many unsuccessful attempts in intelligence collection. However, on this mission one bad strike seemed to follow another. The next morning — standing in line to pay my bill for an extra jug of coffee the innkeeper had provided — I was late leaving the Pension. I had to hail a taxi to make it to Tempelhof and the U.S. Air Force courier flight on time. I did it the usual way, or at least I thought I had: hailing a cruising taxi just as we had learned at the Little Red Schoolhouse, not one waiting at the street corner. And, as usual, I carried my .38-caliber Colt in my trenchcoat pocket. I had with me just a small travel bag — one the Brit who sold it to me called a "grip." The taxi driver appeared to be friendly — talked a blue streak. Eventually his chatter became just a bit too much, and I grew increasingly uneasy.

I did not yet know that in a split second on that nasty cold-wet early morning in February 1955, my .38-caliber Colt and the six copper-coated rounds of ball ammunition in the pocket of my trenchcoat stood between me and a Communist East German dungeon — or worse. I had been trained to expect danger and to react to it in the most violent way. But I also knew that taxi drivers routinely took the shortest routes to Tempelhof Airbase. The shortest way between Berlin-Charlottenburg and Tempelhof led past East Berlin's Potsdamer Platz.

Already a bit leery, I watched the taxi driver closely as he entered Schöneberger Ufer, a shortcut from Charlottenburg to Tempelhof, the one only one city block from East Berlin's Potsdamer Platz. Riding along this section of roadway was always an adrenaline-pumping event. I knew that if the driver made a sudden left turn at Potsdamer Platz, he planned to collect his ten thousand dollars "in gold."

The taxi driver still talked a mile a minute.

Strange, I thought, *why is that guy so nervous?* I watched the entrance to Potsdamer Platz coming up at my left. Suddenly the taxi driver pulled hard to the left turn.

I panicked, shouted "Halt, halt" — stop, stop.

The driver glanced around quickly; he sneered.

By the time I managed to clear my .38 from the trenchcoat pocket, we had already crossed the Landwehr Kanal and were two city blocks from the East German checkpoint. My training took over. Instinctively, as trained, I fired two shots. The first seemed to graze the driver's head; he dropped out of sight. My second shot hit the glass windshield; it shattered. With the driver seemingly incapacitated, the taxi slowed down.

Clutching my grip in one hand and my .38 in the other, I somehow managed to open the door and to roll out of the still-moving taxi. I hit the ground hard, rolling, flipping on the roadway and finally coming to a stuttering halt. My grip skidded into the gutter. The impact with the hard surface had loosened my hold on the revolver, and it slid across the sidewalk, stopping just short of the grass-covered area beyond. The taxi rolled toward the East German checkpoint. Just a hundred yards or so short of it — still in West Berlin territory — the taxi lightly bumped into a *Litfaßsäule* — an old concrete advertising pillar — and stopped.

All was quiet.

I looked toward the East German checkpoint. Two VOPOs stood at their posts with raised PPShs, their Soviet-made submachine-guns, frozen, seemingly uncertain as to what was happening. I glanced toward Schöneberger Ufer; there was no one there either to witness the event or come to my assistance. I recovered my revolver and my grip. Then I ran, limping and zigzagging, toward Schöneberger Ufer, expecting shortly a burst of East German submachine-gun fire. Still clutching my gear, I made it, breathing heavily, my right hand and right leg throbbing, into the West Berlin street. There I took cover, leaning against the wall of one of the leftover World War II ruins. After a few seconds, maybe a minute, I realized that I was still clutching my .38. I quickly shoved it into the pocket of my trenchcoat and forced myself to think rationally once again.

I had incapacitated — maybe worse — that taxi driver. But no one except the two East German VOPOs had observed the incident. I looked around expecting crowds to assemble, police and ambulances to converge, people to shout, sirens to wail, horns to blow.

Nothing.

All was quiet except for the occasional truck or car rumbling past me on Schöneberger Ufer. Finally I rose, still in pain, and managed, just barely, to stand erect. I brushed the dirt from the trenchcoat; there was a rip in the right sleeve. My right arm must have hit the dirty road first; that's how I had lost the grip on my .38. I looked around. Seeing nothing that indicated commotion, I decided to walk, slowly at first, along Schöneberger Ufer toward Tempelhof. My initial goal was to get out of the immediate area as quickly as possible; I also wanted to ease, or at least to get used to, the shooting pains in my right arm and leg. Finally, I reached the environmental cover of a bus stop. I dared not sit down, afraid that I'd never get up again. I checked the posted bus route list; Tempelhof was on the scheduled bus run. I remembered having bought a weekly bus fare ticket the previous day. With my throbbing hand, I carefully pulled it from my wallet — and waited.

The sun started peeking through the clouds. To my right a few sparrows fought on the sidewalk for a morsel. A seagull — it must have gotten lost from the Wannsee — joined the fight for the crumb, and won. A slight breeze bent the grasses on the strip between the sidewalk and the street. Far to the west I heard the sounds of a vibrant city.

I looked around.

I was alive. Damn it, life was good.

The screeching brakes of the bus brought me back to reality. The sign blinking brightly above the driver announced "Tempelhof." I entered, the driver greeted me with a friendly "good morning," and the nearly empty bus roared on its way.

I arrived just in time to board the C-47 transport for Frankfurt-on-Main.

Not Quite According to the Rules

Frankfurt-on-Main
I.G. Farben Hochhaus
February 1955

Initially I thought to include the incident report in my "no-show" contact report for Ops, but on the return flight to Rhine-Main Airbase, I started to have doubts. I remembered the "loose-lips" major's wife and how this story would spin out of control. I worried especially about Ann Marie and how the incident would impact her. Her worries were already at a heightened level. I mulled this over and just before the courier flight landed, I decided not to mention it at all. Before anything was said I first had to discuss this with Fred Herz. I could trust him to keep it confidential.

On the way into town, my support agent asked what I had happened to my arm. I told him that I had tripped on a curbstone and scraped my arm — not exactly a lie. He thought that maybe it would be best to have a medic look at the scrape, and we went directly to Frankfurt's U.S. Army 97th General Hospital. The X-rays revealed no broken bones. The physician's assistant cleaned my arm, hand and leg lacerations, bandaged them, and gave me a tetanus shot "just for good measure." Then we drove to headquarters. I wanted to get reoriented before I told Ann Marie about the injury. I sat in one of the sixth-floor offices for another half-hour to collect my thoughts. Then I went home.

When Ann Marie saw my injured arm, she turned pale. I told her that I had slipped and fallen — again, not exactly a lie — and that I had a tetanus shot just for good measure. I just could not have her worry more than necessary.

For some reasons I was not at all stressed; I felt rather great. It must have reassured Ann Marie, because, most unusually after a mission, I devoured a breakfast of ham and eggs Ann Marie had prepared with relish.

Later that morning I was back at headquarters to write my "no-show" contact report. Still later, I sat for a long time staring out of the sixth-floor office window seeing, but not seeing, the rebuilding of the city of Frankfurt, a city emerging from its ashes. I became convinced that I was correct in not reporting the incident. I thought, *A hell of a decision for a young guy to make. But self-preservation is always number one.*

Almost ashamed, I realized that I had acted without even the slightest hesitation or remorse.

The taxi driver? Fuck him.

To further ease my conscience, I walked into Fred's office. He was overjoyed to see me. Over coffee we talked about family, about Frankfurt's reconstruction, and more. Then I told Fred about my dilemma, about the taxi driver, and about not having officially reported the incident because of the gossip that would invariably arise, and that for Ann Marie's sake I had decided to falsify my contact report.

Fred, always the unorthodox gentleman, smiled, "You are correct. Some things are best left unsaid." He added, "But this time I am glad you were armed, because that was close, too damned close." I tried to dismiss it with, "Well, I have to be lucky, I just don't have your good nose for trouble."

Fred chuckled.

"What clinched it was the son of a bitch turned and smirked at me when I ordered him to stop. He thought he had that ten thousand already in the bank."

Fred suggested he would check through Berlin's newspapers to see if there were any mention of an incident on Potsdamer Strasse.

A few days later he called. "Guess what?" he asked, and without waiting for an answer he continued, "A Berlin taxi driver reported that he must have fallen asleep at the end of his night shift and that he had bumped into a *Litfaßsäule* on Potsdamer Strasse. He claimed to have injured his head hitting the windshield. Nothing about getting robbed or shot. That bastard had kidnapping in mind and tries a cover-up."

Fred chuckled, "I think we are clear, and that bastard has learned a lesson."

CERAMICS?

Hotel-Restaurant Kleiner Riesen
Koblenz, West Germany
Autumn 1955

When the Old Man had assigned the S&T task to SpecOps 3, we had not realized how difficult it would be recruiting new sources who had access to East Germany's scientific and technical community. During the course of the next year we established a network of agents probing East Germany for sophisticated scientific and technical testing or research facilities, those that were thought to be suited to assist Soviet technology. We received some unanticipated help from a Dutch "walk-in."[68]

For the case officer, a walk-in can be a most frustrating, time-consuming event. I recalled the old colonel at the Little Red Schoolhouse lecturing about walk-ins — one of his favorite topics. According to him, a walk-in could be the best, but was most often the worst thing that could ever happen to an intelligence officer.

"Gentlemen," the colonel would shout, waving his wooden pointer like a saber, "a walk-in could become your worst nightmare; the worst that ever happens to you and to our organization." He explained that a walk-in could be a "dangle," a false defector from the other side's counter-intelligence service. He mentioned the British MI6, the German *Amt, Ausland/Abwehr,* the Soviet GRU[69] and KGB as being the most proficient in dangling a false defector. They had used dangles for centuries.

"Beware!" he shouted, "a walk-in could ruin your entire career."

An overt U.S. Army Intelligence office in Mainz-on-Rhine called our liaison officer; they had a "Dutchman who claimed to be in contact with an East German scientist who was willing to work for the *Amerikaners.*

Since SpecOps 3 was our only element interested in S&T information, this contact landed on my desk, I drove to Mainz to meet the Dutchman.

Ceramics?

One of my former classmates from the Little Red Schoolhouse was our contact at Mainz. He introduced me to the Henrick, the Dutchman, as George Trenker. My classmate had arranged for a room in his office where the Dutchman and I could talk. According to Henrick, the East German traveled between Berlin and Amsterdam and between Amsterdam and Koblenz-on-Rhine to exchange information that would benefit both East Germany and Holland. Henrick had known the East German for some three years and said that it was only family connection that had kept the East German from fleeing to the West. He identified the East German as Hans Kansdorff living in Cottbus, a city southeast of Berlin, and as a man working on ceramics. I informed Henrick that I would have to check with my office and asked how I could contact him. He gave me his Amsterdam office telephone number. I thanked Henrick for the information and we parted. I told my former classmate that I was not sure whether or not the Dutchman and his East German contact would be of interest to the G2 in the Pentagon, but that my office would send him a "Letter of Appreciation" for his effort.

Ops, back at the I.G. Farben Hochhaus, looked in the EEI[70]—his "shopping list," and thought that "ceramics" were of interest.

A few days later I called Henrick. He informed me that Kansdorff was in his office and asked if I wanted to talk with him.

On the telephone, and since time was of the essence, and since it seemed just right, although is was against all security regulations, I arranged to meet Kansdorff in Koblenz.

Thus, on a beautiful August afternoon, I drove in heavy traffic an hour westward to Wiesbaden and then north along the Rhine River to Koblenz—a fantastic, refreshing drive. For me the Rhine River Valley had always offered one of the world's most beautiful vistas. I arrived in Koblenz just in time for lunch. Since I had not been in this city for a while I made a little area reconnaissance, starting at the *Hotel Kleiner Riesen* on Kaiserin-Augusta Anlagen 18, where I had arranged to meet Kansdorff. I checked inside. The hotel reminded me of a large, overgrown, informal chalet. It had several lounges well suited for private conferences, and it was away from town traffic, peaceful, with a small-town atmosphere. From there I expanded my reconnaissance into a four- block area surrounding the hotel; I wanted to be sure I knew every nook and cranny because this was strictly a "Blind Treff" where the potential source had not been vetted. The hotel was one of the few hotels in central Koblenz; it sat directly on the banks of the Rhine. Its rooms were close enough to view the boats as they drifted past. Unfortunately, for security reasons, I could not stay there. I thought that after conferring with Kansdorff I would leave town, making sure I was not followed, and then stay somewhere south of the city.

Toward evening, I parked my car three blocks from the hotel and sat on a park bench reading the *Der Spiegel* magazine I had purchased during my "reconnaissance." From the park bench I had a good view of the hotel's entrance. Less than 30 minutes later I spotted a man walking slowly toward the entrance. He had a folded newspaper tucked under his left arm and an umbrella in his right hand. I had told Kansdorff to carry the umbrella no matter what the weather was — he had followed my directions. He glanced left and right, and then continued into the next street. I had told Kansdorff to circle the block once. I wanted to be sure he had not been followed. I saw Kansdorff again approaching the hotel entrance. He looked around, looked in my direction, and entered the hotel lobby. I waited a few minutes to see everything was normal, then I rose and walked leisurely across the street into the hotel.

I saw Kansdorff standing in the rear of the lobby and walked up to him. "I am Mr. Trenker. We spoke on the telephone."

He nodded, stood up straight, clicked his heels ever so lightly, bowed, and said, "Kansdorff; it is a pleasure."

I was only slightly amused by Kansdorff's old-fashioned introduction, but he seemed at ease with it. I motioned toward one of the lounges and waited for Kansdorff to enter. Three of the nooks had men and women in business attire; I picked one away from those, one that guaranteed more privacy.

I ordered drinks and made myself comfortable. Kansdorff seemed a bit uncomfortable. I started the conversation by telling him how glad I was that he had agreed to meet. Then I asked him why he had told Henrick of his willingness to provide information to the Americans.

Kansdorff stuttered and turned a light pink. Finally he spoke of his dislike for the East German regime and his personal position that prevented him from coming over to the West; he had a wife with a large family living around Cottbus, and his own parents also lived near him. His mother was not well; collectively, all this forced him to remain in East Germany.

This was part of the information our Source Control Officer required for the initial contact form, Form 1. I then asked about access to scientific and technical information. Kansdorff stated that his office did testing on all sorts of ceramics, especially in connection with heat resistance and shielding qualities for electrical transmissions. He gave me the name and address of his bureau and the name of his boss.

I then asked him if he would let me copy data from his *Kennkarte*. He consented, and I recorded the rest of the information that would complete my source's Form 1.

I then informed Kansdorff of our contact procedures — his in particular differed from that of our regular sources, because he traveled into Holland and West Germany on government business.

Kansdorff then asked — he seemed embarrassed — how much he would get for the information he could provide.

I told him that all collected information was evaluated by analysts, and that payment depended on amount and quality provided. I also told him that we were reluctant to pay cash since it had been our experience that this often led to arrest of the informant.

"However," I said, "if this will become a long-time arrangement, we will set up an account, a no-name account, in a neutral country to which only you, or a person designated by you, will have access."

He nodded in agreement. "I don't need money now, but may need it later. And if it is secure, then I will have a nest egg. I like that."

I asked him when he would be again in Holland or West Germany so that we could arrange a meeting.

"Actually," he replied, "that I cannot tell. I travel only when my boss orders me to meet the Dutch or German ceramics specialists."

"I will give you a post office box address in Frankfurt-on-Main. I would prefer about a two- or three-days' advance notice. If you come to Koblenz it would be convenient for us to meet either at this hotel, or if you prefer in one of your choice."

A little later we walked into the restaurant and ordered Hungarian goulash with fine Rheinländer rye bread and two steins of Warsteiner. Over the second round of beer I explained the one-way contact arrangement. That if we were to meet at Hotel-Restaurant Kleiner Riesen, all he needed to send was a plain postcard with time and date. Otherwise, a picture postcard with dates and places; the picture designated the place of the Treff; the date was always three days added to the date Kansdorff wrote on the postcard. And again, since I was always at liberty to travel and he was not, Kansdorff would arranged the approximate date for the next Treff according to his timetable and availability.

I thought this was about as much as I would tell Kansdorff for this initial meeting. I asked if he had any other questions. He did not, and we said our goodbyes.

Kansdorff left. I waited a bit and then decided that I needed to stretch my legs anyway; I walked to my car the long way around the hotel while making certain he had not acquired a tail.

Although it was late, I decided to return to Frankfurt and sleep in my own bed; I would arrive home about 2 A.M.

Problem in the Floor Wax Business

Frankfurt-on-Main, West Germany
Kirchner Strasse
Late 1955

The day had come when I had to disappoint the Old Man. The first bad news was that I would have to "Form Six"[71]— terminate — Waxman and his proprietary. The second bad news was that the Old Man would lose his Opel, the vehicle "blessed and baptized in German."

The wholesale floor wax business had grown by leaps and bounds. From my brief visits it appeared that we had a legitimate proprietary and that all was well.

Close to a year after we had purchased the Opel, Anton asked to meet with me over a cup of coffee at a nearby hole-in-the-wall coffee shop. We settled down and after a few sips I asked, "What's this all about, Anton? I thought you had coffee in the office."

"Herr Trenker," he said, "I am sorry to tell you this, but we could be in real trouble."

"Who? What do you mean 'we'?"

"The business. When you and Manfred first talked me into working in this wax business as a sort of overseer, either you or Manfred said that this business, because it is connected to U.S. Intelligence, must be clean. I think it was you who said 'cleaner than a hound's tooth.'"

He looked at me questioningly. "Right?" Anton used the American expression.

"Right," I agreed. It always bothered me just a little bit when Anton called my old mentor by his real name. But, of course, I knew that they had been pre–World War II classmates at one of Frankfurt's Gymnasiums.

"Everything went great for the first five or six months." He paused for a moment. "Well, before I continue, let me explain, you know we have three grades of wax, industrial, medium quality, and high-gloss quality?"

I nodded.

"Okay. A few months ago I noticed our sales in high-gloss quality increasing, and the sales of our medium quality decreasing." He looked questioningly at me.

"So?" I asked. I still did not know where this conversation was leading.

"Without us purchasing more high-gloss quality wax, but purchasing the usual amount of medium quality wax."

"Oh, shit. Don't tell me that sonofabitch is filling high-gloss containers with medium quality wax?"

"You got it. I probably would have missed it, but a few weeks ago I had a casual conversation with one of our high-quality wax customers who complimented me for being so cost-conscious, giving a small discount for empty wax containers. I really did not know what to say, but then the customer mentioned that the Herr Baron came by every month to pick up empty containers."

"Oh shit. I can't believe that."

"Neither could I, but I then looked in the books and sure enough, many, not all, but many of these buyers were getting a three-percent discount. None of the buyers of lesser grades are getting discounts."

"Oh, shit. I got to tell the Old Man. He is gonna be pissed. He likes that car, blessed and baptized in German."

"What do want me to do?

"Nothing. Just act as if you had not noticed anything. I think I might have to bring in an accountant from headquarters."

I thought for a moment. "Tell me, does Waxman come in during the evening or at night? I mean to the office?"

"No. He knocks off at five in the afternoon, or before. I come in on Saturday, but he never comes in on weekends."

"If I need you," I contemplated, "you are going to be available late in the evening, right?"

"No problem," replied Anton. "Any time."

"Okay. I'll get back to you. First I've got to talk to the Old Man. God, I hate to do this to him. He was so happy with the wax business. He thought nothing could go wrong with it."

I hurried back to headquarters and asked to see the Old Man. When I told him my sad story, he asked, "What are you going to do about it?"

"Sir, I thought the first thing to do is to have our Fiscal Officer look at all the invoices and the other paperwork."

"Money Bags?" The Old Man looked at my startled face and laughed, "Isn't that what everyone calls him?"

"Yes ... yes, sir." I stuttered.

"But Money Bags can't read German."

"Well, sir, I have the inside man who told me the story. He speaks fluent English. He and the captain can work together ... if you give the okay. Sir?"

"Well, Money Bags will love it. That will be the first time he has ever gone on a clandestine operation. He'll be tickled pink." He turned around and called into his outer office, "Caroline, will you tell Money Bags to come as soon as he can?"

"Yes, sir," replied Caroline, the Old Man's secretary.

I thought, *Does everyone know who Money Bags is?*

Almost immediately the fiscal captain appeared. When he saw me he looked worried. I thought, *He probably thinks I am getting the ax.*

After the Old Man had explained the situation, he appeared much relieved. He enthusiastically agreed to go on his first clandestine operation. The Old Man discouraged him from taking a sidearm on this operation. "Maybe next time, when there is something brewing in Berlin," the Old Man placated him.

When we had completed the preliminary arrangements, I asked the Fiscal Officer, "What cover name do you use?"

"How about —" he paused dramatically, and then looked at me with a twinkle in his eye. "How about Money Bags?"

There was a pause. Then the Old Man and the captain laughed as if they had pulled one of their better jokes on me. And, in some respects, they had.

I arranged with Anton to meet Money Bags the next Friday about 8 P.M. Anton was the work force of the office. He did all the wholesale ordering and selling, all the invoices, and all the wax office correspondence. He also did all the loading and unloading at the warehouse. Anton pulled out the files and translated them.

Some two hours later the captain had enough evidence to convince the Old Man that we indeed had a fouled proprietary, something no intelligence agency can afford to have.

The next Monday morning, after the customary staff meeting, the Old Man gave the orders to "Form Six" the wax proprietary. This time I met Anton at his house. "Anton," I suggested, "make noises of having a better job offer across town. Give him two weeks' notice, and then slide gracefully out of the wax business. Your next job will be with us. I will arrange for office spaces in the northern outskirts. It means a bit of a longer ride for you, but we can use you in spotting sources and making the initial recruiting contact."

I thought for a moment. "I think you should talk with Manfred. Get his advice. The job I have is a bit dicey."

"Dicey?" Anton asked.

"Yeah," I replied. "There is a certain degree of danger involved in the initial contact. You will always have an armed back-up man near you. I cleared it with the Old Man; I want you to 'bird-dog' one of my guys, a blond giant. He is called Chuck Sattler; you will work for him as a recruiter."

I looked at Anton, wondering what his response would be.

"But I want you to talk with Manfred before you agree. Then I think we can maybe get another office in a few weeks and you and Sattler can move into that place."

Anton looked relieved.

I continued, "Once you are out of the business..."

Another thought occurred to me. "I mean, you are secure, right? Waxman does not know your real name?"

"Nope, he knows me as Anton. He is a sort of arrogant bastard; he never really cared to get to know me better. He is far too concerned with his own standings in the business community to be concerned about anything else. That arrogant shit."

"Great. Let it be. Now comes the hard part. But that's my problem."

Three or four weeks after Anton had said his goodbyes, I told Waxman that I thought his business, being as good as it was, could continue without my monthly stipend. He was somewhat shocked, but I told him that as a reward for all the good work he had done for us he could be now totally independent, the sole owner of the business. I also told him that he could sublease the second room of the office.

Waxman became irritated when he realized that I was cutting him loose and divorcing him from my operation. He said that he was not sure whether the business could survive without the stipend, and that this termination, on such short notice, was totally unfair. I got the impression that he wanted to ride the gravy train as long as possible. As Anton had told Fred some time ago, this guy was a mercenary. Still, I was trying to disassociate myself on friendly terms when Waxman suddenly said, "Well, Herr Trenker, I think that is totally unfair. I wonder what the local authorities would say if they heard about this whole thing?"

I had expected this from Waxman and was prepared. I looked him in the eye. "Did I hear you correctly? If I did, it sounded like blackmail to me. Let me ask you one question: Have you ever known of anyone who has blackmailed an intelligence agent and lived to tell about it?"

He started to breath hard; I noticed a nervous flicker in his eyes; he blanched. I thought, *Gotcha!*

I turned, walked out of the office and slammed shut the door.

It was the last I ever heard of Waxman.

Contact Lost

Safehouse
Northwest Frankfurt-on-Main
Late 1955

Our S&T collection seemed to have gone sour. Our sources had queried their friends and colleagues on advanced scientific and technical research that could benefit the Soviet Union, but all they found was mundane, run-of-the-mill research mostly benefiting the housing construction industry.

We had lost contact with the single source I had recruited in Koblenz, the East German Hans Kansdorff of Cottbus. He supposedly was involved in research of certain qualities in ceramics that had advanced heat resistance and some other traits — the G2 in the Pentagon had "ceramics" in his EEI; thus I had eagerly awaited communications from him to meet in Koblenz, or any place convenient.

Not having heard from Kansdorff, I finally contacted the walk-in Henrick, the Dutchman, who was Kansdorff's associate. According to Henrick, he had not seen Kansdorff in more than two months. When I called Henrick, he said, "No word from Kansdorff, but I have the feeling something has gone wrong." Then he mentioned that another East German scientist had visited his ceramics laboratory. When queried, that East German claimed not to know anyone by the name Kansdorff.

I asked Henrick if that East German worked in the same laboratory as Kansdorff. Henrick said, "Yes."

I notified Source Control, and it sent a search request via our liaison officer in the Pentagon to the Library of Congress to search through East German newspapers for the whereabouts of Kansdorff. Several weeks later we received a reply: This name has not appeared in any official East German media. This was odd, unless Kansdorff had gotten cold feet. Usually when East German counterintelligence caught, or had thought they had caught, one of their countrymen spying for the Western powers, they made a big to-do, publishing not only the name and circumstances of the "spy," but even his photo and photos of the approximate operational area of the American "spy-master."

I met with the Source Control Officer. We decided to extend the open source research for Kansdorff for another three months, and if we did not hear from the DIA[72] open source research element, or from Kansdorff, at the end of three months, we would drop him from our source rolls — a Form six event. More than four months thereafter, we did not receive any news on Kansdorff.

Whereabouts of Kansdorff remained undetermined.

Code Name "The Shepherd"

Bad Homburg-vor-der Höhe, West Germany
Kurpark Restaurant
Mid-1955

Somehow SpecOps 3 had inherited a no longer active source living in Bad Homburg-vor-der-Höhe, a renowned spa a short distance north of Frankfurt-on-Main. Most agent teams in our organization conducted what was called "a source maintenance program." This source was a retired *Kriegsmarine* officer with good contacts along the North and Baltic Sea coasts. For reasons unknown to us, the retired naval officer had the codename "The Shepherd." We inherited The Shepherd because he lived near our safehouse.

Bad Homburg was a spa known for its "healing" springs dispersed over beautiful lawns of the *Kurpark*, the spa's large garden. Central Europeans have an affinity for drinking the most awful-smelling sulfur water, as well as other waters rich in a variety of minerals. Bad Homburg had been the place where both the Kaiser and his cousin, Nikolaus II, the Czar of all the Russias, vacationed together before the big blowout that later became known as "The Great War" or "The World War." The Czar had even built a small Russian orthodox chapel complete with the typical onion-shaped steeple in the Kurpark.

SpecOps 3's contact with The Shepherd was more of a caretaker function than an operational one. I, or one of my guys, would visit the old gentleman once a month, have lunch in one of the fashionable restaurants, and present him with a bottle of Bourbon and a box of his favorite hand-rolled cigars, made by a little cigar maker in Ybor City, an enclave of Tampa, Florida, the home of the finest Cuban cigar makers in the United States. I thought I would never re-deploy this source or use him in any of my clandestine operations; it was one of many wrong assessments I made in this strange profession.

During one of our morning meetings in late 1954, Ops mentioned that G-2 Washington had transmitted a request to assist Naval Intelligence col-

The man code-named "The Shepherd."

lectors with a collection problem. Someone chuckled in the rear of the room, "Ha, the navy has collection problems?" Then one of the Order of Battle (OB) collectors asked, "So, what else is new? We don't have any problems?" Another OB collector asked, "We have navy people here in Frankfurt? What are they doing here? They ought to be up in Hamburg or Lübeck where they at least can smell saltwater." As the request was kicked around the table it became obvious that no one wanted to accept the task. At the end of the meeting Ops asked me to stay for a chat. The others filed out of the room to retire to the cafeteria for their traditional morning coffee and donuts. Ops sat down across the table from me. "I wonder if you could take that action. It falls into your area of responsibility."

"Captain," I laughed, "everything no one else wants falls into my area of responsibility."

"Well, that's just about right. So, how about you at least talking to those guys? They have an office in a side street about a block from your former safehouse at Eschersheimer Landstrasse. Talk to them and see what their problem is." He paused, then handed me a note. "Here is a name, the address, and telephone number. The Old Man said to give it a try, at least to make it look good, make it look as if we are cooperating with the navy."

"Okay, sir. How much time should I spend on that project?"

"Don't let it interfere with your regular operation, but try to help them out. First find out what their problem is."

"All right, sir." I looked at the note and thought, *I might as well call right now to get it out of the way.*

I parked my car about a block from the navy safehouse. The safehouse was in a U.S. dependant quarters area. I rang the doorbell. A tall, slender, bespectacled man opened the door.

I flashed my fancy credentials and introduced myself. "I am Special Agent Thamm from army special operations. I called just a few minutes ago."

"Oh yes, please come in." The gentleman introduced himself as "Doctor Wilhelm." He searched through his wallet and produced an AGO[73] card, U.S. government identification, with the name Frederick Wilhelm. After we made ourselves comfortable in the living quarters, he told me about his mission, the difficulty he had recruiting sources, and his problems keeping his name out of the East German newspapers.

"Hold on a moment." I started to wonder what kind of intelligence operation the navy was running in Europe. "Let's go through this once more, but from back to front. What do you mean by keeping your name out of the East German newspapers?" He looked perplexed. "Well, my name has been mentioned in *Neues Deutschland*[74] on several occasions."

Still puzzled, I asked, "Which name?"

"Well, my name, Frederick Wilhelm. Each time they write that I was an American spy trying to subvert the will of the German people."

"I still don't understand how your real name got into *Neues Deutschland*."

'What do you mean *real name?*"

"Don't you have a cover name?"

"Cover name?"

"Sure. Here, let me show you." I pulled out my phony Northern Area Command I.D. card. "This proves beyond any doubt that I am what I am not. I mean I can change my name at the drop of a hat."

"How did you get this?"

"Oh boy." I paused trying to gather my thoughts, "I think we … eh, you have a problem."

Doctor Wilhelm nodded and then asked whether I wanted some refreshments.

I said, "Coffee is fine."

He disappeared into the kitchen. I thought that this would take longer than anticipated and took off my jacket. Doctor Wilhelm reappeared with a tray that had on it a pot, two cups and cream and sugar. He nearly dropped the tray when he saw my gun holster on my belt. He was startled. "Are you a police officer?"

"No, why?"

"You are armed."

"All the time. This is a nasty business." I smiled, "I operate near the East German border and those guys on the other side don't have a sense of humor."

I then asked him if he had ever attended the Little Red Schoolhouse at Camp King, or any other intelligence school.

He had not. He said that he was a professor of languages and linguistics at Georgetown University in Washington, DC, on sabbatical leave to the navy, that the navy wanted someone who spoke German fluently, and that he fitted their bill. He mentioned that his nominal boss was a navy lieutenant commander who also served as liaison officer to the U.S. embassy in Bonn. In Frankfurt he was more or less the boss. He had three navy petty officers and a yeoman to help write reports "and that sort of thing."

I interrupted, "But what is your mission?"

"Well, to gather intelligence on Soviet, Polish and East German naval activities, their ships, technical characteristics of naval combatants, harbor installations, coastal areas suitable for landing operations, all that sort of thing."

"Does your job include recruiting penetration sources — folks from the other side?"

"Well, yes."

It turned out Doctor Wilhelm had navy *carte blanche* to operate clandestinely collecting naval intelligence information covering all of Eastern Europe. Unfortunately, his single qualification for navy clan-ops was fluency in the German language. I briefly sketched out clandestine operations in general and U.S. Army clandestine operations in particular.

He listened, totally amazed.

"This does sound like a spy story," he gasped. After about an hour of questions and answers I told Doctor Wilhelm that I would have to go back to my office to consult with my operations officer. I promised that I would visit again in a few days.

I returned to the I.G. Farben building and reported my conversation to Ops. When I had finished my report the captain looked at me incredulously and asked, "You've got to be kidding, right?"

"Sir, I wish I were. That poor fellow doesn't have a clue. The navy dropped him off here in Frankfurt, gave him an office, some administrative help and let him fend for himself. I almost feel sorry for him."

"Is there anything we can do to help?"

"I thought about this on my way here. I have the old *Kriegsmarine* officer living in Bad Homburg. He has been inactive for a while, but still has good contacts along the Baltic."

"Okay. But...?" Ops was skeptical.

I cautioned, "I can't let the navy operate him; they would get him killed in a New York second, but I could have The Shepherd..."

"The Shepherd?" Ops interrupted.

"Yeah, that's his code name. I could have him contact some of his old *Kriegsmarine* friends and turn the information over to the good doctor."

Ops was still doubtful. "Let's talk to the Old Man first."

We walked across the hall into the Old Man's office. Ops explained the situation and my objections to allowing Navy to run The Shepherd.

The Old Man agreed, "Let's do it. I want the navy to pay for the whole op. I want navy to write the IRs, but I insist on the byline 'Information gathered from a cooperating U.S. Army source' on every IR that comes from us. Is that understood?"

The Old Man always gave fast and decisive orders. He told Ops to fix up Money Bags with a shoulder holster and a .38 revolver. The Old Man laughed. "Just to show the Navy we are in a dangerous business."

Doctor Wilhelm appreciated our help. He agreed to finance the operation. He and Money Bags finalized an agreement regarding the transfer of funds. In my *Memo for the Record* I made it clear that Doctor Wilhelm was not to intrude into our operation because he did not have the expertise to conduct clandestine operations. I then called Bad Homburg and arranged to get together with the old gentleman. We met for lunch in the Kurpark Restaurant. After lunch, while sipping our beers, I said, "Herr Schäfer, what would you say if I asked you to reactivate a few of your old contacts?"

He smiled, "Ah, Herr Trenker, life in Bad Homburg is wonderful." He paused for another sip of beer, then added, "But boring. My wife has her garden club, but I have no hobbies. I walk once in a while to the Kurpark to watch the health nuts treading water in the basins. It amuses me. They look so serious, like a bunch of storks stalking frogs."

He looked up and smiled. "I think I have too much free time on my hands." He paused, "Yes, in answer to your question, yes, I would enjoy it."

He paused again, looking dreamily into the distance. "And I think my friends also would enjoy a little travel and excitement."

"Herr Schäfer." I attempted to bring the old gentleman back to earth. "I have an interested party that needs information on Soviet, Polish and East German naval matters, as well as on harbors and beaches suitable for troop landing."

"Don't tell me that your party wants to invade East Germany?" The Shepherd laughed.

"I don't think so, but you know how bureaucracy works; every boss wants to have all the answers just in case his boss should ask."

The old gentleman smiled. "Some things never change." He paused again, thinking. "Landing beaches, huh? I have a lady, the widow of one of my academy classmates, living in Stralsund. They used to have a weekend house on the Isle of Rügen ... may still have it. You know, the East Germans are so paranoid. All the folks living along the coast, or within some five or ten kilometers of the coast, must have two identifications, one the regular *Kennkarte*, the other another photo ID permitting travel into this *Sperrzone*.[75] She has those two IDs; she would be ideal, and..." He interrupted himself. "Oh, yes, she is a bird watcher and an excellent photographer. She has a hobby that could come in handy in this operation."

We started planning and scheming as if the operation was already in progress. I could see that Herr Schäfer—now it suddenly dawned on me: *the code name The Shepherd, it's a translation of Herr Schäfer's name; Schäfer=Shepherd, of course*. This realization had distracted me for a moment, when I heard Herr Schäfer say, "Harbors? I have several wartime subordinates, much younger than me, who now captain tramp steamers, cargo ships that ply the Baltic. Maybe we could do something there."

Again we went through several scenarios and finally settled on photography of harbors. Herr Schäfer thought the best way to photograph a harbor was from the bridge of the ship. "It's high up and has a commanding view."

But no matter how hard we tried we could not think of a way to shoot photos without the East German pilot and the *Volkspolizei*[76] escort becoming aware of it. After another beer the problem seemed to be someone else's. I told him not to worry; I would get some of our experts figure out how not to get us into trouble with the Commie police. I told The Shepherd that I would call him as soon as I had an answer to the photography problem, and that in the meantime he should establish contact with his old friends. I said, "You and I can meet them either in Berlin or up north; Hamburg or Lübeck. Whatever is easiest for them."

We shook hands and I watch the old gentleman as he walked out of the Kurpark. The Shepherd seemed transformed. He walked toward his apartment with a new spring in his gait. But I wondered just how much of my time would have to be devoted to this operation. I thought the time had come to let Rudolf Schramm, the latest addition to my team, have a free hand in escorting The Shepherd.

Corporal Schramm had the cover name Rudy Scharff—for some reason he had insisted on having two "Fs" in his name. He was a 25-year-old draftee, a German-born electronic engineer drafted from his civilian position at Schlumberger, an American oil well electronic testing concern. Schramm, old for a draftee, was the richest corporal I have ever encountered. Schlumberger paid him the difference between his corporal's pay and his civilian salary.

Schramm had almost flunked out of the training course at the Little Red Schoolhouse. He had an unpleasant encounter during the surveillance-training phase. A Volkswagen driver almost hit him in a crosswalk in Bad Homburg. In Germany, where pedestrians always have the right-of-way, this was very serious traffic violation. Before the local police arrived, Schramm got into a shouting confrontation with the driver. It ended with Schramm punching a dent in the door of the Volkswagen with his fist. The trouble was resolved, the police citing the Volkswagen driver with a traffic violation and Schramm paying for the damage to the automobile. There was a hearing before the local U.S. Army provost marshal with the German police officer testifying in Schramm's behalf.

With a warning in his 201-file,[77] Schramm became one of my crew.

Whenever he told the story he started out saying, "You know, it was one of the reason I came to America; them goddamned arrogant Germans just piss me off." Then he really vented his scorn. "That bastard actually started to curse me for being in the crosswalk, but I'll tell you, that cop set him straight. It may have cost me a few bucks to have the dent taken out of his goddamned VW, but that SOB walked a few weeks while he attended traffic school."

He would stop for a moment then add with an embarrassed grin, "Man, I thought I had broken my wrist when I punched that goddamned VW."

Although Schramm had a bit of a hot temper, he became a trusted case officer. Whenever possible, he accompanied me to the pistol range. In due time he became a very good shooter and I used him often as security backup whenever one of my contacts was of less than honorable character.

A few weeks after my meeting with The Shepherd, Frank (no last name), one of the technicians from "The Hobby Shop"[78] asked me to stop by — he had something for me. And indeed he had. At a junkyard he had bought a ship's position lantern. "Looked at a bunch of them. Different ones. Think I can modify any of them in a few minutes. Must get aboard ship." He had a habit of talking in chopped-up sentences. Frank turned the lantern back and forth, even upside down.

He called my attention to a small glass-covered hole in the sidewall of the lantern. "Optical glass," he said proudly. "I call it 'magic eye.' Tried it out with a regular camera. Works like a charm. Hardly any distortion at all. Can install it in minutes."

He paused to take a deep breath. I thought he had not talked this much in a month.

"Fastenings are perfect," he continued. " No wiggle at all."

I marveled, "Great job."

He interrupted me. "Not finished." Then he said that someone, meaning I, would have to find a camera that could be remote-activated from someplace on the bridge, or the bridge wing of the ship. "Need a battery-driven camera ... maybe movie camera."

He looked at me questioningly. "Remote control? Can't find one."

"Let me see what we can do," I replied. "Give me some dimensions of the thing you need. I will have one of my guys look for whatever you need."

The technician looked relieved. "Right away. Have it right here. Looked through all the catalogues. Nothing..." he trailed off.

"Anton, I have a job for you." The security watch NCO and Anton, formerly of our wax business proprietary, were the only ones at the safehouse; everyone else was on the road. I explained what I needed in camera equipment. We were experts on still cameras, but novices when it came to remote control or remote-control movie cameras. Anton spent the rest of the day on the telephone. He was a man with a system. First he called every photographic equipment center in Frankfurt-on-Main. Then he worked the surrounding area, and then he went out-of-area, first the industrialized northern Germany, then from Wiesbaden south. By five in the afternoon he had covered all of southern Germany and Switzerland — nothing.

"Mr. Trenker," he lamented, "You are going to have one hell of a telephone bill next month."

"No problem, Anton. Why don't you get a fresh start tomorrow morning." I kidded him, "I think you are getting hoarse talking to half of Europe."

He laughed.

The following morning Anton arrived exuberant; he came with promising news. "I talked to my next-door neighbor, a real photo nut. He thinks a small manufacturer in Graz, Austria, makes what we need." He picked up the telephone and called operator assistance Graz, Austria. Shortly before noon I heard him shout, "Got it, by God, I got it." He had reached the manufacturer of the battery-powered camera and requested advertisements with specifications for all his battery-powered cameras to be sent to one of our post office boxes. Four days later, when the literature arrived, I carried it to the "Hobby Shop." Frank ordered the proper one for testing. A week later the "Hobby Shop" ordered a dozen cameras — Navy footed the bill, of course. Frank prepared brackets for the cameras and made them ready for installation. Once The Shepherd had recruited a tramp steamer captain, The Shepherd gave me the type and nomenclature of the captain's position lanterns. Frank purchased three used lanterns of the exact type and nomenclature for testing. He would install one camera on the starboard side — The Shepherd suggested that we train the captain or one of his designees to operate it.

I had decided to accompany The Shepherd on his initial contact trip to meet all his sources. Later, l would split the operation into two, the seaborne one at Hamburg/Lübeck and the coastal one at Berlin. Once operational, The Shepherd would handle all shipboard transactions at Hamburg/Lübeck. He would bring Frank, or one of the other technicians, aboard ship to install the equipment. Schramm/Scharff would accompany him to provide security.

The Shepherd had many friends in the coastal area and enjoyed seeing them again, taking them out to dinner, playing a little bit of the big shot with Uncle Sam's Navy money — all for a good cause.

Later, once all the recruiting was done, I would introduce Anton, our only German national contact employee, to The Shepherd's Berlin sources — I used Special Agent Carl Schenck/Sattler as a cutout so that Anton and The Shepherd would never meet. Schenck and Anton would handle the widow from Stralsund and others who came into Berlin for debriefing. I wanted to keep The Shepherd and Anton apart so that neither could be compromised. Schenck would oversee the Berlin operation, and I would then be free to once again answer "Special requests from the Commander."

Several weeks later I visited Doctor Wilhelm to explain the operation. I brought him to the Hobby Shop to show what his money had bought. He was totally amazed. He wanted to go along to help install the first camera on the ship. I was afraid that this would happen. I danced around the subject. Finally, I made up a story about security violation, possible compromise, danger, etc. It discouraged the good doctor.

Some months after I had initially met Doctor Wilhelm, The Shepherd, accompanied by Schramm and Frank, rode the express train to Hamburg. Since Frank was not an agent, I first had to clear his deployment with Ops. Our Operations Officer, who usually was a "by-the-book" kind of fellow, declared Frank a "temporary duty special agent," a designator that did not exist. Money Bags had declared this designator "feasible" and I dressed Frank in appropriate seaman's regalia. In the meantime, Schramm, with The Shepherd's help, briefed Frank on shipboard behavior — right is starboard, left is port.

Three days later Schramm reported that Frank had been true to his word. He had installed "magic eye" late at night with only the ship's captain and the captain's wife on board. The Shepherd had arranged it all. They had loaded the first reel of film, and the ship left on schedule; it was to return to Lübeck in three weeks.

When it did, The Shepherd and Schramm, who had been trained by the technician in servicing the camera, exchanged the first reel of film for a new one. Our photo lab developed the film and made several hundred still photo prints, and I made Doctor Wilhelm his first present. A few days later he came to our I.G. Farben headquarters and presented the Old Man with a copy of his first really productive IR; it had the byline "**Information gathered from a cooperating U.S. Army source**" prominently in heavy print in the first paragraph. The Old Man was happy. During the next six months Frank installed cameras in three additional tramp steamers plying the Baltic. It started a long and prosperous cooperation between Army and Navy, with Navy paying the bills.

ANOTHER BUSY DAY IN BERLIN

Berlin/Dahlem, West Berlin
Clayallee
Mid-1955

Once again I got word that the Old Man wanted to see me. I drove to the I.G. Farben building, parked my car in the Officers Club parking lot and leisurely walked through the gardens to the east entrance. The eastern lobby of the building had a pair of those strange elevator-escalator combinations called *Paternoster*, after the unending prayer ritual, a set of two continuously moving "vertical escalators." Two sets of boxes, about six by six by eight feet, rose and lowered people from one floor to the next without stopping. Each box could accommodate two persons comfortably, or four agile GIs; the last two had to be really quick to enter or exit. Most Americans — well, most folks who had never seen one of these contraptions were reluctant to use it. However, once tried they found the *Paternoster* a very efficient way getting from one floor to the next.

I walked past the MP guard at the door and hopped into the *Paternoster*. I nodded to the guard on the sixth floor, who greeted me with, "The Old Man wants to see you."

"I know. What's up?"

"I don't have the slightest," he answered as I walked along the corridor to the Old Man's office. Caroline, the boss's secretary, gave me a cup of coffee and indicated that the Old Man would see me in a minute or two.

"What's going on?" I asked.

"Some kind of problem in Berlin," she answered, but before she could continue the Old Man opened the door to his office and beckoned me to come into his office.

"We have a little job for you and the boys." The Old Man was never one for small talk. "Seems that a German photographer is giving trouble to the boys in Berlin." He described the location of one of the safehouses on a side street off Clayallee.

"It seems that this damned photographer wants to take photos of everyone going into and coming out of the safehouse. The guys in Berlin don't quite know what to do about it. See if you can help them persuade the photographer to take a hike."

"That's it, sir?" I asked in surprise.

"Yes. Can you do it?"

"Yes, sir. I'll take one of my boys along. Maybe we can talk the photographer into changing his location."

"I think they tried that already."

I pondered the situation, not quite knowing what the Old Man wanted. "Maybe I we can be more persuasive, sir?" I hoped for some sort of guidance.

The Old Man just smiled, "That's what I had hoped you would say. Take a couple of days, but make that guy go away."

"Yes, sir," I said, and the Old Man dismissed me.

Caroline smiled as I walked past her desk. "You will take care of the Old Man's problem?"

I returned her smile. "I hope so," I said, not quite knowing what the solution to the problem might be.

The next morning Carl Schenck and I flew out of Rhine/Main Air Force Base to Berlin. Joseph Milewski, our sergeant major, and my support agent had arranged for us to be picked up at Tempelhof. Harold, the agent-in-charge of the safehouse, himself drove the car. On the way to Clayallee he briefed us. "I tried everything, including money, but that sonofabitch won't leave the area. I even deployed one of my German police contacts to check out the man, but the sonofabitch has a city license and my cop friend can't do shit."

Harold explained that there was nothing much to photograph. "We don't have any tourists in this area. There is damned little pedestrian traffic, nothing where that sonofabitch could make a living. We all think, shit no; I know the STASI pays the bastard to scare away my walk-ins. He is ruining my main business; he is killing my operation."

The more Harold became excited over "that sonofabitch," the faster he drove through town. Finally, after I assured him that Schenck and I would take care of his problem, he drove in a more leisurely fashion down Clayallee. Clayallee was a broad avenue in the Berlin-Dahlem borough named by a grateful Berlin citizenry in honor of General Lucius D. Clay.

Harold said, "Watch here, just a few blocks before the Onkel Tom's Hütte U-Bahn station, you'll see that rotten SOB."

Schenck and I perused the area. We were in the outskirts of Berlin. There was hardly any noticeable bomb damage. We saw well-kept gardens; long stretches between houses; a rich neighborhood. I also noticed very little traffic, very few pedestrians — unusual for most German suburbs. Harold explained, "Mostly American families live around here."

Suddenly he pointed. "There is that SOB."

I saw a rather shabbily dressed man in his late thirties or early forties standing near a large box camera mounted on an old-fashioned heavy wooden tripod. The camera pointed across the street. "See," exploded Harold. "He has that goddamned camera pointing right at my safehouse. There ain't nobody walking around here to be photographed, except maybe one of my potential walk-ins."

He sputtered once again, "That no-good rotten SOB."

Harold drove around the block and then from the alley into the garage of his safehouse. He had arranged for Schenck and me to stay at his place. He had three guest rooms on the second floor and two in the attic. Schenck and I settled in. I made myself comfortable on the second floor, Schenck in the attic. Schenck had brought with him a set of good field glasses and a camera for, as he said, "show and tell for the Old Man." From his attic room he would study and photograph the photographer.

"Schenck, you watch that SOB. He has a regular routine," said Harold, looking at his watch, "In about ten minutes he will get his bag from the box he is sitting on and bring out a bottle of beer and a couple of sandwiches. Then he'll sit in the box and have lunch. A little later he'll go the U-Bahn station to take a crap, and then he'll be sitting on his goddamned box till dark. He is a persistent SOB; I'll say that much for him."

Harold and his crew were practically unemployed because the photographer scared everyone away from the safehouse.

I walked up to Schenck's room. Schenck snickered, "Harold is right. This guy is sitting on his box eating his lunch. He really seems to enjoy what he is doing. He's got Harold by the balls."

"What in hell do you mean 'by the balls'?" I asked. "He isn't doing anything but sitting there feeding his face."

"Yeah," Schenck laughed, still studying the photographer. "But he is doing a good job doing nothing. No one from the other side would dare to walk into this place. Not with this big camera looking at him." Schenck snickered again, "Harold is going bananas." Schenck always had a weird sense of humor. He seemed to enjoy Harold's dilemma. Then I remembered, Schenck had worked for Harold. They had some kind of disagreement and Harold had asked that Schenck be returned to the headquarters agent pool — not a career-enhancing move for any agent. I inherited Schenck on a sort of probationary basis. But Schenck and my guys got along all right. He became one of my most reliable case officers. He accepted every assignment cheerfully, was innovative, fearless, and because of his large stature, he could be intimidating — in fact, we all thought he would make a damned good candidate for the "Hollywood" Waffen-SS.

I assumed he just might have been bored doing the routine walk-in job. *Well,* I thought, *there is nothing routine in SpecOps.*

After a while Schenck handed me the glasses. "Here, see if you can think a way to get rid of the asshole." I studied Clayallee, the pedestrian traffic — or the lack of it. What cars there were drove at a fast clip. I had already thought of one way, maybe the best way, of getting rid of the photographer, to scare him away from this site. The Old Man had not been specific on what action I ought to take, but it was clear that he wanted me to solve Harold's problem.

"Carl, what do you think if we ran over that SOB — or at least his tripod?"

Schenck laughed, "When?"

"Tomorrow morning after 'rush hour.' I want you to time the vehicular traffic. If it is as meager as it is now, there should not be any witnesses."

"You mean to kill the asshole?"

"No, just to scare him away. Make him think we tried to kill him. We'll wait for a gap in the traffic and then run over the tripod — hopefully without injuring the photographer."

Through the field glasses I minutely searched the area. I saw a wide avenue bordered on each side by a bicycle path. Young trees grew between the bicycle path and a broad gravel- and sand-based sidewalk. A moderately low curb, I estimated it to be less than four inches high, separated the bicycle path from the street. The photographer's tripod sat with two of its legs on the bicycle path and one almost in line with the trees. The photographer had placed his black case, probably a photographer's case that also contained his lunch and his beer ration, some two or three feet from the tripod toward the sidewalk.

I discussed the situation with Schenck. We knew that the photographer had every right, and the legal license, to be where he was. On the other hand, he had no valid reason to be there — there were no tourists in need of his services. To us it was obvious that he worked either for the GRU[79] or the STASI. Harold had tried to remove him legitimately through his Berlin Police contacts — unsuccessfully. It was now up to us to convince him that it would be best if he moved and never returned. We talked long and in detail about what our next action should be and came to the conclusion that the only solution to that particular problem was an action, maybe illegal, but effective: run over all three legs of the tripod-mounted camera and hope the photographer had enough sense to jump out of the way.

Schenck suggested that we not tell Harold of our plan, "Let him *zappeln*[80] a little." Schenck had a habit of throwing in a German word every once in a while for effect.

We had one advantage: in Berlin we were still occupation forces and had nearly dictatorial power. Our action would be swift, completed in seconds, and we would be difficult to trace. I decided to sleep on the plan and act on it if we were still certain it was the best, or the only, solution to Harold's problem.

Once the decision was made, Schenck and I waited until dusk to walk through the neighborhood and reconnoiter the roads and byways, inspect the streets that could possible screen our approach and departure—Fred Herz's lesson of area reconnaissance never forgotten. I wanted to measure the heights of the curbstone that I would have to mount. We stopped some three or four blocks from where the photographer usually positioned his tripod. I walked along the bicycle path, checked the curbstone, especially the heights of the curb, even felt it with my hand. My estimate was correct: the curb had a smooth, rounded corner and measured less than four inches.

"Piece of cake, Carl," I said. "Tomorrow we will find out how good our offensive driving course in O'gau really was; it should be much less hazardous than slipping on that slimy parking lot."

Harold was a bit puzzled by our relaxed attitude. He kept asking about our plans, but I told him the less he knew, the better off he'd be; the less he could tell later—should anyone ask questions. Harold took us out to dinner—I think he paid for it out of his own pocket—and with him we toured the neighborhood once more. Traffic was sparse on Clayallee during the evening hours.

Later, in Schenck's upstairs abode, I repeated my earlier assessment. "Piece of cake. Tomorrow evening we'll be on the courier flight back to Frankfurt." Schenck agreed. We went to bed sure that this would be another successful special operation that complied fully with "Special requests from the Commanding Officer."

The next morning Schenck came down from his perch on the third floor for breakfast. Harold's whole crew was there. Everyone expected a progress report. Several of the men asked, "What can you do that we could not?"

"All I can tell you," I said, "is that by noon you will no longer have a photographer looking at your safehouse."

After breakfast Schenck returned to his perch. I followed. "Anything different?"

"Nothing; the guy is true to form. He put his tripod into the exact place he had yesterday. He is sitting on his goddamned box eating something—I think it's his second breakfast. If you are ready, so am I."

I cornered Harold. "I want one of your old black Opels. Take off all the license plates. Make sure it's gassed up, and don't ask any questions."

For a moment Harold looked at me as if he had not heard me. Then he shouted to one of his guys to prepare the vehicle. I told Harold that Schenck and I want to be at Tempelhof for the afternoon flight to Frankfurt. He had one of his support officers make the arrangements. He said that a car would be waiting to take Schenck and me to Tempelhof whenever we were ready.

In the meantime Schenck was again on his third-floor perch observing the scene. I walked upstairs for one last look. "Nothing out of the ordinary," reported Schenck. "He had his breakfast and is sitting on his box doing nothing—as usual."

"Okay, Carl," I said, "it's apple-picking time." We walked downstairs and into the garage. Schenck slid into the right seat and I got behind the steering wheel. The old Opel started with a roar. One of Harold's guys opened the garage door and I backed the car into the alley. I aimed the Opel away from Clayallee. I wanted to take the long way around several blocks toward the west on Clayallee to get some distance driving eastward; I needed the extra time so that I could adjust the timing of the run to avoid any vehicular and pedestrian traffic. I entered Clayallee some four long blocks from the photographer. As I slowed and turned into the street I saw only one other car. There was not a single pedestrian on either side of the wide boulevard as I accelerated the Opel. The photographer still sat on his box watching the safehouse as I hopped the old Opel over the curbstone onto the bicycle path and slammed on the gas pedal. In the first few hundred feet I was in third gear going about sixty MPH. Still going about sixty I sped toward the photographer and his tripod. He heard the roar of the engine, looked to his left, saw the car hurtling toward him on the bicycle path. Momentarily confused, he sat frozen on his box. Then, as the Opel was within maybe fifty feet, he jumped off his box as if rocket-propelled and threw himself out of the path of the Opel onto the sidewalk. A split second later my Opel hit the tripod with sufficient force to toss the instrument up and over the car. We sped away.

Schenck started to laugh.

Three or more blocks down Clayallee I slowed to cruising speed and turned left into one of the side roads that Schenck and I had reconnoitered the previous evening. In less than five minutes we would be back inside the garage. Schenck, still laughing, said, "You should have seen that asshole skidding on the sidewalk gravel. I bet he won't forget this. I bet he won't be back. God, you almost hit that guy."

"No, I saw him pop up like a rocket. I would have missed him either way. All I wanted was to wreck his camera and to scare the shit out of him. I think we succeeded on both counts."

We took a leisurely cruise through the side streets of the beautiful Dahlem neighborhood. "Harold sure picked himself a great place to live and work," I said.

"Yeah," replied Schenck, "except for that asshole photographer."

"Correction," I laughed. "I think the term is former asshole photographer."

Schenck laughed, "I sure as hell hope so. If that guy comes back we might have to be more adamant."

"Adamant?" I smiled. "Carl, you always like to use obscure words. Next time we might have to actually run him over."

"That's what I meant when I said adamant," laughed the blond giant.

As we came through the back door of the safehouse Harold came toward us. "What happened? Did something go wrong? How come you are back so soon?"

Now I had to laugh. "Take a look outside. See if your friend is still taking pictures."

Harold looked perplexed. "You mean he is gone?"

"He is, or he will be momentarily. I think your troubles are over. Have your guy drive us to Tempelhof. Take the old Opel to the motor pool and have the bumper repainted."

Harold, still breathing hard, waved to one of his special agents, "Take those guys to Tempelhof in the good Opel and have someone take the old one to the motor pool to have the front bumper repainted." He then shook our hands. "I can't thank you enough."

I bushed it off. "Let the Old Man know if your photographer returns. I don't think he will. If he does, next time he'll have a closer shave."

That evening we landed in Frankfurt. One of our support agents picked us up at the airbase. As we wheeled toward town he said, "The Old Man is happy. He wants to see you first thing in the morning."

Schenck laughed. "Another job well done courtesy of SpecOps 3."

Reorganization: The New Boss

Berlin/Neukölln, West Berlin
Schierker Strasse
Late 1955

In 1955, after Austria had regained its sovereignty, Jack Heisser, one of the Old Man's acquaintances, transferred into our unit. Jack was a somewhat rotund man who, at least outwardly, appeared to be a jolly guy. In reality he was tough as nails, both physically and when it came to making tough decisions. He was an avid hunter who, while working in Austria, had endeared himself with the *Gemsbock* Society of chamois and mountain goat hunters. His friends claimed he could out-climb a *Gemsbock*. He quickly took charge of all three of the special operations units.

Soon after Jack Heisser arrived, SpecOps 3 received a new target. It was one of Jack's purported specialties: defector inducement, i.e. to convince Soviet military personnel stationed in East Germany to desert, to come over to West Germany. This program had two goals: first, to gain access to Soviet occupation forces' internal information; and second, to lower the morale of their military. According to Jack, the operation was simple: we would gain access to Soviet soldiers via their German girlfriends. Since the Soviets were not permitted to marry their girlfriends, the girls would convince them to come to West Germany, where they could live happily ever after.

According to Jack, "It's a piece of cake."

To assist in this venture, my team received an additional member, a Pfc. named John Mackintosh, a philosophy graduate, a draftee from a prestigious East Coast university. He was single and thus became one of two support agents who lived in the safehouse. I put Mackintosh in charge of security. He made the daily "burn run,"[81] scheduled automobile maintenance, and was responsible for the physical security of the safehouse. He also "roughed out" our intelligence reports and source contacts reports and reviewed fiscal reports before they went to headquarters. He seemed to enjoy this job; he walked around the safehouse with his government-issue Colt .45 automatic in his shoulder holster. The other team members started a rumor that Mackintosh slept with the .45 strapped over his pajamas.

With the new mission, Jack Heisser advised us to spread a wide net of informants, totally separate and fully dedicated to that operation. He did not want our other networks contaminated by this operation. The very concept of a wide net was in total contradiction to a long-held clandestine collection *modus operandi* that dictated strict compartmentalization. The instructors at the Little Red Schoolhouse taught that only strict compartmentalization assured a certain degree of survivability for the U.S. agent and his source. This new type of operation increased the chance of compromising the entire operation exponentially. The change in *modus operandi* led to extensive discussions between Heisser, the case officers, and Ops. With the informant net considerably enlarged — with the number of direct-contact informants rising to forty and beyond — case officer security would become a serious concern.

Heisser insisted that we form teams of at least one backup security agent to cover each defector inducement Treff. He reviewed the security plans for each Treff in detail. Heisser advised that each team train and always work together. After some trial and error, we came to the conclusion that the case officer or officers acting as backup security would cover the Treff very discreetly so that the source was unaware of the security agents' presence. Heisser advised that we all have a single tactic: should a case officer exit a Treff walking in front of the East German informant, it would be the signal that a compromise had occurred, that a kidnapping was in progress. It meant the case officer was in extremis; he was no longer armed and definitely under the control of an East German double agent. In that case the security agent would maneuver himself into position where the case officer and the double agent had to pass in close proximity. The recognition signal for the imminent demise of the East German was a folded newspaper in the hand of the security agent; it concealed a .38-caliber revolver. As soon as the case officer passed the security agent, the security agent would kill the East German. Normal procedure called for at least two shots into the heart region.

The case officers practiced this maneuver at the U.S. Army pistol range in the Frankfurt-on-Main area until each was confident of the other's reaction. A silhouette target and, to demonstrate the seriousness of this operation, live ammunition was used in this training. Thus backup security agent and case officer became an inseparable team.

Anton, Fred Herz's old high school classmate and the only German national working in one of my safehouses, had a distant relative, a Berlin City police officer. Heisser had the Berlin cop probed by several security systems, among them the CIC.[82] Heisser had also discreetly queried one of his private contacts in the Berlin Police Office of Internal Affairs; he then declared Anton's distant relative, now codenamed "Alibar," trustworthy.

I wanted to vet Alibar personally because he seemed to have many useful family members and former high school friends still living in East Berlin and East Germany. Anton and I flew to Berlin to meet our potential source. Alibar was about Anton's age — in the early forties, tall, somewhat heavy, but with a powerful way about him. He was a large man; he looked like a typical New York City cop.

Anton had arranged for us to meet at Alibar's house; he lived near Tempelhof Airbase. Alibar greeted us like old friends. His wife had a fresh pot of coffee on the stove, and we sat around the kitchen table, almost in a very *gemütlich* kind of family way, discussing the potential value of this type of operation. When I explained the details of our operation to Alibar he nodded in agreement, but then remarked, "Mr. Trenker, the goal is good, but the execution will be difficult."

We agreed. In essence, it was what we had already determined.

"True," Alibar continued, "if we can succeed, it will shake up Karlshorst,[83] but I am sure you know that Soviet privates go into town always escorted by senior NCOs or even junior officers. They must meet girls on the sly — forbidden — when they go over the perimeter fence at night. The only Soviets permitted to go unescorted are senior NCOs and officers."

"My assessment exactly," I replied, "but we have our orders and you know how it is..."

Alibar nodded. "Some things never change."

"But," he continued, "back to business. I have several acquaintances — all men my age — who in turn have friends and neighbors who do business with those Soviets. I have one old friend who owns a pub. His wife cooks some simple meals, mostly soup and sandwiches. Those Soviets who manage to sneak off come to his place with their German girlfriends to eat."

He paused. "Well, actually, to get out of sight, get off the street, so that they are not observed by senior officers or," he chuckled, "worse yet, by the officers' wives."

"Well," I replied, "that at least looks promising. Can you, I mean, are you able and willing to contact that man and attempt to establish some sort of liaison?"

"I can. He visits West Berlin about once a month. He always stops here for a cup of coffee. How do you want me to handle this?"

I looked at Anton. "Why don't you explain it? I have some business to take care of. I'll meet you in front of Tempelhof about four this afternoon."

Anton agreed. We had arranged this vetting process before we left Frankfurt, and our meeting would take place in a small tavern near the airport. I thought it would be less stressful all around without me. Aside from that, I wanted to be just a distant observer of this operation; Anton and Special Agent Carl Schenck would be handling the Berlin end of the operation.

Anton and Carl Schenck had worked together for several months; they had become a team. Schenck had covered Anton during several dicey Treffs. To be close to the action, we decided to establish a safehouse in Berlin. Heisser knew of a suitable apartment in the Neukölln borough of Berlin, on Schierker Strasse. It was a rather noisy place almost directly under one of Tempelhof Airbase's glide paths, but Carl Schenck and Anton would use it for short periods when Alibar signaled that he had a potential source coming into Berlin.

In less than three months, with Alibar's help, we had established an independent net. Unfortunately almost the entire net hinged on Alibar. Jack Heisser agreed that it may be risky, but it was as he said: "A calculated risk I am willing to take."

Heisser cautioned us that a calculated risk did not mean that we should be careless. "Be friendly to everyone, but trust no one. In this business you live longer that way." This was in essence the same advice Fred Herz would have given, and indeed it was, and had to be, a risky operation. To have any success at all we needed many contacts to scout for German girls dating Soviet soldiers. Heisser estimated that we would need between thirty and forty main contacts. Each contact would have to develop numerous connections of his own inside East Germany. Theoretically, we were supposed to run these third-hand contacts through SCO. After some heated discussions, the SCO dropped that demand—he too admitted that this would have been a difficult if not impossible task.

Carl Schenck opined, "Yes, it's one thing to convincing the girls, but to convince their boyfriends to leave the workers' paradise is a totally different matter." We all agreed with that assessment. Even in the beginning, this appeared to be one of those missions dreamed up by a bunch of headquarters eggheads who had never moved through the murky clandestine world.

We used Alibar, the Berlin cop, strictly as a contact recruiter. We paid him handsomely, mostly with American cigarettes and whisky—thus saving hard-to-get cash. Several times Alibar cautioned us that a particular contact had a criminal record, but was otherwise dependable.

"He'll do anything for money," he told Carl Schenck. Toward the end of the year we had over forty East German prime sources operational. From what we could ascertain, altogether we had between one hundred and two hundred — we never were sure of the numbers — East Germans involved in the operation.

Heisser was happy; he relieved my team of most other duties so that we could concentrate all our efforts to, as he always said, "get a few of these lovesick puppies into our compound."

During the past year Carl Schenck and Anton had become a good team. Rudolph Schramm acted as my security agent. We had a goodly number of promising leads; we came as close to getting a defector as meeting some of the Soviet soldiers' girlfriends. However, not a single one of these girls was ever able to convince her boyfriend to defect.

After I had devoted more than a year to the effort, I turned over the job to Schenck. Schenck had already directed most of the activity of the defector group, and since my tour of duty was slowly coming to an end, I wanted to close all the loops. I had to turn over the proprietary business to one of my case officers, Henry Vogel, cover name "Hans Volker." He had served as my assistant with Mecklenburger's advertisement and travel agency, to service that proprietary. He had from time to time supplied Mecklenburger with American advertisement magazines, special paintbrushes, and artist paints.

For the past year Mecklenburger's atelier had been self-supporting; there was just the normal liaison, or maintenance, to do. Really, for Vogel, this would be just a part-time job. The tourist business into Czechoslovakia continued unabated and undetected — everyone considered the rolling post office a success.

My biggest concern was The Shepherd, our old sailor. Ops suggested transferring the old sailor to the navy, but Heisser and I objected vigorously. Heisser suggested either letting The Shepherd retire or retaining him as a SpecOps 3 contact agent. Heisser lamented, "These amateur navy spooks will get that old fellow killed in no time."

On the way out of the Ops office I gratefully shook Heisser's hand. I did not want the navy to somehow snag the old sailor; he deserved better than to get killed through sloppy source handling. I had suggested either releasing or assigning The Shepherd to one of my recently arrived agents. Unfortunately, Rudolph Schramm, or Rudy Scharff— Scharff with two "Fs," The Shepherd's old case officer, had already returned to his high-paying civilian job with Schlumberger oil prospecting. Heisser suggested letting Frank Mackenzie, aka Franz Neuhammer, a civilian case officer, take care of The Shepherd. In spite of his Scottish last name Mackenzie spoke German like a native; his German-born mother had taught him to speak the High German of the North Sea coastal area. He was a tall, lanky fellow who wore black horn-rimmed glasses — the lenses thick like the bottoms of Coke bottles. Mackenzie proved to be a good choice. He blended into the Hamburg/Lübeck area as if he had lived there all his life.

Wasted Effort

Berlin/Charlottenburg/Tiergarten, West Berlin
Meinekestrasse
Late 1955

This was "Alternate Treff Day." It was another busy late afternoon along the Ku'damm. I was early. I wanted to have enough time for the mandated security procedure. It would take just short of an hour to be sure I had not been spotted, that I had no East German tail. I waited for the bus. When it arrived I swung aboard the bus just as it started to leave—I thought, *Stupid instructions*. The conductor, very helpful, reached behind my back to assist.

I remembered another time, more than a year ago, an embarrassing moment at almost the same location. I was the last to hop on the bus just as the driver revved up the engine. Then another friendly, helpful conductor reached behind my back to assist. He gave me a strange look, because he had felt my .38-caliber revolver that I carried in a shoulder holster. I whispered "Polizei," and he gave me an all-knowing wink, as in, "We both work for the same city government." After that incident I stored the shoulder holster in my office safe and carried my revolver either in a spring-loaded holster on the left side of my belt, or just loosely in my overcoat pocket; not as sexy as a shoulder holster, but much handier—when I thought I was in danger I could feel the reassuring cold steel in my hand.

The evening chill had started to penetrate my cheap suit. Those German trousers just didn't hold the crease worth a damn and, when wet from rain, they smelled like old potato sacks. I should have worn my trenchcoat and looked like a real spy, but the weather forecaster had not mentioned rain. After the obligatory "security" round trip through Berlin's Charlottenburg borough, I arrived back at the Ku'damm. Since I still was a bit early I walked two blocks to Meinekestrasse, the site of the Treff, to check out the rubble cleanup. Doktor Hermann had taught me well. "Always reconnoiter the area," he advised. "Remember, you are the Pointman, except you don't have an infantry squad following you."

On Meinekestrasse I saw that work crews had successfully stabilized some of the once beautiful old buildings that phosphorus bombs had burned and gutted. Only the outer walls remained, but they were apparently in good enough condition to be retained as the buildings' outer facades; steel I-beams, along with huge braces, connected all four walls. In a few years the weather would have deteriorated these walls and they would have become victims of the wrecker's ball. I tried to imagine what these ruins would look like after restoration.

The Brandenburg Gate, the far end of my op. area. The author at left, with his support agent.

Well, I thought, *once the workers do their job I will have to find another escape route.* With that thought in mind I casually returned to the Ku'damm, made a slow U-turn, and returned to Meinekestrasse and walked a block away from the Ku'damm to a good spot from which I could observe Landser's approach. I pretended to peruse store windows while waiting. I looked at my wristwatch. Five minutes were up.

I thought, *Should I leave or take a chance? To hell with those damned instructions. I'll give Landser another five minutes.*

Waiting in the wet drizzle was getting to be very uncomfortable. Housewives and returning workers with what Americans derogatorily called their *Schnitzelbags*— imitation leather briefcases with the permanent smell of sandwiches and lunchmeat — crowded the street. A few working girls looked me over as a potential early customer. They finally ignored me in favor of more important-looking executives hurrying from offices along the famous avenue.

Among the swaying wave of humanity I finally spotted a bent, gaunt figure walking with a slight limp.

Landser stopped under the nearest street lamp and lit a drooping, hand-rolled cigarette. The yellow flare of his match flickered across his hands, his narrow lips and the sharp beak of his nose. The flame emphasized the sunken eyes hidden under gray brows. He had followed the prescribed Treff procedure to the letter: approach slowly, ascertain that recognition is established, and pass. I felt only the slightest hesitation as he walked past me. He would turn left into Uhlandstrasse and walk toward Hohenzollernplatz. Now it was my turn to check whether he had picked up a tail. My adrenaline started pumping, but everything appeared normal. Nothing appeared to be out of the ordinary. No one seemed to pay even the slightest attention to either Landser or me. I mentally counted the steps until he was at least halfway down the street. Before I turned to follow, I cast one last searching glance in the direction from which he had come. This was vital. Once I turned to follow I could not easily check for a tail. I hesitated, uncertain, and looked around once again. No one was following. Finally, I turned into the street toward the rendezvous. Meinekestrasse was a tunnel of trees. It was late afternoon — dusk — the yellow light from street lamps cast their reflections on the wet pavement. Here and there a brightly lit grocery store or butcher shop window added a bit of light, and small, rectangular illuminated signs in first-floor windows advertised the various tourist homes or *Pensionen*; they let the latecomer know that there were still rooms available with *Frühstück mit Ei* — continental breakfast with one hard-boiled egg.

Now that I had turned I stepped forward trying to appear confident, even a bit cocky, or brave; today I carried my confidence on the left side of my belt in a spring-loaded holster: my .38-caliber Colt Police Special revolver loaded with six copper-coated rounds of ball ammunition. About half a block away Landser approached the Treff — *Becker's Gaststätte, mit Eigener Schlächterei* — Becker's restaurant with its own butcher shop, next door; to the "hometown folk" a sign for good, wholesome food. I caught up with Landser as he opened the door of the restaurant. Loud, friendly noises of a typical good neighborhood bar-restaurant, and the smoke from cheap German cigarette and pipe tobacco, engulfed us. The *Gaststube*, the eating area, was filled to capacity, but the owner waved us in, pointing to a just-vacated table at the far wall near the toilets. The rough, unpainted wooden floor was clean, but had decade-old stains from spilled beer. The smell of oiled wood shavings, spilled beer, sauerkraut, and roasted sausage accompanying the tobacco smoke gave the *Gaststube* that all familiar, all *gemütlich*, comfortable, relaxing atmosphere.

The smell of oiled wood is a common occurrence in Central Europe. Every morning the owner, or one of his helpers, swept the floor of the restaurant meticulously with oiled wood shavings spread evenly over the bare-wood floor. The oiled shavings were then swept onto a shovel to be saved for the next day.

Heavy tables and chairs sat pushed against the three walls; a stand-up bar dominated the fourth wall — no stools; it had a brass rail brightly polished by generations of workers and housewives. A collection of lamps — no two alike — gave enough light to see food and drink through clouds of tobacco smoke. Through the blue-gray haze we spotted the empty table. Although it was *gemütlich*, my eyes darted between the front door and the hallway leading to the toilets. From previous visits I knew that an exit led from the rear of the bar, past the toilets, through the long hallway into a drab courtyard. From there, a path led through the ruin of an apartment house to Fasanenstrasse; it was an effective way to leave unobserved, to dodge a tail. I had eaten here before. The restaurant owner's wife brought an order of beer, goulash, and thick slices of black bread. The warmth of the stove, the friendly banter between groups of patrons, and the red paprika in the goulash relaxed body and soul. I queried Landser on route and approach — standard operating procedure.

"Herr Trenker," he said between bites, "the postcard came almost too late to make a plausible excuse leaving the office. Luckily I have an aunt in Neuruppin, so the round-trip rail pass gave me an excuse to travel through Berlin-Ostbahnhof."

Between beer, bread and goulash Landser made his security approach report. "I got out at Ostbahnhof, walked on Koppenstrasse toward Stalinallee, that's the old Grosse Frankfurter Strasse. You know, it's hard to believe, but that old borough, Friedrichshain, is still fifty percent bombed-out. Even now, almost ten years after the war, they have not even removed the ruins. Anyway, I walked north on Koppenstrasse, then turned left into Singerstrasse. Just to make sure that I had not picked up some goons, I went around that little park at Andreasplatz and made a goat leg into Kleine Andreasstrasse. Then up Krautstrasse to Strausberger Platz U-Bahn station. I took the long way 'round over Alexanderplatz, switched trains, went to Gleisdreieck, and hopped the second train to Uhlandstrasse."

He paused for another heaping spoon of goulash, then continued, "When I got there, I followed your advice and first walked north, stopped at the little tobacco store to buy some good West German tobacco. I'll still use the East German cigarette paper, but the tobacco sure tastes a hell of a lot better than that Russian Makhorka. Goddamn tobacco stems, hardly any leaf tobacco in it."

He took a deep sip from the beer stein. "Well, we lost the war and I guess Makhorka is Stalin's revenge. Anyway, when you spotted me, I was just lighting my first good cigarette — couldn't you tell?"

"Not in that crowd of people. I almost missed seeing you. That long way around may be a little time-consuming, but I sure feel better. You never know when one of those STASI assholes wants to buy a good pair of jackboots in West Berlin and recognizes a fellow East German. How many times have both you and Doktor Hermann told me that in this business you only get to make one mistake, then it's twenty years at Bautzen?"

Landser nodded in agreement.

While we ate I outlined the walk to the secure meeting place. We finished the goulash, wiped the plates with pieces of black bread and emptied our beer steins. Landser went to the men's room while I paid the bill. We met at the back door of the restaurant. Only one weak light bulb illuminated the courtyard. Garbage cans lined two of the walls. The path led through one of the ruins, a shortcut, to the Fasanenstrasse exit. As a precaution I carried my .38-caliber revolver in my right hand, hidden by the coat sleeve. It was dark and dangerous territory. We reached Fasanenstrasse without incident. The street was empty — it was suppertime, and all good Germans take their supper hour seriously. I returned my revolver to the holster.

In early afternoon I had rented two rooms at the Hotel-Pension Atlanta at Fasanenstrasse 74. For 9 Deutsche Mark per room per night I got clean, warm rooms and *Frühstück-mit-Ei*. I had engaged the landlady in conversation. We talked about the weather, politics, the soon-to-end occupation — at least in West Germany — and life in Berlin. After a while the landlady pushed the registration form back into the stack on the desk. I knew that if I waited long enough I did not have to fill out the police visitor's registration form. Without a form the landlady did not have to pay the tourist tax — a little extra money in her pocket — and I avoided automatic registration at Berlin's Visitors Police Department.

I had arrived with two suitcases and deposited one in each room. For Landser I had some underwear, a pair of dry, warm trousers, shirt and sweater — all made in East Germany — in the suitcase. Landser was anxious to get out of his wet clothing; it looked and smelled worse than mine. While Landser dressed, I asked the landlady for a pot of coffee. When Landser entered the room, I was already at the window with a steaming cup. Landser filled the other cup, and after a few careful sips, he said, "This coffee will put me back on my feet again. It's like getting a new lease on life." He lit one of my Philip Morris cigarettes, and we settled down for the debriefing.

I had the feeling that it would be another frustrating event. Landser reported that he had found absolutely no evidence of any sophisticated scientific and technical testing or research, not even plans for anything out of the ordinary. I knew from others who had also queried friends and acquaintances far and wide that none had ever heard of East Germany having any interest in anything except rebuilding apartment houses and factories damaged during the last big debacle — and paying war reparations to their "Soviet Friends." I had concluded some time ago that this S&T collection was a wasted effort.

Landser reported that he and many others were engaged in designing pre-fabricated sections of walls, interior as well as exterior, so that common laborers could assemble buildings without having to undergo training as stone masons or bricklayers.

Landser laughed. "The big shots in East Berlin can't keep master masons in East Germany; most of them have left for greener pastures. Now they are going to build prefabricated apartment houses. I wonder how that's going to work?"

All our sources involved in this S&T collection effort had reported similar information: East Germany, they said, was concentrating on solving its housing shortage, a result of Allied bombings and exacerbated by the departure of skilled craftsmen to West Germany. It was not exactly the research and development into high technology that we had expected. Our sources had rummaged throughout East Germany for several years — unsuccessfully; they had found absolutely no evidence of advanced research and development, especially in weapons and weapon systems — or, Landser's specialty: advanced metallurgy — titanium. In essence this particular collection effort brought few results. Apparently Communist East Germany, still struggling to rebuild its economy while having to pay heavy reparations, had only sufficient resources to solve her immediate needs. For the case officers of SpecOps 3 it was a very disheartening period.

After more than a year of frustration the Old Man canceled this assignment. We asked no questions and gladly disassembled our informant net.

I met Landser one last time to turn him over to my old friend Fred Herz, who had originally recruited Landser. For me it was a bittersweet occasion, because I knew that in just a few months I would return to the United States. Lander would once again report on Soviet military rail transport movements across the Neisse River, and Doktor Hermann, his old handler, would handle the reporting.

Landser departed shortly after Fred had made arrangements for the next Treff.

Fred and I decided to have a late dinner at the Kempinski Hotel to celebrate the turnover. As always, we performed the counter-surveillance routine, first walking along Meinekestrasse, then turning into the Kurfürstendamm. Fred stopped at a large antique store window, supposedly admiring the display, but actually checking whether or not we had picked up an East German goon. He remained viewing the display somewhat longer than necessary, then pointed. "You must buy those two glasses." I looked; in the display were a glass beer stein with "Schneekoppe"[84] in old German writing below a painting of the weather station and auxiliary building, and a wineglass with an identical painting, but somewhat smaller.

I knew I just had to purchase those two glasses.

As we entered the store, the air of old surrounded us. Upon my inquiry the proprietor retrieved the glasses from the display. Below the building on the amber-colored glass I saw chunks of anthracite coal — one of Silesia's treasures. The beer stein had two little chunks of coal missing, but it did not matter; these two glasses reminded me of the home my family had lost.

Back at the hotel, after we had completed our "shake the tail" routine, I thanked Fred for spotting this wonderful memento.

"We all must have bits of stuff that makes us recall moments of days gone by. You have seen my photos, my glassware, my stuff; all reminders of Frankfurt, my former home. None of them are my family's, you know that. But all these things have some sort of meaning, for me an anchor, some sort of tie to the days when I was a happy young man living in Frankfurt. That's why I thought you ought to have those two glasses."

Fred had never shown such sentimentality before; it surprised me. I knew the Nazis had killed his mother and father, but I had not realized that the little things, things Fred called "stuff," were so important to him. Now, these two Silesian glasses in my attaché case brought back old memories, memories I had forced into forgetfulness long ago.

"Fred, as you know, Christmas 1955 will be my last Christmas in Germany."

He nodded.

"There was another time when Christmas was the last one my family and I had spent in the only home I had ever known."

Again he nodded.

"As you already know, unlike you and Martha, I am not a practicing Christian, I am just a traditionalist who celebrates Christmas the same ways as my ancestors celebrated it two millennia ago, first as winter solstice, then in celebration — a holiday."

Fred looked at me, questioning, "How can you celebrate Christmas without Christ?"

I had thought about this many times, but now I verbalized it for the first time, "It's the holiday I celebrate: solstice. It happens to be around the end of December — the twenty-first to be exact. It's a joyous celebration. It's rebirth of the world, rebirth of nature, the coming of the growing season. Very important for those of us who tended the land. It's the future of mankind, of food for the next year, it's life itself. It has nothing to do with Christianity."

"So?" Fred looked impassioned.

"Fred, when I worked on the captured German records and saw what the Nazis did to others, a feeling of utter betrayal grew inside me. I felt betrayed by all those who supported this movement. But I felt especially betrayed by my Protestant ministers who had led me and my folks down the garden path, who had never stood up to the Nazis. I remember how our pastor led his congregation in prayer to save the Führer so that he could lead us to the *Endsieg*, to final victory. The Catholics were no better; they, all of them, had misled us, the believers. They should have stood up collectively and denounced that bastard and his Nazi minions. As true believers, these ministers, these priests, to demonstrate their true belief, should have become martyrs. But no, they prayed and made the rest of us pray as if Hitler were the new Christ. No, I can never forget nor forgive what the Christian clergy did to us; they were our shepherds, and they misled their flock."

"But," Fred interjected, "as a good Christian you must forgive the sinners."

"Oh? And how did that save your parents and the other German Jews, all good Germans, and many like your parents actually practicing Christians? How did it save those good Germans from the Nazi gas chambers? No, Fred, I can never forgive the Christian clergy for never standing up to the Nazis. I suppose your forgiving those makes you a better Christian than most."

Fred looked at me as if he had never met me, or as if he had seen a new me.

"You still have a Christmas tree, no?" Fred's question was rhetoric, he had visited my family the previous Christmas.

"Yes, but in name only. And don't we call it *Tannenbaum*[85] instead of Christmas tree? For me, the traditionalist, the *Tannenbaum* is the symbol of rebirth, of life's renewal."

I paused in reflection as I recalled my last Christmas in Silesia.

The Last Christmas in Silesia

Soviet Kolkhoz
Jauer or Jawor, Poland
Christmas 1945

The winter 1945–46 was a bitterly cold one. My entire clan still worked as slave laborers on my grandfather's former farm, now the *Kolkhoz* that raised food for the local Soviet Army *Kommandantura*. Although we had cut and stolen much wood, most was destined for the *Kommandantura*. To survive we also cut and burned the supporting beams from our — but no longer our — barns. We also split wood from ammunition boxes and anything else flammable; we even shared it with our Soviet guard detachment.

On Christmas Eve my mother decided to cut the pine tree, the one of two our father had mailed in 1939 from the Western Front. Father's Silesian 461st Infantry Regiment had transferred after the Polish Campaign to the Western Front, and he served there at a listening post far in front of the main line. Father and his comrades had dug shelters, earthen bunkers. They reinforced these bunkers with heavy logs, covered everything with a thick cover of earth, and then camouflaged it all with small pine trees. Just before Christmas a note from the Post office asked us to pick up a package; it contained two small Christmas tree seedlings — one for my sister Helga, and one for me. I planted the seedlings, sister Helga's in our vegetable garden, mine at our Preuss Opa's grave site. Helga's tree grew better than mine; it had grown into a most beautiful tree. Just before the holidays I walked into the garden in front of the farm and cut down Helga's tree. That *Tannenbaum* was absolutely the finest that had ever graced a home. We celebrated the birth of Christ — even some of our guards joined our activity.

As we had envisioned, it was to be our last Christmas in the land my family had tilled for generations.

NEW TASK—
BUILD A BOLTHOLE[86]

I.G. Farben Hochhaus
Frankfurt, West Germany
1956

The Ops called me and relayed a message from the Old Man, who was in a meeting in Washington, DC. Ops said that the Old Man and Source Control wanted to have at least one "bolthole" in the Görlitz area, that the Old Man had already discussed this with Special Agent Fred Herz, and that Herz had agreed to release Heinz Schwertfeger, code-named Landser, if Landser would be agreeable to the task.

I had not seen Fred for some time and wanted to touch base with him; actually, I wanted to be sure that Fred did not mind transferring one of his old sources. I also wanted to get an update on Landser and to see whether or not Landser had ever spoken about his wife, because a bolthole operator must have a wife that is agreeable to the operation since both the source and his live-in companion will become bolthole operators.

Fred, always the singleton, the lone case officer, now had an office on the sixth floor of the I.G. Farben Hochhaus. I called him, we met, he was overjoyed to see me. Over coffee we talked about family, about Frankfurt and reconstruction. Then we turned to the business at hand. Fred suggested if I were to invite both Landser and his wife into this operation, I ought to schedule a meeting somewhere in Austria, near the Czech border.

"Landser and his wife Lieselotte, 'Liesschen,' once before vacationed in Czechoslovakia. And," Fred said, "they can get into Czechoslovakia, and from there into Austria, without too much trouble. It just takes a couple of bottles of Scotch to make the Czechs guarding the crossing into Austria agreeable."

According to Fred, the guards would think it was a black-market deal. "Aside from that, there is a lot of black-market trading between the Czechs and the Austrians and the Czechs appreciate the booze."

Fred used his contact procedure to arrange the meeting. Landser agreed to drive his Trabant, an offspring of the pre–World War II DKW — a minicar still produced in West Germany. The Trabant was Landser's "dream car."

The plan called for Landser to make reservations at a hotel in Ceske Budejovice, in Czechoslovakia, some miles north of the Austrian town of Freistadt, our Treff location.

Fred had arranged for the recognition meeting in Freistadt on the city's main square in front of the Rathaus — the city hall.

Life Is a Gamble

Freistadt, Austria
March 1956

On a misty day in late March 1976, Special Agent Carl Schenck, aka Chuck Sattler, and I "toured" Freistadt. We had driven the previous day from Frankfurt to Linz, on the Danube River. We overnighted in Linz and arrived in Freistadt at midmorning.

Freistadt, a charming, medieval town, is watched over by the *Alte Burg*, the Old Castle. The town is surrounded by a green space, the *Stadtgraben*, the original moat before the city wall. We parked the car behind the *Stadtpfarrkirche*, a church adjacent to the city square, and made ourselves comfortable at a sidewalk café from which we had a commanding view of city hall and the square.

Reading the local newspaper, still fastened in the old-fashioned way on a wooden rod, courtesy of the café, and sipping our coffees, Schenck and I conversed in German, commenting on the beauty of this idyllic place, the weather, and politics. Others around us all seemed to know each other; new arrivals greeted everyone, shaking hands, slapping shoulders, and conversing between reading their newspapers. We seemed to be the only two outsiders.

A little before noon, Schenck motioned to a Trabant entering the city square. Everyone looked up; everyone seemed to know it was an East German car — it rattled, it coughed, and it trailed a plume of smoke worse than any diesel truck.

Schenck called over the waiter and paid the bill. We then walked toward the *Stadtpfarrkirche* and our car. The driver of the Trabant apparently took this as a signal to follow.

Landser did a double-take when he spotted me as he exited the Trabant. While his wife climbed out of their car, Landser walked toward me with outstretched hands.

"Herr Trenker," he managed to gasp, "not in my wildest dreams would I have ever expected to see you again."

He introduced me to his wife Liesschen, and I introduced Schenck as Chuck Sattler. We decided to stretch our legs a bit before eating lunch. Landser and I walked toward the *Stadtgraben*; Schenck and Liesschen Schwertfeger followed. Landser wanted to know what I had been doing.

I told him that I was now in a new organization that was mainly concerned with protecting endangered East German informants. I thought that this was the right time to broach the topic of converting Schwertfeger from a railroad watcher, who reported on Soviet troop and equipment movements from and to East Germany, to a bolthole operator.

"I talked this over with Herr Doktor Hermann," I said, "and he was agreeable, but only if you thought it was right."

Schwertfeger wanted to know what that would entail, and I told him that only highly trusted agents in extremis were told to go to a certain address to seek temporary asylum. They would stay there only a day or two and then an "exit party" would extract them.

"To protect you, the exit party will not know your address. The endangered individual will go to a previously arranged Treff location for pickup."

Then I told him that his wife should be willing to operate the bolthole, that it was not without some danger, and that she had to be totally briefed on the operation, because she would become the "keeper" of the asylum seeker. I also told him that Chuck Sattler would most likely be the man in charge of the bolthole operation.

"Not to worry about Liesschen," Landser replied, "she knows all about my activities and has watched trains for me while I was at work."

"Yes, Herr Schwertfeger," I said, "but this is a little different than just watching and reporting. This means hiding a person."

Landser thought about this a while and then said, "Look, let me talk to her. See what she thinks about this."

We changed places: Liesschen Schwertfeger and her husband walked in front, and Schenck and I followed. The mist had lifted, and walking in the shade of trees along the *Stadtgraben* was invigorating.

The Schwertfegers debated for some time. Finally, they stopped and Liesschen told me that if only highly trusted agents would be allowed to know of the bolthole, she felt obliged to grant them safe haven.

I warned her that there always would be the possibility that the asylum seeker had been tailed by the STASI.

Liesschen Schwertfeger replied, "Herr Trenker, life is a gamble. Sometimes you win, sometimes you lose, but if the odds are in your favor, you win more often than you lose."

I agreed. I thought, *This is one short speech I must remember.*

After a wonderful lunch, Schenck, Landser and I arranged the details. I told of the must-dos and the absolutely must-not-dos — all associated with the security of the bolthole and its operators. I also reminded Schwertfeger of his no-name account in Liechtenstein that Herr Doktor Hermann had established and that my organization would pay a monthly stipend into this account. I asked if the Schwertfegers had any other questions or concerns, and when they acknowledged that they thought we had covered everything, I said, "Everything, except for the Scotch we have in the car. I think Herr Schwertfeger can be generous, and the border guards will love him."

Schenck laughed. Together we walked to the *Stadtpfarrkirche* parking lot and, after a long goodbye, the Trabant departed in a cloud of oily smoke.

Back in Frankfurt I reported the details of out newly established bolthole. The Old Man, who had returned from Washington during our foray into Austria, was overjoyed.

"Mr. Thamm," he said, "I haven't told you, but this is our only bolthole in all of East Germany. Good job."

I suggested that all this was only possible because Special Agent Fred Herz had recruited a very capable source.

The Old Man said he would mention that during the next morning meeting.

A few days later Money Bags had completed all the details, arranging the deposits in Landser's no-name account a bank in the Principality of Liechtenstein. He directed me to make the initial cash payment into this account. Later payments would be made by an automatic deposit system.

END OF TOUR OF DUTY

Frankfurt-am Main
I.G. Farben Hochhaus
May 1956

My three years of overseas assignment ended in May 1956. The Old Man had asked me to extend for another three years, but Ann Marie and I wanted to get back to the "Land of the round door-knobs," as the GIs lovingly called America. I had not seen my parents and my sister Helga all this time. While we were overseas, my frugal parents had purchased a small townhouse in the Glover Park district of Washington, DC, one we were eager to see. I hated to leave this utterly fascinating job, but I also may have subconsciously realized that I had suffered "burn-out." The constant danger, the long hours, the pressure of living multiple lives had taken its toll. I longed for the company of men I could trust, to once again be a soldier in the United States Army.

Much was left to do before my departure. SpecOps 3 ran swift and smooth, but the German police liaison needed to be continued. Frank Mackenzie took this additional assignment. I introduced him to Oberinspektor Hanke. It seemed as if Mackenzie and Hanke hit it off well from the very beginning when Mackenzie mentioned that his mother was originally from East Prussia, but had been raised in the Hamburg area. Hanke then told that his father was originally from Königsberg, East Prussia; he had been stationed in Silesia. There he had married and remained in Löwenberg where the young Hanke was born; another important link in the liaison chain for SpecOps 3.

As a final act, Money Bags and I completed auditing my operational funds and expenditures. Money Bags mentioned that for the rest of my army career, my 201 File—the personnel record—would be classified Confidential.

"You will find," the fiscal officer chuckled, "that your next personnel officer will resent this, but those agent payment receipts and payment documentations will remain part of your records."

Trust, and the Bad Apple

West Germany
The 1950s

Much of clandestine operation is based on trust: trust among case officers, the operations managers, source control, the fiscal and security officers. To control, even to oversee, the travel of the case officers, the contact expenses, the sources recruited, and the information collected is extremely difficult. There are certain control and security measures built into the overall clandestine operation, but when is comes right down to the details, trust is a major component. As Fred Herz had told me eons ago, "Even in this business there is a certain integrity that must be observed."

Also, although it was never so mentioned at the Little Red Schoolhouse, there also grows a certain amount of trust, sometimes even friendship, between case officer and source—all, or in part, connected to survivability. One of the instructors at the Little Red Schoolhouse had cautioned us regarding money, or as he said, "Uncle Sam's dough." They also implied, maybe in not so many words, that even with all the personnel and personal security exercised in clandestine services, there must be first and foremost a bond of trust: trust in the individual, and trust in the organization—trust that if the case officer acts correctly, then the organization will back him to the hilt.

Truth be told, we had very few bad apples in our organization, or in my former unit, the 513th MIG. Part of our good security was the long vetting and screening processes all agents had undergone. For example, only five or six from my class of some sixty Army Intelligence personnel at the Little Red Schoolhouse passed the final muster. I am convinced that the old colonel, our "headmaster" of the class, had much to do with that selection.

However, in every barrel...

We had a few very embarrassing events happen, where that trust was violated. These were damaging not only from the national security point of view — although some had indeed severely damaged national security — but damaging to the security of case officers and their sources. Indeed, when we case officers were "on the street," when we were most often alone, we were then most vulnerable. Our security, our lives, depended on total maintenance of all aspects of personnel, personal, and operational security. One bad apple in the barrel can kill, and we had a few bad apples our organization.

One incident occurred in the mid–1950s. It was a very public, embarrassing event that involved our organization. We had a safehouse in Würzburg that, according to *The Overseas Weekly* (*OW*) — a sensational tabloid, also known to most everyone as the *Oversexed Weekly*— was operated by a Mr. Walker. Most of us knew the safehouse on "Eisenmann Strasse" as a sweet deal: easy living, involving little travel and hardly any physical danger for those operating it.

OW reported that the Communist East German propaganda machine had proudly displayed a "returnee" who, it claimed, fled to the East Zone with information stolen from American CIC headquarters here [a misnomer — it was actually MI, a Military Intelligence house]. According to *OW*, "The man the East Germans displayed at last week's press conference was 34-year-old Horst Hesse. He claimed he had been employed in the American CI office at No. 4 Eisenmann Str. Chief function of the office, he told reporters, was the screening of refugees from the East and 'enlisting of American agents.' Hesse said he went from East to West Germany in 1953, went to work for the CIC, and then defected to the East in May of this year. As a sign of good faith, he said, he brought a safe chock-full of important information 'about American agents in East Germany.' Hesse displayed some of the material supposedly stolen from CI headquarters here. Reporters noted most of the material consisted of phony press cards and ordinary blank identification card forms. Last May, East German Minister-President Otto Grotewohl announced that a former American employee had brought stolen information, which had led to the arrest of '137 American agents.' The Army has denied that anything was ever stolen from the Würzburg headquarters. To Grotewohl's statement, USAREUR replied: 'We don't regard Grotewohl as a reliable source of information.' This week the Army added that nobody by the name of Horst Hesse was ever employed by American Intelligence in Europe. A German newspaper reports that 'Hesse's immediate superior, a Mr. Walker, has been fired.' The Army replied that nobody by that name has been fired by the CI in Würzburg or anywhere else."

Of course, any records search would have revealed that we did not have a "Mister Walker" employed, and that, if he existed at all, he was not fired by the CI in Würzburg or anywhere else, and that Horst Hesse did not work for the CIC.

OW further reported, "Besides giving German newspapers columns of speculative news stories, the cloak-and-dagger affair has had one other immediate result: the house on Eisenmann Strasse now stands empty. The Americans who used to circulate in and out have disappeared and nobody seems to know where they have gone."

Very evident was that someone, the unknown Mr. Walker, had severely violated the trust placed in him. What had actually happened was even worse than reported by the *OW*. The special agents at the "House on Eisenmann Strasse" had gotten extremely careless. One of my acquaintances, who had investigated this horrendous security violation, told me that the whole crew of the safehouse had gone to dinner and had left the former East German source, Horst Hesse, alone and "in charge of the safehouse"—a case of extremely misplaced trust on their part. Apparently this had happened before, and Horst Hesse had arranged with several East German STASI officers to steal the office safe. After the Americans had left to dine, the Germans had backed up a small truck to a window of the office in which the safe was located. Then they had rammed the heavy safe—the safe was on rollers—through the wall below the window and into the truck bed. Thereafter, and long before the Americans had discovered it, they had casually driven the short distance from Würzburg to the East German crossing point.

From the STASI point of view, a brilliant intelligence operation; for our unit a highly embarrassing event.

I learned of a far more serious break of security many years after I had retired from the world of falsehood and betrayal.

It came as a horrendous aftershock to learn that one of my former colleagues at the 513th Military Intelligence Group had become a KGB source, that he had betrayed his adopted country and all members serving in U.S. Intelligence; it was former Sergeant First Class George Trofimoff—later U.S. Army Reserve Colonel George Trofimoff.

From official records: "George Trofimoff was born in Germany to Russian émigrés and became a naturalized United States citizen in 1951. He enlisted in the United States Army in 1948 and received a commission in the United States Army Reserve in 1956, and retired from the United States Army Reserve with the rank of Colonel in 1987."[87]

"From 1959 through 1994, Trofimoff was employed by the United States Army as a civilian working in military intelligence, serving primarily in Germany. Throughout his career with the United States Army, Trofimoff held SECRET and TOP SECRET clearances, and received periodic briefings and acknowledged his responsibilities in handling classified information."

Trofimoff was one of the interrogators who had worked with me in the chalet at Camp King, Oberursel.

Of the few bad apples in U.S. Army Military Intelligence's barrel,[88] George Trofimoff was among the worst. The details of this espionage offered here are drawn from a wide variety of published news sources and the actual federal indictment at the United States District Court, Middle District of Florida, Tampa Division, in June 2000.[89] "Trofimoff spent his career in military intelligence. He was so far above suspicion that he was put in charge of a house in Nuremberg, Germany, where American intelligence would interview defectors from the Soviet Union. The interrogation center contained a library of classified information, everything the U.S. knew about the Soviet Union that interrogators used in questioning defectors."[90]

Then, in 1992, the event occurred that all traitors fear most: a defector from the other side spilled the beans. For us, the priority in all interrogations of defectors from other intelligence services was counterintelligence, i.e. what type of information is funneled from U.S. sources into the foreign system? A KGB[91] clerk named Vasili Mitrokhin reported that one of the American interrogation centers had an inside spy, and Mitrokhin had proof. He handed over KGB records that showed that 50,000 pages of classified documents were taken from Joint Interrogation Center (JIC) in Nuremberg.

Retired Colonel George Trofimoff was arrested in June 2000 in Florida and charged with espionage. Trofimoff was the highest-ranking U.S. military officer ever charged with espionage. The espionage of Trofimoff covered a span of 25 years.

The *Orlando Sentinel*[92] reported that during that time Trofimoff was paid $250,000 to $300,000. Thirty-two overt acts of conspiracy were cited in the indictment.

After retirement Trofimoff had purchased a home in a gated community in Melbourne, Florida. His address was 1427 Patriot Drive, rather ironic for a Soviet spy. At the time of his arrest, Trofimoff worked bagging groceries at the local Publix, a grocery chain with numerous stores in Florida. It has also been reported that Trofimoff appeared to live beyond his economic means and had five marriages over the course of his life.

Trust, misplaced trust, allowed Trofimoff to associate with high KGB staff, where he had discussed his duties with a KGB flag officer. Internal security, as well as the Army's Counter Intelligence Corps (CIC), failed to detect that Trofimoff vacationed as a KGB guest at a Crimean resort. A disastrous happening for U.S. Intelligence; a brilliant coup for the KGB.

Trofimoff was found guilty and sentenced to life in prison.

Order, Counterorder

Home, Sweet Home
Alexandria, Virginia
1956

When asked, I had requested reassignment to Headquarters Company, U.S. Army, South Post Fort Myer, Arlington 8, Virginia, for duty with the German Military Document Section, Captured Records Branch.

As so often in the military, "for the benefit of the service," the army denied my request and gave me orders to report to the "Casual Detachment 3420 Service Unit, Fort Bragg, North Carolina." I read and reread the orders. I thought, *Fort Bragg, North Carolina, what in hell is that? Is there someone trying to screw me?*

Being an old soldier and having had, against all odds, orders previously changed, I thought, *Don't screw with me.* I had fully expected to return to the Pentagon, or at least to the Washington, DC, area. I still do not know what this was all about, but I knew that I had an ace in the hole — I had a good friend, Iggy Ernst, my old sergeant major in the Pentagon, and he wanted me back in the army document exploitation business. I wrote to him a letter and enclosed a copy of the orders. Then I waited.

Less than a month later, to someone's surprise, I received another set of orders, and, lo and behold, the amended orders assigned me to "Hqs. Co. United States Army, for duty with," well, the Pentagon, of course — the power of old sergeant majors. I am sure someone in Headquarters Northern Area Command wondered … or maybe not. Every old soldier knows that old sergeant majors run the U.S. Army.

After long goodbyes, the army packed our household goods; we "cleared quarters," a cumbersome, often unpleasant procedure. I finally traded my long hair for a good military haircut and, dressed in my best Class A uniform, I departed for home.

Back on U.S. soil. Life on top of the hill — Summerville Hill, Alexandria, Virginia. The author with wife Ann Marie and children (left to right) Renita, Erik and Erwin.

Before leaving Germany I had harbored some concerns about how I would handle the transition from being the Man Called Trenker to Sergeant First Class Gerhardt B. Thamm. I should not have worried. During my absence the German Military Document Section had been enlarged to include other foreign document collections. All my old friends were waiting, and I once again worked with Master Sergeant Alois Himsl, the ingenious Minnesota farmer's son. It did not take long to get used to the soldier's routine; I once again reported for the Wednesday morning company formation on the street between the old wooden barracks and attended the once-a-month training session on Wednesday. I especially enjoyed the "pass-in-review" parades on the North Post Fort Myer parade grounds that had, long before World War I, seen the first landing and takeoff of a military aircraft. It felt good to be back in the womb, to be back among men I could trust; it felt good to once again be a soldier. And it felt good to live a normal family life in Virginia.

While I was in Europe, the mission of the Captured Records Branch had changed the emphasis of research from Soviet studies to military history. We supported the U.S. Army's Military History Branch. Later we assisted in gathering evidence for ongoing war crimes prosecutions. The Army G2 transferred our unit to the Army's Adjutant General's Office (TAGO); that in turn attached us to the National Archives in Washington, DC. There we started preparation to return most of the captured German records to the *Bundesarchiv* in Koblenz, Germany. Later, I met several interesting foreign researchers: British, French and, most interesting, two Germans.

In 1960, a Dr. Alfred Wagner from the *Bundesarchiv* in Koblenz and Freiherr Fabian von Schlabrendorff arrived at the records depository in Alexandria, Virginia, to assess the collections and work out the details for the transfer of the captured documents to the Federal German Republic. In addition to his official role as Wagner's assistant, Schlabrendorff was also engaged in a private research project to find information relating to the March 13, 1943, assassination attempt on Adolf Hitler. The former German Major von Schlabrendorff and his superior, General Henning von Tresckow, were the architects of this assassination attempt. Before World War II Schlabrendorff had been a barrister; long after my association with him he became a judge on the German Supreme Court.

Because researchers could not enter the document storage area, my sergeant major assigned me to assist the two researchers. I was thoroughly acquainted with the thousands upon thousands of records stored in this facility. After I learned of Schlabrendorff's main interest, I brought records that he may otherwise have missed in searching through our somewhat crude card files.

Schlabrendorff was somewhat average in stature, height and looks: a quiet man wearing steel-rimmed glasses. All in all, a seemingly ordinary man—not what one would imagine if conjuring up a picture of a would-be assassin. But as I perused the Gestapo files I realized he was a man of extraordinary courage and unbelievable determination. Although he was born in Saxony, he came from an old Prussian family living in Silesia. When Schlabrendorff discovered that we had the Prussian aspect in common, he seemed to relax just a little bit.

In days gone by I had been a Prussian. For centuries, my ancestors had served Prussian kings and German emperors. My grandfather's city farm in Jauer, Silesia had the nomenclature "*Lehngut*." Under old Prussian laws and traditions, as an owner of a *Lehngut* my grandfather was obligated to serve the king in time of war, along with two of his horses and a horse handler. During the Great War my grandfather, two of his sons, two of his horses, and one of his horse handlers served the emperor on the Western Front. I had spent my early life living on my grandfather's estate in Jauer, Silesia, some twenty miles from Kreisau county where *Operation Walküre*, aka Operation Valkyrie, was conceived—where German generals had gathered to plan the removal of Hitler, Germany's head of state.

Initially the conspirators had planned to arrest Hitler and then, via the German Reserve Army, remove the Nazi hierarchy from power. On September 3, 1939, the day France and Great Britain entered the war against Germany, Schlabrendorff notified George Ogilvic Forbes, British Secret Service representative in Germany, working out of the British embassy in Berlin, of German Colonel-General von Hammerstein-Equard's plan to arrest Hitler while he visited troops on the Western Front. This attempt failed, and so did the one in March 1943.

Many of our discussions took place while Dr. Wagner and Schlabrendorff joined another sergeant and me during our brown-bag lunches in the archives depository, known today as the "Old Torpedo Factory." During one of our conversations, Schlabrendorff mentioned that even in the late 1950s a segment of the German population considered him and the other members of the *Kreisauer Kreis*[93] — the group that had plotted to kill Hitler — traitors, betrayers of the defenders of the fatherland. This thought intrigued me, because I had been a member of the U.S. Army of Occupation, Germany, in the early 1950s. During that time I had never heard that opinion expressed by any German I had met.

Schlabrendorff dismissed it simply with, "Ah, Sergeant Thamm, of course not. *You* are an American."

Working with the captured German records, I had known of the many attempts to kill Hitler, of the conspiracy within the *Oberkommando der Wehrmacht*, the German High Command, but had never heard of Schlabrendorff or his superior, General Henning von Tresckow. Now I had almost daily lunch with one from the inner circle of conspirators, with the man who, in March 1943, had actually given an unwitting courier an explosive device meant to kill the Führer, to explode over Russian territory. Schlabrendorff discovered later that "everything had worked as expected. The glass encasing the chemical fuse with the corrosive fluid had been broken, the chemical had eaten through the wire, the firing pin had been released and had struck forward — but the detonator had not ignited! One of the few duds that slipped past a British inspection was responsible for the fact that Hitler did not die on March 13, 1943."[94]

* * * * *

In July 1960 the Adjutant General, Headquarters, U.S. Army, decided that our small group of German linguists had completed the exploitation of captured documents. The army dissolved the organization and transferred all the military members to various intelligence and security elements. I received orders to report to the Central U.S. Registry in the Pentagon. Central Registry was a document security operation that received and distributed classified documents from NATO and other global defense alliance elements. It sounded very exciting, but in essence we were glorified letter carriers. We had a wonderful officer in charge, a Lieutenant Colonel John Manfre. We worked in a vault on the first floor of the Pentagon. As the new man in the unit it was my duty to pick up the classified mail from the Department of State classified mailroom. I rode an army sedan from the Pentagon motor pool from the Pentagon's River Entrance into Washington, DC, and brought a duffel bag full of highly classified mail to our office. There we opened the sealed bag, signed for its content and then distributed it, using a very efficient document number, to the various armed forces classified document registries, just as mail carriers deliver mail. In essence, it was an easy job with much free time. But after about a year in this unit I became bored. Colonel Manfre urged me to stay, but I told him that I wanted something a bit more interesting, and he reluctantly approve my transfer to the U.S. Army Security Agency in Fort Meade, Maryland. It meant changing from a comfortable commute from our house in Alexandria, Virginia to a long haul — all before the infamous Washington Beltway had been completed — to Fort Meade.

I came into a unit that later became the 410th U.S. Army Security Agency Special Operations Unit (410th USASA SPECOPS). There I again met a few of my former Captured Records Branch comrades. The 410th had highly qualified voice transcribers — some native Russian, Polish, and German speakers. I was granted my wish; it was exciting work.

The Later Years

The 1970s and 1980s
Fort Meade, MD,
West Germany,
and Alexandria, VA

During my last tour of duty with the U.S. Army Security Agency (USASA), I had nine permanent duty transfers/changes of station, two in Germany during my last three years in the Army. Time and the army had taken their toll on both me and my family. I had reluctantly made the decision to retire from the army when I realized that pressures of a growing family and limited promotion possibilities meant that I needed to return stateside and find a more conventional career field.

Also, and unfortunately, some months into my last overseas assignment, Ann Marie, for reasons unclear to me, announced that she no longer wanted to be associated with me. She spent much time in bed. In addition to my job, I had to manage the household. I cooked, cleaned and took care of Ann Marie and the children. To add to our misery, the army decided to transfer me in-country from Frankfurt-on-Main to the USASA Base Herzogenaurach (Herzo Base), near the Czech-East German border, where I was nominally in charge of a section of the 411th U.S. Army Security Agency Special Operations Unit.

While at Herzo Base, our son Erik lived in a dormitory in Frankfurt so that he could attend Frankfurt American high school; our two younger children remained with me in Herzogenaurach. Our 16-year-old daughter Renita attended the Nuremberg American middle school, and our 11-year-old son Erwin attended American grade school in Nuremberg. By now Ann Marie had been ill for some eighteen months, and a few months before I was scheduled to retire and return to the U.S. in 1968, she decided that for health reasons she needed to return to her family in Minnesota immediately.

Preparing for retirement, and the move back to the USA as a single parent, was both stressful and exhausting. Just the infamous "Clearing Quarters" — every service person will understand that term — was highly stressful. My daughter Renita had problems of her own and was no help in preparing the apartment for departure. I had to clean the entire apartment, remove all stains and picture-hanging marks from the walls.

Luckily, I had two German inspectors, and after a bit of chit-chat in German — and two bottles of bourbon — they declared the quarters fit for my departure.

Because our home in Alexandria, Virginia, was still occupied by renters, upon our June 1968 return to the States we stayed temporarily with my parents in Washington, DC.

A few years later Ann Marie and I parted our ways via a mutually agreed-upon divorce.

Several years after I had retired from Army Intelligence, I married Suanne Elizabeth Zuzel of Dunkirk and Silver Creek, New York. Suanne was an executive in the Library of Congress. Suanne became my Rock of Gibraltar. She is my best friend, my lover, my wife, and she made my third life worth living.

POSTSCRIPT

Old Spooks...

Many years ago one of the instructors at the clandestine case officer training center at Camp King, Oberursel, Germany, told us, "Foreign intrigue gets into your blood, and the intelligence service will call on you time and again. And, no matter how often you promise yourself not to answer the call—you will; time and again." I remembered that when I joined Naval Intelligence in 1970 and the Defense Intelligence Agency (DIA) in 1985. During those years I learned new trades; I became an intelligence analyst in Naval Intelligence and a HUMINT Operations Officer at DIA. In those capacities I would travel into foreign lands where I would encounter danger from the known and the unknown. As the former case officer, the prima donna of the clandestine world, I could not escape that lure.

Shortly after I had retired from the Defense Intelligence Agency in 1987, a defense consultant firm, aka "Beltway Bandit," hired me. For the next four years, along with my partner Louis Zammarella, I presented counterespionage security briefings to personnel in the Office of the Secretary of Defense, and the Office of the Chairman of the Joint Chiefs of Staff in the Pentagon.

In 1994 Suanne took early retirement from the Library of Congress; she and I moved to Fernandina Beach, a lovely little town on Amelia Island, a barrier island on the northeastern shore of Florida.

*****

I now question whether it was paranoia or security concerns, but the intelligence services had strongly discouraged, or at least severely restricted, private contact between its agents and foreign friends. After many years in government service I have come to the conclusion that it was bureaucratic inertia that pushed the dictum, "Restrict your correspondence to close relatives, and even here only to *Christmas card relationships.*"

Every contact with a foreigner had to be listed in detail in the *Standard*

Postscript

"The Man Called Trenker" in retirement, 2004.

Form 86 Security Investigation Data for Sensitive Position. Most of us assumed that the mere listing of too many foreign contacts would preclude getting a security clearance.

In essence: No security clearance, no job.

Having "subverted" numerous persons to betray their countries, I have yet to recruit one because he or she had merely corresponded with a friend. In security nothing is as important as personal integrity and love of country. Over the past several thousand years intelligence operatives have developed "Penetration Indicators" for persons thought to be susceptible to subversion; these indicators are used by all the intelligence services. Case officers seek persons who have access to their nation's innermost secrets and who are in dire need of money. A person in great financial difficulties facing the loss of the family home, bankruptcy, or family separation may become subject to recruitment. An intelligence agent can help this person out of these difficulties, but for a price: betrayal. Case officers also watch for the "talker and the bragger." With a little prodding he or she will tell the case officer either wittingly or unwittingly many highly confidential details just to enhance the bragger's importance, just to prove the bragger's expertise. Of course, case officers have it easy with those in the category of *greed and conceit.* Their greed for money and dreams of becoming master spies cause them to betray their country.

Old Spooks never die, they...

NOTES

1. Proprietaries: businesses operated for and by intelligence agencies.
2. So called because if the rifleman did not have a Panzerfaust when attacked by tanks, it was "hallelujah." See *The Hallelujah Weapon*, Gerhardt B. Thamm, Armed Forces Journal International, May 1987, pp. 84–86.
3. Gerhardt B. Thamm, *Boy Soldier: A German Teenager at the Nazi Twilight* (Jefferson, NC, and London: McFarland, 2000).
4. Schuhmine — explosives in a small wooden box with a single trip fuse.
5. Collective farm.
6. Kommandantura, the local area commander.
7. German farmers from the Swabian and Baden principalities had migrated to the Volga region during czarist days.
8. SS *Marine Tiger*, 12,420 GRT, Single Screw, Geared Turbine, 17 knots max. speed. Built 1945 by Kaiser Co., Vancouver, Washington for War Shipping Administration as a C4-S-A3 Transport. 1947: Chartered by United States Lines. 1949. Handed over to U.S. Maritime Commission, and laid up. 1966: Sold to Litton Industries. Lengthened and converted into the Contain Ship Oakland. 1988: Sold for breaking up, but wrecked off Vietnam. Source: Anthony Cooke, *Emigrant Ships*. (London SE 10 8 JL: Carmania).
9. Victory in Europe.
10. Foreign Armies, East; the intelligence branch that dealt with the Soviet Army. After the war Gehlen directed the Bundes Nachrichten Dienst (BND), the intelligence service of the German Federal Republic.
11. German Armed Forces High Command.
12. Leitz, a trade name for a gray-black hardcover archive folder with a label at the back and a metal-framed hole at the bottom to facilitate pulling the folder from the shelf.
13. Evaluation Site West.
14. The Luftwaffe's Transient Camp, Air, West.
15. For interesting reading see: Raymond F. Toliver's *The Interrogator: The Story of Hanns Joachim Scharff, Master Interrogator of the Luftwaffe*. (Atglen, PA: Schiffer Military History, 1997).
16. Raymond F. Toliver, *The Interrogator: The Story of Hanns Joachim Scharff, Master Interrogator of the Luftwaffe*. (Atglen, PA: Schiffer Military History, 1997).
17. Wilhelm Canaris, head of armed forces intelligence; a longtime naval career officer, he entered the navy in 1905 as a cadet; he was involved in the attempt to kill the Führer and was executed by the Nazis on 9 April 1945 — less than one month before Germany capitulated.
18. German Armed Forces Foreign Intelligence.
19. That meant that had all the files been set upright next to each other the row would have been nineteen miles long.
20. So called because of his occupation before becoming the Nazis' top killer.
21. Die Kleinen hängt man, aber die Großen lässt man laufen.
22. *Military Intelligence: A Picture History*, by Patrick Finnegan. (History Office, U.S. Army Intelligence, 1984), p. 117.

23. Recalled to active duty.
24. "Shorts," artillery shells that exploded short of their intended target.
25. Wilson Quarterly (Autumn 1996).
26. IPW-Interrogator, Prisoner of War.
27. Private First Class (PFC).
28. Rail Transport Office.
29. A three-quarter-ton three-axle vehicle of World War II vintage, akin to today's HUMVEE — only a lot less expensive.
30. Raymond F. Toliver, *The Interrogator—The Story of Hanns Joachim Scharff, Master Interrogator of the Luftwaffe*. (Atglen, PA: Schiffer Military History, 1977).
31. VOPO: Volkspolizei, the garrisoned People's Police.
32. Women's Army Corps.
33. Dangle: A false defector.
34. Bachelor Officers' Quarters.
35. U.S. Army Europe.
36. Recuperation Center.
37. OSS — Office of Strategic Services of World War II fame.
38. Irreverently called by the soldiers, "Christ, I'm Confused."
39. Now called IIR, Intelligence Information Report.
40. Safehouse: a secure place for the personnel and activity of an intelligence operation. The term is often misused for walk-in facilities. See: Walk-in. Another type of safehouse is called bolthole; it is an emergency escape safehouse usually, but not necessarily, in an unfriendly country or region that is operated by a trusted member of the intelligence net.
41. All right.
42. The German equivalent of G.I.
43. Treff— Meeting place, from the German word "treffen," or meeting someone. Used by Soviet, German and U.S. intelligence agents.
44. Subway.
45. Elevated train.
46. Schuhmine — explosives in a small wooden box with a single trip fuse.
47. A wound serious enough for even a German soldier to be discharged — to go home.
48. Ersatzkaffee — a concoction made of roasted barley.
49. Panzergrenadier division, something close to a U.S. armored division.
50. A favorite Nazi propaganda line when Germany lost terrain.
51. The 100th Jäger Division — formerly the 100th Leichte Infantrie Division, which was destroyed at Stalingrad.
52. Hanns Neidhardt, author of *Mit Tanne und Eichenlaub* (*With Fir Tree and Oak Cluster*).
53. The state of an army, its numbers, leaders, organization and equipment — along with its capability.
54. Singleton: An illegal living in the target country directly controlled by the case officer.
55. Post Exchange: the army's general store.
56. A car that today would be called a "sub-compact."
57. Senior Inspector, rating in the area of an army colonel.
58. Fellow countryman.
59. Curiously, Oberinspektor Hanke used my grandfather's word for the British.
60. A one-page, six-paragraph report that contains source number, time and place of meeting, items to report, money dispensed, and time and location of next Treff.
61. Operations Officer.
62. Source Control Officer.
63. A support group of troopers attached to our unit from the Corps of Engineers.
64. Germans who were deported from their ancestral home in the Sudetenland, a part of Czechoslovakia.
65. My grandfather, a wealthy farmer and senior trustee of the local bank, had lifelong friends; they always used the formal form of address. The single exception was reserved for regimental comrades, especially wartime comrades; they, no matter what their current position in society, always addressed each other in the familiar form. It is especially difficult for English speakers because the "you" is phonetically similar to the German familiar "Du."

66. A bastardization of the official acronym for the East German: SSD — Staatssicherheitsdienst — State Security Service.
67. Bautzen, Saxony; near the Czechoslovakia border, site of the infamous Secret State Police high-security prison for traitors and malcontents.
68. Walk-in: an individual who offers his services, or information, to a foreign country.
69. GRU: Glavnoye Razvedyvatelnoye Upravleniye (Soviet Military Intelligence).
70. Essential Elements of Information.
71. Colloquial term: the Source Control Form Number 6 terminated the employment of an A source, a permanent source.
72. Defense Intelligence Agency.
73. AGO, acronym for Adjutant General's Office.
74. The official East German newspaper.
75. Restricted Zone.
76. East German People's Police.
77. Military personnel record.
78. The laboratory that manufactured "toys" for the clandestine service.
79. GRU: Acronym for Glavnoye Razvedyvatelnoye Upravleniye (Soviet Military Intelligence).
80. Zapplen — German for wriggle, fidget — keep in suspense: sweat.
81. Daily trip to headquarters to destroy accumulated classified papers.
82. U.S. Army Counter Intelligence Corps
83. Karlshorst, a suburb of East Berlin and the site of Soviet Forces Headquarters, Germany.
84. Silesia's highest mountain (1,602 meters high).
85. Fir tree.
86. Bolthole: an emergency escape safehouse operated by a trusted source.
87. United States District Court, Middle District of Florida, Tampa Division, June 2000.
88. Jim Gates, *Bad Apples in the Barrel*. CIC Story, Golden Sphinx, Spring 2005.
89. Jim Gates, *Bad Apples in the Barrel*.
90. CBS News, *60 Minutes*, March 27, 2002.
91. KGB: Komitet Gosuderstvennoy Bezopasnosti. (Soviet Committee of State Security).
92. *The Orlando Sentinel* of June 15, 2000.
93. The conspiracy was known as the Kreisauer Kreis (Circle), founded in 1939 by Count Helmuth von Moltke. Most conspirators were either of Prussian nobility or German intellectuals who opposed Hitler. They met — most often on weekends — at the Moltke estate in Kreisau, Silesia. Among the many members of this circle executed were Moltke, Adam von Trott zu Solz, Count Peter York von Wartenburg, Count Friedrich Werner von der Schulenburg, and Count Claus Schenk von Stauffenberg.
94. Schlabrendorff, *The Secret War Against Hitler*. (New York, Toronto, and London: Pitman, 1965).

INDEX

Alibar 182, 183
Altenbuchen 109
American Zone of Occupation, Germany 7, 62
Amt (*Ausland/Abwehr*) 48, 154
Anton 121–123, 143, 145, 158–161, 171, 172, 182; see also Hauser, Anton
Army Intelligence 48
assessing 80
Augsburg 25, 28, 29, 31, 32, 33, 35
Ausland/Abwehr see *Amt*

Bad Homburg (vor-der-Höhe) 66, 164, 167
Bain, Pvt. 63, 71
basic training 40–42
Bauer, Richard 54
Bautzen 138
Berlin 7, 8, 25, 51, 98, 102, 104, 105–107, 115, 116, 138, 147; boroughs 105; East-West border 105, 148, 149
Berlin Airlift 51
black market 7, 8, 31–34, 65–66, 146
"blanket roll" 88
Blomberg 24
Boley, Pvt. 63
bolthole 195, 198, 199, 216
border crossings 117; Forst/Neisse 117; Frankfurt/Oder 117; Görlitz/Neisse 117; Kietz-Küstrin/Oder 117; Neukölln 105
Bremen 35, 64
Bremen-Fegesack 35
Bremerhaven 35, 36, 63
Breslau 110
British Zone of Occupation, Germany 22, 23, 28
Brower, Mr. 43
Bundesbahn 75

Cameron Station, Alexandria, Virginia 44

Camp A.P. Hill, Virginia 51, 52, 54
Camp Kilmer, New Jersey 63
Camp King, Oberursel 62, 63, 66–74, 77, 78
Canaris, Adm. Wilhelm 48, 215
Captain Opinion 82–83
Central Intelligence Agency 46, 79
Ceske Budejovice 196
Charlottenburg 148, 149
Christmas: (1945) 194; (1946) 28, 29; (1947) 35
clandestine case officer training 79–86; assessing 80; counterintelligence 84–85; offensive driving 86; recruiting 80–81; spotting 79–80; surreptitious entry 82–83; vetting 80; walk-ins 81
concentration camps 49
counterintelligence 84–85
courier flight 136, 142, 149
Croatians 17
Cunningham, Billy 38, 39

"Dangle" 68
Dearborn, Michigan 37
deportation from Silesia 21–22
Detmold 22, 23, 24, 75
Detroit 13, 32, 35
Dresden 137, 141
DULAG LUFT WEST see Luftwaffe's Auswertestelle West

"early warning" mission 117, 120
East Berlin 69
East German military defectors 68–69
East German reconstruction 113
East German People's Police see VOPO
East German Revolt, June 17, 1953 69
East German science and technology assignment see S&T task

219

Eastern Front 11, 15, 30, 107, 109
EEI 113–114, 155, 162
Ehrlich, Herr 19, 22, 29
Erholungsheim 72, 75, 78, 79, 84
Ernst, Sgt. Maj. Ignaz "Iggy" 43, 44, 205
Eschersheim 66
Eschersheimer Landstrasse safehouse 118, 120, 134
Essential Elements of Information *see* EEI
ethnic cleansing 18

Fasanenstrasse 139, 189–190
fatherless children from West Berlin 100
Faustpatrone *see* Hallelujah weapon
Field Operations Intelligence (FOI) 97
5th U.S. Army Basic Training Center 40
54th Armored Field Artillery Batallion 40
54th Jäger Regiment 11, 12
First Ukrainian Front 15
Fiscal officer 83–84, 91, 92, 93, 94, 96, 129, 131, 159; *see also* "Money Bags"
513th Military Intelligence Group 62, 63, 65, 67, 72, 73, 201
522nd Military Intelligence Batallion 9, 87
food shortages, post-war Germany 25–27, 29, 31–32
Ford Motor Corporation, Dearborn, Michigan 13, 32, 37
Foreign Armies, East 215; see also *Fremde Heere Ost*
Forst/Neisse 117
Fort Knox, Kentucky 40
Fort Myer, Virginia 42, 50, 55
Fort Riley, Kansas 56, 57, 61, 62, 63, 79
411th U.S. Army Security Agency Special Operations Unit 210
461st Silesian Infantry Division 25, 64, 194
410th U.S. Army Security Agency Special Operations Unit (410th USASA SPECOPS) 209
Frankfurt 64, 65, 66, 73, 77, 78, 87, 91, 122, 124, 127, 144, 153; central rail station 64–65, 116; police headquarters 122, 125, 133; *see also* Frankfurt-on-Main
Frankfurt/Oder 117
Frankfurt-on-Main 7, 47, 62, 86, 87, 90, 92, 99, 121, 129, 145, 148; *see also* Frankfurt
Frankfurter Hof 144, 145
Freistadt 196, 197
Fremde Heere Ost 45, 48; see also Foreign Armies, East 215
"Frenchie" 80
Fussell, Paul 54

Gedächtniskirche, Kaiser Wilhelm 106

Gehlen, Reinhard, General 45, 48
Georgetown University 80, 167
German Jews 91
German license plates 121–125, 133–135
German MLR (Main Line of Resistance) 16
German Military Documents Section *see* GMDS
German postal system 33
German wine 98
Gestapo files 46, 49
GMDS 42, 43, 49, 51, 55, 56, 59, 68, 205, 206
Goethe Strasse 127, 129
Görlitz 22, 195
Görlitz/Neisse 117
Great Depression 13
Gross-Hilligsfeld 25, 26, 34, 35, 77

Hallelujah weapon 12
Halyshin, MSgt. Mike 44
Hameln 26, 34
Hanke, Oberinspektor Eduard 122–125, 133, 200
Hanover 31, 64
Hans 100–103
Hansa Allee 99
Harry 68
Hauptwache Café 144
Hauser, Anton 145
Headquarters Company U. S. Army 42, 52, 55
Heidelberg 69, 113
Heisser, Jack 180–181, 183–184
Henrick, the Dutchman 154, 162
Hermann, Doktor 92, 99, 109, 112, 113, 186
Herz, Manfred "Fred" vii, 47, 89–99, 104–107, 110, 113–114, 116, 117–118, 121, 123, 126–127, 143, 145, 146, 153, 191–193, 195–196; *see also* Hermann, Doktor
Herz, Martha 91, 99, 115
Herzogenaurach 210
Hesse, Horst 202–203
Himsl, Sgt. Alois 44, 45, 46, 55, 206
Hirschberg 95, 110
Hitler, Adolf: assassination attempt 207–208
Hoff, Col. 78
Hoffman, Heinrich 48
Holstad, Sigurd H. vii, 50
Hotel Kleiner Riesen 155
HUMINT 79, 212
Hungarian defector 71

I.G. Farben building 93, 94, 96, 99, 132, 134, 167, 171, 195

Index

Intelligence Reports (IRs) 68, 90, 93, 94, 168
Intelligence School, Fort Riley 56
Irmchen *see* Raasch, Irmgard
Istrup 24, 25, 76
Ivan 20, 22

Jauer 13, 17, 18, 22, 25, 28, 35, 124; combat sector 11, 15; Soviet occupation 18, 19
Jawor *see* Jauer
Joachim (Preuss) 26, 29, 34
Junction City, Kansas 57

Kansdorff, Hans 155, 162–163
Karl-Marx-Strasse 105
Kassel 64, 66
Kennkarte 7, 8, 92, 113, 156, 169
KGB 203–204
Kietz-Küstrin/Oder 117
Klaus (Schindler) 19
Klein-Hilligsfeld 26, 29, 77
Koblenz 155
Korean conflict 51–52, 56
Ku'damm 7, 9, 138, 139, 142, 146, 186, 187
Kuehnel, Ann 37, 39
Kuehnel, Harold vii, 32, 35, 37, 39
Kurfürstendamm *see* Ku'damm
Kurfürstenkeller 142

land navigation training 59, 61–62
Landeshut field hospital 108
Landser 8, 95, 107, 109, 110, 112, 113, 137, 146, 187–191, 195, 197, 199; *see also* Schwertfeger, Corp. Hans
Lee D. Butler Studebaker 101
Lehngut 207
LeVine, Pvt. 63, 65
Liegnitz 23
Lieselotte, Liesschen 195, 198
Lietzenburger Strasse 139
Lippe 23
Liska, Hans 11, 16
Little Red Schoolhouse 72, 73, 78–79, 87, 93, 104, 113, 115, 147, 148, 154, 169, 181, 201
Louisville, Kentucky 40
Löwenberg 124
Lower Silesia 9, 13, 15, 124
Luftwaffe Auswertestelle West 47, 59, 67, 72

Mackenzie, Frank 184–185, 200
Mackintosh, John 180–181
"mailmen" 119
Mainz 154
Manfre, Lt. Col. John 209

SS *Marine Tiger* 36, 37, 215
Mecklenberger 127–129, 130, 131, 132, 136–142, 146, 184
Meinekestrasse 137, 139, 142, 187
Michigan Avenue, Detroit 38
Milewski, Joseph "Joe" vii, 5, 86, 114, 127, 174
MilGeo Collection 46
Mitrokhin, Vasili 204
"Money Bags" 93, 94, 132, 160, 168, 172, 199, 200; *see also* Fiscal officer
money laundering 34
Munich 32

Naval Intelligence, assistance to 165–168
Nazi Party 46
Neisse River 22, 110, 113, 117
Neuhammer, Franz *see* Mackenzie, Frank
Neukölln 105
New York City 36, 63
NOC Ops 81, 127
Non-Official Cover Operations *see* NOC Ops
Northern Area Command 87

Oberammergau 85
Oberkommando der Wehrmacht 45
Oberursel 47, 62, 63, 66
Oder River 15, 113, 117
offensive driving 86
The Old Man 87–88, 89, 91, 120, 121, 123, 125, 127, 128, 129, 130, 131, 143, 146, 158–160, 168, 173–174, 191, 195, 199
100th Jäger Division 11, 12, 16, 95, 107, 110
Ops 89–90, 126, 127, 128, 131, 132, 152, 155, 164, 165, 167–168, 181, 183, 195
orphaned Jewish children 36
Owen, Herb W. 11, 16

Panzerfaust *see* Hallelujah weapon
Panzergrenadier Division 110
Paternoster 173
Paul, Pfc. 63
penetration indicators 213
Pension Imperator 142
Pentagon 42, 43, 44, 51, 209
Pivitsheide 75
Poischwitz 9
"The Pokerface Method" 60–61
Polish defectors 69–71
Posen 13
Potsdam Archives 44, 45, 46, 55
Potsdamer Platz 148, 149
POW interrogation files 46–47
Preuss, Bruno 77
Preuss, Karl 25

Preuss, Willy 25, 26, 29, 77
Preuss Oma 24, 26, 28, 29, 76, 77, 109
Prisoner of War (POW) Interrogation 59, 67–68
proprietary 126, 128; atelier 127–132, 146; rolling post office 130–131; tour bus 130–131; wholesale wax business 143–145, 158–161
Putzker, Herr 111

Raasch, "Aunt" Emma 26, 27, 77
Raasch, Irmgard ("Irmchen") 26, 27, 29, 33, 35, 36, 77
recruiting 39, 80–81
refugees 31
resettlement 23
"Return of U. S. Citizens" program 32
Rhine-Main Air Force Base 116, 142, 152
Rice, Pvt. 41
Ristorante Milano (Frankfurt) 127, 129

S-Bahn 105, 139, 148
Safehouse 91, 216; see also Bolthole
S&T task 146, 154–157, 162, 190
Sattler, Chuck 143, 161, 197; see also Schenck, Carl
Saxony state propaganda office 136
Schade, Wolfgang 19, 21
Schäfer, Herr 164, 165, 168, 169, 171, 172, 184
Scharff, Hanns Joachim "Pokerface" 47–48, 59–60, 62, 68
Scharff, Rudy 169, 179, 184; see also Schramm, Rudolf
Schenck, Carl 143–144, 172, 174, 175–179, 183–184, 197, 199; see also Sattler, Chuck
Scholz, Lothar 15, 16, 18, 19, 20, 21, 22
Schöneberger Ufer 150
Schramm, Rudolf 169, 170, 171, 172, 184; see also Scharff, Rudy
Schumine 17, 107
Schwertfeger, Corp. Hans 16, 95, 107, 108, 109, 195, 198–199; see also Landser
7880th Army Unit, Headquarters 87
7982nd USAREUR Liaison Group 87
The Shepherd see Schäfer, Herr
Silesia 124, 140
Silesian 461st Infantry 25, 194
"Singleton" 117
66th CIC 84
Socialist Unity Party 137
Source Control Officer (SCO) 84, 90, 91, 94, 96, 113, 119, 121, 126, 129, 143, 144, 156, 163, 183, 195
South Post Fort Myer 42

Soviet and East European intelligence collection 117
Soviet POW camps 77, 110, 112
Soviet troop transports 113, 118, 191
Soviet Zone of Occupation, Germany 26, 97
Special Operations Team Number Three see SpecOps 3
SpecOps 3 120, 131, 143, 144, 154, 164, 179, 180, 184, 191, 200
"spook pass" 96
spotting 79–80
Spratt, Jack C. 67
STASI 137, 147, 174, 176, 189, 198, 203
Studebaker Starlight Coupe 101, 102
Stuttgart 84
Sudeten Mountains 15, 16
Sun Tzu 3, 79
surreptitious entry 82–83
Szopiak, SFC Walter "Wally" 43, 57, 58

T-34 medium tank (Soviet) 11
Taunus Mountains 67
Tempelhof airport 105, 137, 148, 149, 151
Thamm, Ann Marie Holstad vii, 50, 71, 77, 99, 100, 101, 102, 103, 115–117, 142, 145, 152–153, 200, 206, 210
Thamm, Arthur 77
Thamm, Erik vii, 50, 71, 77, 99, 100, 101, 206, 210
Thamm, Erna Preuss (mother) 13, 24, 25, 26, 27, 28, 29, 33, 34, 35, 50, 77, 109
Thamm, Erwin (son) vii, 206, 210
Thamm, Erwin Erdmann Erick (father) vii, 13, 14, 25, 28, 29, 31, 32, 33, 34, 35, 50, 77, 194
Thamm, Helga (sister) 14, 24, 26, 27, 28, 50, 77, 194
Thamm, Kläre 75, 76, 77
Thamm, Renita (daughter) vii, 50, 56, 71, 77, 99, 100, 101, 206, 210, 211
Thamm, Suanne Zuzel vii, 211, 212
Thamm family farm 18–22
Thamm Opa 76, 216
3rd Armored Division 40
Torpedo Factory, Alexandria, Virginia 55
train watchers 113, 117–118
Trans-Siberian Railroad 46
Traveler's Aide (New York) 36
Treff 105, 107, 119, 129, 137, 146, 147, 149, 155, 157, 181, 186, 187, 198
Trenker, Georg (George) 7, 8, 92, 109, 116, 122, 128, 129, 141, 147, 156, 161, 168, 171, 182, 198
Trenker, Louis 92
Trenker, Sebastian 17, 92, 95, 107–109, 110

Index

Trofimoff, SFC George 73–74, 203–204
troop movements in East Germany 97
U-Bahn 105, 148
U-2 reconnaissance aircraft navigation and photography 46
Uhlandstrasse 7, 9, 137, 139, 146
Union Station, Washington, D.C. 42
U. S. Army Commissary (Augsburg) 32
U. S. Army Counter Intelligence Corps 84, 182, 204
U. S. Army General School 57–62
U. S. Army Heidelberg headquarters 118, 119
U. S. Army Intelligence 123, 137, 154
U. S. Army Northern Command 9
U. S. Army occupation force 99
U. S. Army Security Agency 210
U. S. Army V Corps 97, 123, 143
U. S. Consulate, Munich 32
U. S. Intelligence Service 124
United States Line 37
USAREUR 69, 119

vetting 80
Vogel, Henry *see* Volker, Hans
Volker, Hans 131, 138, 184

von Schlabrendorff, Fabian 207, 207, 217
VOPO 68, 69, 105, 150
Vorwerkgut 14, 28

"WAC Circle" 100
Wagner, Alfred 207, 208
Wagner, Sgt. George 55
walk-ins 81
Walker, Mister 202–203
Walloons 16
War Department 43
wartime crimes committed by Nazis 46, 48–50
Washington, D.C. 42, 77, 101, 113
"Waxman" 144–145, 158–161
Wehrmacht 11, 12, 14, 15, 49, 85
Wende, SSgt. Walter 43, 44
West, Chief Warrant Officer 100
"Westländer" 127, 128, 131
Wiesbaden 66
Wilhelm, Dr. Frederick 166–167
Wolfgangstrasse 87
Würzburg safehouse 202–203

Zammarella, Louis 212
Zweibrücken 64; Replacement Depot 63

www.ingramcontent.com/pod-product-compliance
Ingram Content Group UK Ltd.
Pitfield, Milton Keynes, MK11 3LW, UK
UKHW041952140426
5217IPUK00015B/756